DATE DUE

MAR. 12 1994	
MAY 1 3 1996	

D1260061

Cuban Americans
Masters of Survival

JOSÉ LLANES

Cuban Americans
Masters of Survival

Abt Books
Cambridge, Massachusetts

Reissued by arrangement with
University Press of America, Inc.
4720 Boston Way
Lanham, MD 20706

Library of Congress Cataloging in Publication Data

Llanes, José, 1947–
   Cuban Americans.

   Bibliography: p.
   Includes index.
   1. Cuban Americans—Social conditions.   2. Cuba—
History—1959–   . I. Title.
E184.C97L55   306'.089687291'073   82-6849
ISBN 0-89011-563-X   AACR2

Printed in the United States of America

Book design by Marianne Rubenstein

A mi padre,
mi madre,
mi esposa,
y a José Martí . . . .
Desterrados todos
por una dictadura u otra.

CONTENTS

Foreword   ix

Acknowledgments   xiii

Introduction: *Masters of Survival*   1

First Wave   5
    The Utility of Virtue   7
    The Decision to Leave   11
    Crashing Upon the Shores of Liberty   29
    The Entrepreneurs   47
    Cochinos   62
    From *Cochinos* to the Missile Crisis   78

Second Wave   87
    Love Is Repaid by Love   89
    Once More Upon the Shores of Liberty   98
    Becoming Cuban-American   122
    Those Left Behind   135

Third Wave   139
    Return to Cuba   141
    The Mad Exodus   147
    The Third Time Upon the Shores of Liberty   159
    A Walk Around Miami   185

Conclusion 195

Epilogue 207

Who's Who 209

About the Method 213

Bibliography 217

Index 231

FOREWORD

Among the nationality groups that comprise the peoples of the United States, only the Native Americans lack recent legends of how they came to inhabit this country, and even their stories, after all, concern a similar theme: how they were forced to relocate. The legends of migration are the primary and unifying folk themes which explain over and over again who we are. The explicitness of each group's legend also tells us of its emerging place in the North American social order. For example, the Mayflower legend became a source of prestige among Massachusetts Bay Colonists, and there are towns in Virginia and the Deep South today where social position and purpose alike are accounted for by genealogical descendents from some and not other immigrants to these shores.

This beautifully written book establishes the already embellished and differentiated legends of the several contemporary migrations of Cubans to the United States. Good scholarship has been invested in monographs on the subject, and thousands of Cuban-American families have composed and handed down their own variations. The stories are recent enough, moreover, to rest on our memories from yesterday's newspapers. In this sense, we know the outlines of the legends, and the sons and daughters know the details of their unique variations. What José Llanes has accomplished, however, surpasses the contributions of scholarship, family storytelling, and journalism. He preserves the individual and family uniquenesses and at the same time discloses the universal, symbolically pertinent, shared patterns of the legends by brilliant use of the ethnographic imagination.

Every reader will share in these stories of the joys and heartbreaks of discovering the United States and of defining oneself within it. The emotions are expressed with freshness because they are within recent memory and with directness because that is part of the Cuban heritage and part of Llanes's genius as a social scientific interviewer, recorder, and insider to the emigration experience.

The legends come with the experiential territory of merging into a nation of immigrants. They also have pungency. They are so current, so much a part of the second half of a war-seared century, and Cuba herself has always been breathtakingly close to the United States.

These legends also signal to us, when they are written this way, that the occasion for incorporating them as markers of enduring permanence and lasting "arrival" have been posted. The Cuban-Americans José Llanes chronicles have demonstrated their mastery of survival. As he notes in celebration; they have also put forth the record of their distinctive inclusion in the North American scene, on their own terms, with their own expressions of relief and outrage, innocence or cunning, and stoical adaptability or sense of mortification.

As with other legends of migration to this land, the Cuban-Americans who speak with such authenticity in this stirring chronicle tend to separate themselves rather deliberately from parts of the historical matrix of their homeland. We have all heard about the voyages out of the Pilgrims and the Puritans, for example, and about the early years of their struggle to survive, just as we learn a little about the forces impelling their journeys. The latter fades a bit, however, whether the legend is of Puritans, Moravians, or even, more recently, of Russian Jews.

Thus, the marvellous tellers of true stories recorded by Llanes in this book give us snippets of Cuban history, ancient or contemporary, in the course of their telling. We hear few echoes of the rapacious depredations of the Spanish colonizers, whose nearly genocidal practices after all defined a part of the Cuban cultural response to invasion, colonization, and tyranny. We hear very little of the defining years of United States control from 1898 to 1909. The shadow of Sergeant Fulgencio Batista falls occasionally across the page, but its length never equals the span of his dictatorial regime which ruled, with occasional elections intervening, from 1933 to the last days of 1959.

This engaging book chronicles the legend of how the first wave of more than 100,000 Cubans left the country in the short period between Batista's flight into exile and Fidel Castro's consolidation of his dictatorship less than two years later. Even the vivid narratives of all but a few of those in the first wave avoid dealing in any depth with the historical nature of what they were fleeing and concentrate instead on the voyage out and on life in the new land.

When I first read the book manuscript, I brought this to the attention of José Llanes, and was reminded by him that the journey and the new life were after all the true *topical agenda* for his interviews—that he was not asking his living historians to reconstruct the Cuban experience itself. This is of course correct and I raise the observation again not to fault the book, which is logically as well as culturally consistent, but to suggest my lingering fascination with what is selected out by legend makers as much as with what is woven in.

For example, the love for Cuba, for distant kin and friends, and for one of the many Cuban ways of life, stands out boldly in the stories told here. The yearning for a return, the maintained identification with Church, profession, or city and village, and the matching of beliefs in liberty and fraternity with United States variations on those ideals—these are all powerfully conveyed. So it is not that Cuba is forgotten. Indeed, for some of Llanes's composite characters, Cuba as they were shaped by it is carried across into life in the States with the fidelity we associate most frequently with some European immigrant sects, though never with the separatism of the Amish or the Hutterites, to be sure. Most of the characters present themselves as skilled at assimilating adaptively in some portions of their new mainland lives and at preserving intact some other portions, as befits proud island peoples voyaging out from an often colonized and nearly always tyrannized society. Others were too young to form sound knowledge about the forces driving their parents to flee.

The exceptional power of this book springs from its steadfastness in presenting to full view the manner of three waves of voyages out and of the inventive modes of adapting to a land close by that had been experienced economically, militarily, politically, and culturally for generations before the voyage had to be made. Yet for all of that, a land that turns out never to quite correspond to what was sensed secondhand at home in Cuba. The power of the book also springs from a realization that it makes accessible to thousands of us, without jargon and without formalistic overlays of social scientific conceptualization, the homemade legends of persons as much like ourselves (and as much unlike ourselves) as our next-door neighbors. In this balanced simplicity, it helps us to rediscover America in these fog-bound days when we want to learn to see ourselves and others more clearly than ever.

We cannot learn from this chronicle whether the courageously determined outmovement of more than a million Cubans was linked with the staging of foreign policy conflicts on that island in the years from 1958 to 1965. It would be poor historical reasoning to imagine alternative conditions under which the first two waves of migrants might have been spared their turbulent journeys, but it is not inappropriate to note that the United States was, along with the Soviet Union, invested in generating the stresses which overwhelmed parts of the Cuban work force as well as parts of the polity. In this respect, then, the Cuban-Americans who have taken root in our midst are now part of us because of what the United States did and did not do in responding to both Batista and Castro.

Finally, José Llanes has made a contribution to social science. His method is a kind of cross between the journalism of Studs Terkel and the approach taken so imaginatively by Oscar Lewis in *Five Families*. As a result, Llanes gives us a book that can be read and believed by any literate person which is at the same time a technical contribution to ethnography: It shows how that method can be used to illuminate great events such as the Cuban migration. Above all, this book engages the imagination, enabling the reader to take the role of the immigrant, and in this sense, it lays a foundation for future social action.

Robert A. Dentler
Cambridge, Massachusetts

Acknowledgments

At the end of the journey, which began 10,000 miles before, I find that I'm indebted to hundreds of people who shared their hard-earned knowledge and experience in order to make the inquiry a success. I can't begin to thank all of those who had a part in this work. In some instances they must remain anonymous, particularly the 187 who gave their life stories—over 800 hours of tape recordings—and who edited and approved the final text. To my 187 collaborators, now my friends, I want to extend my deepest gratitude and respect. Without you there would be no story to tell.

I've wanted to write about us [the Cubans in the U.S.] for a long time, but for one good reason or another excuse, the twin resources of time and opportunity to publish failed to materialize. Or so it was until the Winter of 1980 when Abt Books, in the person of Publisher, Clark Abt, made all my excuses disappear by lending the necessary financial and professional support to the venture. Along with Abt Books came the sensitivity of Editor-in-Chief, Robert Erwin, who saw in the first draft the potential that a father sees in the child's first creative work, and pressed forth with a mixture of guidance and encouragement that made the final product suit his high standards. I also gratefully acknowledge the editorial work of Tori Alexander and the production and editorial management of Nancy Miner.

There were 11 key informants who helped me find the puzzle pieces which completed the picture I set out to construct. Among them are Professors Alma Flor Ada, Román de la Campa, Esther B. Gonzalez, Luis Laosa, Carmelo Mesa-Lago, Lisandro

Perez, and Alejandro Portes. Their published research, personal collections of Cuban material, and knowledge of individuals who should be part of the research gave me my start. Then Josefa Bolaños and Rudy García in Miami and Mike Callahan in Boston went to work, helping me pore through archival data in search of a question or in pursuit of an answer. At the end, there were 5,000 pages of transcripts and notes to be translated and typed, and I was fortunate to find Consuelo Espinosa, Mary Greene, and Jean Landreth ready to help make it all come about.

My colleagues, the social scientists whose experience with social phenomena and "outsider" views of the Cuban-Americans, provide the essential objectivity for which a work of this nature must strive, came to my rescue at the juncture of the second draft of the manuscript. Professors Joshua Fishman, Karen Seashore Louis, Roberto Alvarez, and Steve Arvizu questioned and clarified my own assumptions and ideas, building upon the data with an essential layer of analytical skepticism, leading to insight and wisdom.

But still, the work needed to find its place among the works of other immigrants who have sought to tell about themselves and their groups. This perspective came from the son of an immigrant and one of the nation's leading social thinkers, Robert Dentler. He turned the manuscript into metaphor and made me see its place in the history of the Cuban-Americans. This is the task of a mentor and as his apprentice I give him thanks.

The journey of the inquiry concludes where all things begin and end, with the home and family, and in my case, an extended family as well. The Mulherns of South Carolina, the Molines of Tallahassee, the Garcías of Miami, and the del Portillos of California, all of whom I call family, fed and housed me in the journey, allowing me to use their homes as my own. And my wife, Dr. Celia Barberena, to whom this book is dedicated. She knows the lonely labor invested in this work as no one else does and she shares in that investment.

Thanks also to Ediciones Vitral Inc., New York City, and Grupo Areito for permission to reprint excerpts from *Contra viento y marea*. And to Dr. Leonardo Fernández-Marcané and Associated International Translators, Miami, for permission to reprint "Recuerdo Vital" by Luisa Gil, which originally appeared in the book *20 Cuentistas Cubanos*.

And last, but not least, to my new friend and earnest collaborator, Frank Soler, and his marvelous magazine *Miami Mensual* for building bridges for Cubans which will last a lifetime.

Cuban Americans
Masters of Survival

Introduction

Masters of Survival

This is a book about Cubans living in the United States. It is based on the life stories of 187 of them who were selected by me to compose a demographically representative sample of the rest of us.* I am one of those Cubans and there are over a million more.

I decided to write this book because in 1980 there was no other work in English which had endeavored to reveal the life and thought of the Cubans as residents and citizens of the United States. This is why a cultural ethnography of the Cuban-American social group as viewed by the group and told through their own words, was undertaken.

Early in 1970 a paper by Lourdes Casal on the social-psychology of Cubans in exile (Casal, 1970) awakened in me an interest in the social dynamics of the group to which I belonged. In the margin of that paper I had written three questions which, ten years later, would form the basic core of research questions for the cultural ethnography. I wondered in 1970 how the Cuban exile compared with other political refugees, how they compared with each other on the basis of their time of arrival in the U.S., and to what extent we shared com-

*See "About the Method", page 213.

mon views of our role in the U.S. Since 1970 a great deal of literature has emerged from Cuban scientists as well as other American and British scientists on the life of Cuban-Americans. This information, most of it dealing with micro-processes of our social interactions—our psychological health, our financial and institutional achievements or our political views—saw the light in over one hundred journals and magazines. Each study or article revealed another element of knowledge and brought new understanding to the central issues with which I was concerned. But it would not be until 1980 that the time became available for me to undertake a firsthand look at a geographically diverse and demographically representative group of Cuban-Americans.

1980 was the year of the third Cuban wave of immigration to the U.S. The events of those days threatened to eclipse all other events in the social history of the Cuban-Americans. The press brought to light the horrors of the exodus, the presence of many mental patients and convicted criminals among the new group. The response of the American public, damning and apprehensive, was based on these stories and no others. Unnoticed by the mass media were a thousand or more stories of bravery and sacrifice which served to balance the grim concerns that these were different Cubans than the ones we had seen before, Cubans sent by Fidel to hurt and burden the American society. The Open Arms policy became the Keep Them Away policy as the political advantage to the U.S. of a massive flight from communist rule was outweighed by the political disadvantage of giving refuge to those Fidel did not wish to have around. This was not a correct view. There was a need to look back in time, to the 21 years of Cuban political immigration, before a complete portrait of the Cuban-Americans could be painted. This was the task I undertook.

At first the job seemed insurmountable and later it got worse. My first task was to compose a sample which in retrospect would provide a well-balanced picture. It is up to the reader to judge whether this balance has been attained, but from my perspective, the insider perspective of a member of the group, there is a certain imbalance within the whole group, and it is this imbalance that I have sought to portray. For the most part Cuban-Americans are politically conservative and their views contain a predominance of those symbols more commonly associated with right-wing political causes in the U.S.

We are also imbued—in lesser quantities—with a politically liberal attitude toward bilingualism, self-determination, and freedom of speech, issues that touch us deeply and are key to our survival. My job was to become immersed in these symbols and to select for the reader the words of those who best expressed them. The 187 people who agreed to participate in this study are more than just subjects in a research project. They are, in fact, my collaborators. I found and interviewed them in a great variety of settings: at their homes in opulence and poverty, at work in Army barracks or executive suites, on the streets, in restaurants, in universities of a dozen cities and states, and some in jail, where they faced indefinite incarceration, their freedom still to come.

Interpreting the words of my collaborators was like staring at a Polaroid picture as it emerges from the camera. As the first basic colors rush to find their places in the light-impregnated negative, so do the first basic themes of Cuban-American symbolic interaction become visible in the symbols they discuss. *Libertad,* [freedom], was the basic color red, the first principle of the human seeking refuge in the United States.

Libertad is the symbol of individual self-determination. It resonates well with the American principles of individuality and liberty. This resonance frees the behaviors repressed during the time in Cuba and it legitimizes both our virtues and our excesses. *Fraternidad,* [brotherhood], was the basic color blue. It blended with *libertad* red to form the outlines of the individualistic themes of the national transplantees, just as it had before for the Jews and the Italians.

Fraternidad is the symbolic armor of our collective survival, the bond that makes liberty productive, our guarantee of security. Those who share in the symbolic interaction of the majority of Cubans, cluster geographically, economically, and socially, even though social, economic, and racial differentiations persist.

Thus *libertad* is psychic permission to act and survive, *fraternidad* is the willful pursuit of group security, which is also physical survival. And finally, as the negative blended the yellows and greens, so the stories began to reveal the true nature of the ordeal, the same ordeal as for those who came before us to these shores, *supervivencia,* [the quest for survival].

The cultural motivation of life, its loudest theme and therefore the basis of most of the symbols and behavior of my collaborators, emerge from a willful pursuit of survival. Yet survival for them involves more than the basic needs for food and shelter. Survival means living in freedom; maintaining family, clan, and community; contributing to the challenges of the society and sharing in its rewards.

In the path of survival Cuban-Americans have crafted a common attitude to life in the United States, an attitude that accounts for the patterns of discrimination present in the society. This will to survive and attitude toward survival transcends the wrongful harm they have suffered, and helps them pursue lives with freedom of individual expression and self-actualization.

I interviewed a Cuban man who knew he would die within a few months, and asked him to tell me what label I could place on this our own group that would define our basic symbolic theme during these first 20 years of emigration from our homeland. The man has since died but his words spoken candidly will live in my mind forever. *"Son maestros de supervivencia,"* [We are masters of survival.] he said with a smile and he is right.

The people I spoke to came to the U.S. to survive and once here were put to the test once again, and again they survived. They are in deed no more and no less than they are in symbol. They are *masters of survival.*

In order to tell you their stories and remain faithful to my promise that they would remain anonymous, I have constructed from their conversations and writings 58 characters and have given them fictitious names and noncorresponding life histories. Each character, therefore, is a composite of one or more of my collaborators. Their words were faithfully recorded and translated. I believe they have told me the truth as they see it. Each of them is responsible for what is said by the characters, and no one but me is responsible for deciding what to include or exclude from what was said.

The Utility of Virtue
La utilidad de la virtud

Tengo fe en el mejoramiento humano, en la vida futura, en la utilidad de la virtud y en tí.

I have faith in human improvement, in future life, in the utility of virtue, and in you.

José Martí, 1892, from a dedication in his book for his son, *Ismaelillo*

The Utility of Virtue

The reason that there are over a million Cubans in the United States today is that, beginning in 1959, a massive and perhaps irreversible social change began to take place in Cuba.

The basic facts of this social change are fairly well known to the majority of North Americans. The corrupt and sometimes cruel dictatorship of Fulgencio Batista had dominated the political and economic life of the island of Cuba for seven years and, with help from the United States, had instituted an oppressive social system to which, by the end of 1958, most Cubans found themselves bitterly opposed.

They joined the revolutionary movement called the 26th of July, and each in his or her own way began to contribute toward the forcible overthrow of the bloody dictator.

Fidel Castro emerged as the popular leader and the masses rallied to his side. On January 1, 1959, Fulgencio Batista went into exile and the most profound social change in the history of Cuba began to evolve.

Of course, there had been Cubans in the United States long before Fidel was born. Many businessmen had come here in the late 1800s seeking larger markets in a politically stable environment. Among them were the Cubans who began the U.S. cigar industry and who still produce the finest handmade cigars in the United States. There were also some political refugees, like poet José Martí, who fought Spanish colonialism from New York and Ybor City only to die on the battlefield before seeing his country born. But our numbers in the United States before the revolution of 1959 never exceeded 100,000.

There is no doubt that Fidel and the revolution he still leads have produced important cultural change in Cuba. The revolution has resulted in the exodus of 691,000 people, half of them trained and skilled. There has been a complete social transformation on the island—from capitalism to socialism, from caste politics to party politics. Once the center of American influence in Latin America, Cuba has become its nemesis.

At the same time, the United States has become more Cuban. To the environments Cuban-Americans occupy we have brought our culture and have sought to make it compatible with the goals and truths of the culture we have found.

In order to better understand the nature of this immigration, it would be helpful to classify it in terms of the time of its arrival to the United States.

In chronological terms, the Cuban migration to the United States, which encompasses the period 1959–1980, can be divided into roughly three parts or, more appropriately, three waves. The First Wave began sweeping large numbers of Cubans to American shores when Fidel took over on New Year's Day of 1959. It ended with the Cuban Missile Crisis of October 1962. While it lasted, it brought to the United States 280,000 Cubans. Between the end of the First Wave and the beginning of the Second Wave three years later, fewer than 3,000 Cubans entered the United States. The Cuban Missile Crisis increased the tensions between the two countries, and the Cuban government cancelled all residents' exits, except for official visits to other countries. Cuba was shut tight, and no one could get in or out.

The Second Wave of Cuban refugees began arriving in the United States in 1965, when the U.S. and Cuban governments negotiated an airbridge from Camarioca, Cuba to Miami, Florida. 1,000 Cuban men, women, and children entered the United States via this airlift each week. By the time the flights stopped in December 1973, they had brought an additional 273,000 of us here.

Since then and until 1980, only a small number of Cubans

were allowed to leave the island. In April 1980 political events, leading to the takeover of the Peruvian Embassy in Havana by 10,000 Cubans who wanted to leave the country, precipitated the Third Wave. Between April and September of 1980, before the exodus was halted, approximately 125,000 Cubans escaped to the United States.

The 1960 U.S. census, conducted when the First Wave had just begun, counted 124,416 Cuban-Americans, including 79,150 native-born people and 45,266 born in the United States of Cuban parentage. Ten years later the 1970 census found 560,628 Cubans, of whom 439,048 were born in Cuba and 121,580 were born in the United States. Adding those who were here prior to 1959 those who came in between the three waves and those who came in on the Third Wave, the number of Cubans and Americans of Cuban descent currently residing in the United States exceeds one million people.

Demographically, the First Wave of Cuban-Americans was quite homogeneous. Its members were mostly white (94 percent), middle-aged (an average age of thirty-four years) and well educated (an average of fourteen years of schooling). Their political values were also homogeneous and similar to those of the conservatives in the American Republican party.

While the First Wave was relatively small, as migrations to the United States go, the circumstances of their exodus from Cuba and their undertakings here brought them some early notoriety. These people were considered tangible proof that the United States was siding with the "right-thinking" group of Cubans. Members of the First Wave engaged in heroic escapes, worked hard, showed great resiliency, kept their homes and families in good order, and shared the American view of the Cold War. In addition, they shared with their American hosts a respect for the essential symbol, the "utility of virtue."

The revolutionary conflict that had caused the exodus to the United States was seen by the First Wave as an ideological conflict between Marxist communism and Jeffersonian capitalism. Refugees of the early years believed there was no other reason for the revolution, and that Russian-led Marxism would be its only possible outcome. This attitude fit neatly with the prevailing American political climate of the late 1950s and early 1960s and was reflected in American foreign policy during those periods.

But the Cuban-American symbolism went beyond political attitudes in paralleling American values. The symbolism of virtue, the Greek *arete,* which Homer used to describe excellence of any kind, was an intrinsic cultural characteristic of the First Wave. Virtue is useful as a characteristic of man, as is social structure and morality, because with virtue man reaps the rewards of the society, dominates the social structure, and dictates its morality. This basic conceptual affinity with American values gave Cubans of the First Wave an immediate *entreé* to the host society.

The First Wave was also economically productive for the United States. The immigrants were educated, adapted to the work ethic, and ready to participate in a system of private incentives. Some brought capital, and others had friends, social contacts, or colleagues in the United States. A few came alone, without any economic resources, or too young to survive on their own. But most did survive. Though they never thought they would stay in the United States for the rest of their lives, most are more or less resigned to it now. And yet, they will never stop searching for a way to get back.

Once I heard an American sociologist proudly refer to the First Wave as "the most genuinely patriotic group of Americans that have never been citizens of the United States." Some of my collaborators would agree with that statement; others would argue its merit. But in the interviews and life histories that follow, all embrace in one way or another the ideal of the survival of self through arete, and the survival of freedom. These are the dual principles upon which America was founded.

The Decision to Leave

Jorge Mendieta was waiting for me at his office on the campus of a New York state university, and told me how apprehensive he was about discussing Cuba in personal terms. As a professor he had the comfort of being able to discuss the subject from a detached perspective. That is how he began to answer my questions about Cuba and freedom.

Jorge Mendieta: There is no question that the main preoccupation of the Cuban people of my generation, as well as every generation since the Ten Year War, was the pursuit of freedom. *Libertad.* Independence. We have never achieved that, so it is always our central preoccupation and our fondest hope.

Revolution is like a passion which builds up inside a nation. I see it build up in the United States every four years, but here we have an election to throw the rascals out. [He laughs.] In Cuba the system has room only for armed overthrow, which is much less predictable and desirable. I was a congressman during Batista's presidency in Cuba. There was much government corruption, but you did not have to take part in it if you did not want to. We had begun to enjoy some of the fruits of democracy. People could and did petition the government for redress.

He recited an enumeration of the freedoms he said Cubans had enjoyed in the government of which he had been a part. When he concluded he sank deep into his leather chair and looked out the window to the snow-covered campus that surrounded us.

Jorge Mendieta: This thing with Fidel was different. He sacrificed the country, ostensibly to speed up its social progress, but in fact to put it under armed guard. Of course this is hindsight, which some people say is 20-20. But when I first heard that Batista had left—I was in our house at Varadero Beach—I was very quiet for many days. There was no reason for my apprehension, really. I was a practicing attorney, and everyone thought I could survive, would be left alone. But something told me to get out and face the hardship of exile rather than risk what was to come. Most people thought I was crazy. In seven days I liquidated what assets I could and left with my family for Switzerland.

Within a year, two of my partners in the law firm had left for the United States and the third one was in jail on political charges in Cuba. He got forty years at hard labor and died in prison, at the Principe. I was fortunate to have left as soon as my instincts told me about Fidel.

Jorge Mendieta was among the first to leave for ideological reasons. Few Cubans without close political ties to Batista or the military wanted to get out of the country when the revolution began, even though it was relatively simple to go into exile then. Fidel had adopted the policy that those "counter-revolutionaries" who left the country would not be able to oppose him effectively. He pressured people who were thinking of leaving to leave sooner or with fewer resources by expropriating their "ill-gotten gains," mobilizing public opinion against them or threatening them with imprisonment.

But the main exodus of the First Wave did not begin until 1960. It started in the spring, sped up in the summer, and had assumed the proportions of mass flight by the end of the year. Among the spring refugees were the older, establishment politicians of the pre-Batista era who had survived under Batista's dictatorship. They were people like Manuel Antonio de Varona, the former premier. Later in 1960 the nationalization of American-owned businesses, followed by the expropriation of Cuban-owned businesses, led to huge financial losses for the entrepreneurial class and the major financial institutions. Almost everyone associated with these empires of business and finance left Cuba then.

The closing of private universities and secondary schools, which drove out hundreds of teachers, began in 1961. The new communist party's takeover of the old communist party's trade unions added many of their formerly pro-Fidel officials to the stream flowing out. Other professionals and some intellectuals followed. Eventually, members of Fidel's own 26th of July Movement began to sour on the regime, and many of them fled to the United States, including some of Fidel's appointees; the former minister of public works, Manuel Ray; the former minister of finance, Rufo Lopez Fresquet; and the former president of the National Bank of Cuba, Felipe Pazos.

By 1961, exits from Cuba were tightly controlled: Over 100,000 political refugees had gathered in the United States. This was only a fraction of the people who had tried to get out of Cuba but could not. If all who wanted to leave had been able to do so, the figure might easily have reached a quarter of a million, an incredible number for an island which in 1959 had a total population of about 6 million.

Miguel Taboada, now a semi-retired taxi driver in Los Angeles, was, before 1959, the chauffeur to Martha Batista, the dictator's wife, whose portrait hangs in the living room of his modest apartment beside a picture of his deceased parents.

Miguel Taboada: I remember where I was when I heard the *Generalísimo* was about to leave. I was standing by the car I used to drive for the *Generalísimo*'s wife, a wonderful and warm woman, very kind to everyone in my family. She told me that they [the Batista family] were leaving Cuba. She gave me an envelope with some dollars in it and the name of a man who would make arrangements for my family if we had to leave. I drove them to the airport. It was a very sad experience. Since I had no job after they left, we

moved close to Trinidad [a small town in south-central
Cuba] to the mountains where my brother had a coffee
plantation and where we had been born. It is a place so
small it does not even have a name. Two years later, in
1961, I heard the G-2 [Fidel's secret police] were looking for
me. They went to see my brother and they almost found
me too, but I was working in the *campiña* [the fields], and
the G-2 had left by the time I came back.

They [the G-2] said I had stolen some property from
the government in Havana. Havana [he repeats, shaking
his head] . . . I had not been to Havana since 1959. I didn't
know what was going on. I called the number I had gotten
from the *señora* the day she left. The man told us to meet
him at Plaza de Bibijagua on the Isle of Pines. There we
were picked up by a motorboat and headed north. We ran
into a U.S. Coast Guard vessel which took us to Miami.

Miguel Taboada could not see why Fidel wanted him, but by
now a cloud of terror had formed around the rumored abuses of Fidel's Revolutionary Army. Stalinist-type purges of public and private
institutions sent shock waves through the Establishment and the revolution began to take on overtones of religious fervor as the mass im-
plementation of their ideals was pursued.

Eduardo Lopez is fifty-nine years old and chain smokes Kent cig-
arettes in his small cubicle at a New York newspaper.

Eduardo Lopez: My life seemed to be coming to an end just
about the time Fidel came to power in Cuba. I was dying
from a liver disease—cancer of the liver—and was hospitalized for two years. I recovered and I think I am now
cured. During those first thirteen months of Fidel [1959–
60], when I lay in the hospital bed all day long watching
Fidel on television every night, night after night, I picked
up on who Fidel was and what he wanted to do. I developed a respect for what he *could* do, given his abilities as
a public speaker, his lies, and his rhetorical positions.

Many people were hypnotized by him into staying
with the government longer than their own instincts told

them to. His voice blared morning, noon, and night, on radio and television, and then when they installed the loudspeakers on the streets, you did not even have to turn a radio on. You heard Fidel's voice as you were walking down the street or playing with your children in the park. The speeches would be broadcast over and over again, interrupted by applause that turned into a frenzied, mass St. Vitus dance. Everybody jumped up and down, shouting, *"Gracias Fidel, Gracias Fidel, Gracias Fidel."*

I was a very detached observer from my deathbed—or what I thought was my deathbed—looking at these people who would surely have to contend with this dangerous man, Fidel, and not caring about it. I was going to die anyway.

Then I began to recover—the doctors have never been able to tell me how it happened. At the same time, when I understood that I would not die, I began to panic. I had lived in Argentina under Perón. As a matter of fact I am married to an Argentine, and we both thought that Fidel had more control of the mobs than Perón. It was very frightening to me. As a man who had worked as a journalist, I knew the power of his rhetoric. After I recovered fully, I said to my wife, "Let's go. I'm not going to die here." We went to Mexico.

Much of the mobility afforded members of the First Wave came about because in the 1950s Cuba had evolved an economic system which was responsible for the creation of a comparatively large middle class. This was the second group to feel the impact of the changes Fidel made. Though the existence of a relatively large and economically powerful middle class was most unusual for Latin America, in 1958, the year before Fidel came to power, the Cuban middle class had 235,000 heads of household, amounting to nearly 25 percent of the population. Some 6,000 of these were employed as civil servants, 90,000 as business people, 86,000 as technical personnel, and 53,000 as professionals with advanced university degrees.

In 1958 these numbers represented 33 percent of Cuba's economically active population—a larger middle class group, proportionally, than any other Latin American nation. Nonetheless, in 1959 the inequities between this 33 percent and the other 67 percent of the working population were vast and still growing.

About 200,000 heads of household lived in rural areas of Cuba on rented land, most of which was not suitable for agricultural production. About half of these people were living on the land illegally, squatters who relied upon the seasonal work of the sugar factories for income. Education was not accessible, and no health facilities were available in most rural areas. The average individual income of this group was less than 5 percent of that of the middle class—approximately $85 per year. And their average lifespan was 45 years. These were the people who stood to gain the most from the revolution.

Between the middle class and the very poor was a group I call the lower middle class. Its members were mostly urban and were educated only to the point of literacy. They were at the mercy of the corrupt pre-Castro political world. The lower middle class was potentially the largest politically vocal group in favor of Fidel. Its members were targeted to become the first beneficiaries of Fidel's policies of wealth redistribution and were therefore his earliest converts. But the massive political change eventually touched everyone, regardless of income or political perspective.

Esteban García was a truck driver who lived in Santa Clara, a provincial capital in central Cuba. He is illiterate, having had to work for the support of his family since the age of nine. Fidel's programs benefited him culturally and economically but he rejected those benefits for what appears to be purely ethical reasons.

Esteban Garcia: I saw Fidel not so much as an economic liberator, because in the end I wanted only what I earned and did not want what belonged to someone else, but as a liberator from the subjugation of a corrupt political system. And, particularly in the last few months of Batista, when people were killed because they were with the revolution, I wanted freedom from that. I saw Fidel as someone who would bring things back to normal. Other people didn't see it that way. They wanted to take what the rich had. But I figured they had earned it just like I did. I didn't want anyone to take what was mine, and I did not want anything that wasn't mine.

Martha Losada was a university student in Havana and came from a lower class family who had worked themselves into a small catering business, which enabled Martha to pursue higher education.

Martha Losada: I did want the economic change to take place. It was a shameful situation. There was widespread illiteracy and malnutrition, and people in million-dollar houses were enjoying the afternoon breeze on their private beaches. No. I couldn't live with that.

Eventually the economic change [brought about by the revolution] began to affect our family. My father's business was taken away under a nationalization law. People we knew who were lazy and had never worked moved into our house and took over my father's business.

Sylvia Gonzalez was a debutante in Cuba's upper-class society the year before the revolution.

Sylvia Gonzalez: I didn't know that there was poverty in Cuba. I seldom went out of the house, except to go to school, which was in the same neighborhood, and to my friends' houses. Then we went in cars, and we never went through the bad neighborhoods. I feel like an idiot telling you this, but until I was fifteen I didn't know poor people existed and had never to my knowledge met a poor person. Was that part of the problem?

Carmen Bolaños was more aware than Sylvia of what was at stake in the revolution. While she was only sixteen then, she rejected the values of her middle class home during the early months of the revolution, identifying with Fidel and his liberators as a teenager would with a rock group.

Carmen Bolaños: At first I remember dressing in red and black [the colors of the revolution], singing revolutionary songs. I saw the rebels come down [from the mountains]. We danced with them in the streets and collected autographs. I had one from Ché and one from Camilo. They stopped at a house around the block. All the children looked at them with big eyes.

I never thought it would end up like Batista—worse than Batista. All I could think of was here were these people who risked their lives for my freedom, and this was something I was unwilling to do for myself. When push came to shove, we moved to the United States instead of going to the mountains and fighting like Fidel and his men had.

She followed her family unwillingly into exile, feeling that she was abandoning Cuba in its hour of need, and at the same time beginning to share in the fear for their lives her family articulated around her. I asked her about her last memories of Cuba.

Carmen Bolaños: I remember the airport. It was full of people and very confusing. The worst was coming into *la pecera* [the fishbowl, a glass-enclosed holding area for those waiting to leave for the United States]. Outside *la pecera* we cried as we said goodbye to my father. My sister said goodbye to her boyfriend.

The whole family, including cousins and uncles, went to the airport together. The night before we had gone to a restaurant that served lobster. In the restaurant we talked with people who knew us and knew we were leaving the next day. They scared us with stories about what might happen at the airport—how they were going to undress us and touch us, but nothing like that happened.

When we arrived at the airport, they put us in *la pecera*. At that point no one could talk to us, not even my grandparents, but they could see us and we could sometimes see them. We went single file past the *milicianos* [members of the Cuban militia]. There were questions about what we were taking out of the country. Then we went outside to the runway, where they looked inside our luggage, then back inside *la pecera,* where people were either quietly crying or immobile. Everyone was afraid that the trip would be cancelled at the last minute. I didn't know whether to look at my fellow would-be expatriates or my relatives outside the glass—my father, my mother crying, trying to cover her tears. That was a day full of tears.

That was the first day I saw a man cry. First my father, then a young man who was sitting beside me. I remember he had blue eyes. I remember a young child with a Miami address written on a piece of cardboard strung around her neck. People were somber and silent, looking at the floor. Everyone was crying silently. This lasted until we took off. Then, all at once, I don't know how, everybody began to weep very loudly. I looked back through the window at Cuba disappearing on the horizon. I was crying and very afraid; I felt *desamparada* [homeless].

Francisco Maceo is sixty-eight years old. Next year he will retire from the fish store he owns in Tampa. In 1962, the first time he went out to sea, he crossed the ninety miles between Cuba and Key West in a very small boat.

Francisco Maceo: Some of the people who left from Mariel [in 1980] took twenty hours to cross the distance in a motorboat. We took twenty days in 1962, my family and me, in a boat with three oars and holes. You want to see it? It is still in Key West, on the lawn of a house where they took us from the hospital. I will give you the address. You tell me how eight people could leave on an eight-foot rowboat and expect to get anywhere. Across the Miami Causeway maybe, but not those stinking, treacherous ninety miles. God was with us. There is no other answer.

I had gone to see Pancho Maceo, as his friends call him, because he had been among the first to risk crossing the waters between Cuba and the U.S. by rowboat. I was curious about why, in the accounts of his journey I found in newspapers, he had been unwilling to discuss his ordeal or the reasons which compelled him to take such a major risk for himself and his family. I had spent three hours in his fish store, sitting behind the counter on a makeshift bench made of empty soda cases, and had not been able to get him to talk about the trip in any but the most general terms. At the end of the day he closed the store, took off his blood-stained apron, and asked his wife to pour us some Spanish brandy. He joked about not being able to smell the brandy because the smell of fish was more powerful, and finally turned to me and asked, "What else can I tell you?" "Tell me about the boat," I said.

Francisco Maceo: It was eight feet long, made of wood, with peeling black paint. When I first saw it, it was upside down on the beach near an old abandoned pier and a house where they cured fish. My father and I turned it over. It was dry inside but rotten in parts. There was no way we could all fit in, no cover, no keel to speak of.

But we had to leave. We had no choice. For many weeks we had talked about leaving Cuba, and when the notice came that only I could [get the U.S. visa waiver], we lost our morale as a family and began to disintegrate. I went to the church at Cienfuegos that day, and I prayed on my knees for three hours. God said to me to take a boat and go. God told me [his eyes begin to water] what to take and where I would find the boat. My heart began to pound, like it's doing now [he takes my hand and places it on his chest], as if I was having a heart attack, but I also felt strong and certain. It took all night to walk back to Palmira, and I arrived at our house at dawn. I got everybody together and told them what I had heard, where the boat would be waiting, and what supplies to take.

My family was immediately convinced by my certainty. My father went with me to see the boat. It was just where God said—I said—it would be, but it was not what we expected. We went back home without saying a word. I was sure I had created the fantasy in my own mind that God had spoken to me. My father had more faith but did not say anything. When we got back, we learned that the G-2 had come looking for us. They had left, but we knew they would be back. We found out from the neighbors that the G-2 knew we were planning to leave by boat. They wanted to put me in jail. The only person, other than my family, who knew my plans was the father confessor at the church where I had prayed. I don't know who *me chivateó* [betrayed me]. I'm sure it was no one in the family, and I don't want to think it was the father confessor, but I didn't know who was on the other side of the confessional. You know there is a screen and you cannot see anything. [He pauses and struggles to remember.] When we came back, we brought the supplies and arranged them inside the boat. We didn't know—but we had faith. [He becomes introspective and silent.]

His wife, standing behind him, motions me to continue asking questions. "What did you take with you?" I asked.

Francisco Maceo: The three oars, a first aid kit, about eighteen gallons of water—we lost most of it overboard in high seas—dried fish from the fish house, and a knife. The knife was very interesting. I bought it because—in prayer—I had been told to. My recollection of that moment in the church was that I was told to get a *pescador* [fisherman's] knife. This is a special knife, which I knew nothing about; without it we wouldn't have survived. Then we pushed the boat to the water's edge and drifted off.

He got up as if our interview had ended but his wife intervened once again, this time with a bit of Cuban coffee in small and delicate demi-tasse cups bearing a small replica of the Cuban flag. He was forced to sit down. "Who was on board?" I asked.

Francisco Maceo: My father and mother, my wife Esperanza, my two daughters, and the twin boys. The boys were one and a half then, Carmen was four, and Rosita was six. Carmen was in a coma for most of the trip, at least the last six days or so. You lose track after many days at sea, and it's been so many years. The twins had priority on the water and so did Esperanza. She still had milk and she had been breast-feeding a newborn from her younger sister, who had no milk. Esperanza fed the twins once a day during the trip, but they did not eat much. They seemed to know we were in danger. Everyone knew, after so long, like a cork, trying to row towards the northwest, my father and I taking turns. We had blisters all over our hands, arms, faces. My head was one big blister. We said goodbye many times. When we ran out of food, we thought it would be the end, but we were still alive three days later.

Then we ran out of water. We had no water for two days. That is when the pelican flew close to the boat. My wife says I threw the knife at him and hit him. He fell inside the boat. We survived because of the pelican and the knife I threw at him. The *pescador* knife. [He shakes his head in disbelief.] You know, I don't remember doing this to the pelican. My wife says I did. I don't remember it at all.

I do remember my daughter Carmen's reaction when she woke up from the coma inside the Coast Guard cutter that picked us up. She asked if it was *Nochebuena* [Christmas time] yet. [He laughs.] We all arrived alive, more or less. My father died two days after we touched land of complications created by exposure. He said he had seen us safely to these shores and that this would be our country now. He died quite happily. His death was not sorrowful or pitiful. He smiled and gave us each a blessing, and then he passed away quietly. I cannot tell you any more.

Sergio Espinosa was a high school student when he left Cuba. He is now thirty-five years old and the owner of a large shoe factory in Miami.

Sergio Espinosa: I didn't know why I was being sent to the United States. I mean that truthfully. I was fourteen at the time. My family was with Fidel at first, and then they were not. I was going to a revolutionary army school. Then suddenly there was a change; Fidel was a communist, and I was not, supposedly, a communist—however a fourteen-year-old can interpret that. My mother went to get me at school, which was in the interior of the country, and we returned to Havana. She didn't say much during the trip, except that my father would explain the whole thing to me when we got to Havana. I thought my grandmother had died or something.

My grades in school were very good. I was considered someone with great potential. I wanted to be an army officer and study at West Point, which I knew about through American World War II films and military biographies I used to read. It was more than a childhood dream. I was committed to a military life. I thought that the peace and safety of the world had historically been in the hands of the military. It feels strange to say these things to you twenty years later, but I felt my mission early in life, and I was determined to pursue it. I wanted to be a soldier—one who would maybe someday lead an army.

When my mother and I got to Havana, my father said that I was going to be sent out of Cuba to school in the United States, to a military school in upstate New York. I was filled with anticipation and delight. I thought of it as a great challenge, and began to study English. While we had to remain quiet about it, I did tell a few close friends, and they helped me prepare. I left for the United States in September 1961, but I didn't really know why.

Miranda Martin was living with her parents in Havana and attending Catholic private school. Like Sergio Espinosa she had no clear idea why she was leaving Cuba. Her family, split on the question of Fidel, suffered nonetheless the consequences of the change in the political and economic structure. She is now a public official in New England.

Miranda Martin: My father ran a pathology laboratory, INED [Institución Nacional de Exámen y Diagnóstico], and a preventive medicine clinic, and he volunteered his research services to the revolution. In 1959, during the first national gathering on the anniversary of the 26th of July, close to a million farmers came to Havana to celebrate. My father examined about 500 of them to determine from that sample the health conditions of the farmers in the interior. He did many things like that. He tried to help the government by helping the people directly.

We became aware gradually of the shift in Fidel's policies to the left, but *papi* didn't want to leave Havana, not if there was any chance that he could survive there. My mother, on the other hand, was panicked. What will they do to the children in school? Will they force them to go to communist schools? Finally in August we left.

My grandmother, who lived upstairs from us in Cuba, died at about that time. With her went the most powerful pressure keeping the family in Cuba. She had been ill, and my mother didn't want to leave her behind. When my grandmother died, my father decided to send my mother and me to the United States so I could begin school there in September. Everything was decided during the months of July and August.

We never thought we were going into permanent exile. Then the revolution began to push professionals out. They invented new taxes for private health agencies. My father was certain that they were trying to push him out. He feared he would not be able to leave once they had taken INED by force. Fidel was beginning to feel the impact of the doctors leaving.

My father finally left, with the aid of the American Embassy. He had several patients who worked there. They forged credentials identifying him as a member of INID, which was the government tourist agency and one initial different from INED. He got a U.S. visa and legitimate INID business in the United States. In spite of that, they took him off the airplane three times for interrogation, also to search him, but they finally let him go. My father could have been a great help to Fidel. I will never understand why he eliminated this whole class of people who could have been so helpful to Cuba these past twenty years.

My father arrived in New York and was immediately told that the thing to do was to become a dishwasher until he could take the medical boards. That was really all that was available for him to do. Drew Pearson, the newspaper columnist, had known us in Cuba. He wrote a column about my father, attempting to help him find a professional job in the United States.

Jesús María Laserie was an employee in a Havana casino. He answered my questions about leaving Cuba with analytical clarity, pointing at the social restructuring, the changing values, and the crumbling of his own piece of the pie as the reasons for leaving.

Jesús María Laserie: The exact reason people left Cuba is not really important. There were so many reasons to choose from. Pick any reason and it would be good enough to make you want to leave. You left because circumstances permitted you to leave. Everybody had reasons. Take my case. I had gotten lucky and bought a house. I was afraid someone would come and say that I had worked for Batista and take my house. Nothing had to be proven. There were no real courts, just revolutionary courts.

    If you had children going to school, like I did, you saw that they were being taught revolutionary bullshit and not the real history of the country. You know what I mean? Not about God and family but about Fidel and Celia and that faggot Raul. I didn't want my children exposed to that junk. I was out of a job, since the casino had closed. I was doing things here and there to make money, but it was very difficult to survive. Reasons? I had as many as anyone would need, and not as many as some people I knew.

Jesús María Laserie is right. The particular reasons for leaving Cuba are of little importance. What seems significant is that twenty years later, every member of the First Wave I interviewed remembers the circumstances surrounding the decision to leave with more clarity and emotion than any other event of the same period or since.

    Even those who did not struggle with the decision themselves, but who were led into it, so to speak, by family or circumstance, can recall in detail this crucial moment in their lives. This is true of Sylvia Gonzalez whose sheltered life was turned inside out much before the revolution won control of Cuba.

Sylvia Gonzalez had her fifteenth birthday in the summer of 1958, and was going to be presented to Cuban society. The annual debutante ball was traditionally held at the Havana Yacht Club and attended by what Sylvia calls "party makers, without whom no party is worth its name" and a few uninvited guests. That summer Fidel was planning his final offensive against Batista, and Camilo Cienfuegos was about to start a second front in Las Villas, 200 miles from Havana. Without warning Fidel's urban guerrillas launched a terrorist offensive against the upper class. Its first target was the Havana Yacht Club, where Sylvia sat, demurely waiting her turn to be called up on the stage to hear her virtues told to the audience.

Sylvia Gonzalez: I was sitting on the stage toward the back and at the end of a row of chairs. There was only a curtain as a back wall. I felt a hand on my right calf and then a hand on my mouth. Then everything began to happen at once. Machine guns. My father had armed men all around, and so did my uncle, but the group of twelve *Fidelistas* took over the place. I was their hostage.

I was so remarkably stupid then that I don't know what I thought was going on. Let me tell you the truth. One part of me said that this was all wrong. There was my father almost having a heart attack and my mother fainted. That couldn't be right. But the *Fidelistas* had a great appeal for me. They had a sense of justice, and that couldn't be wrong. Do you see the problem? In those days I also had a wild imagination. I went to a French Catholic school, where crossing one's legs was considered masturbation. And I had never smelled a man before as I smelled the guy [Pablo] who held me throughout the ordeal. I am telling you the truth; I didn't know what to think.

She looked around her terrace where we were sitting and spotted a servant walking toward us with a tray. She remained silent until the servant was outside listening range.

Sylvia Gonzalez: The *Fidelistas* took me away with them. We went by car from the Yacht Club to Marianao, where there was a safe house for the 26th of July Movement. Now they tell me that house is a day care center. I could not bear to see it again. They held me there until the day of liberation—January 1 [1959]. For much of that time, I was with the *Fidelistas* . . . willingly. I have never said that before.

She looked at me struggling to read my reaction to her statement. Pleased, but uncertain by what she found, she continued.

Sylvia Gonzalez: Let me see if I can explain something to you. At the time of the Yacht Club incident there was a person inside me who is now outside, and there was an outside person who is now inside. I had to behave like a nun-to-be in order to please the world around me and survive. The inside person saw the games the boys played and wanted to play with them. But the outside person had to be a source of pride to parents, family, and teachers.

When the *Fidelistas* came, this ambivalence ended. They held me in Marianao. I was brainwashed with their powerful ideology. I read and heard Fidel's speeches, and I read bad translations of American newspaper accounts of Batista's atrocities. My father's name was circled in red ink. They told me the red ink was actually the blood which dripped from his hands. I was hysterical for days. I remember going to sleep sobbing and waking up in a mantle of tears. Finally the *Fidelistas* placed me inside a closet, alone with my thoughts for many days. My imagination did the rest.

She got up from her chair and motioned me to follow. We walked to the end of a pier which extended from her house to the waters of Biscayne Bay and leaned against a large white cabin cruiser tied to the pier.

Sylvia Gonzalez: Ideology and life are one and the same. We must live for the collective "us," and we cannot do it without an ideology. The French Catholic ethic had room for the *Fidelistas*. I decided to live and accepted the ideology in the same act. I did radio work in the final days of my confinement.

On Liberation Day, Pablo took me aside and said I should return home, pretend I had been held captive unwillingly, and face my family. I thought it would be a good idea. Behaving like a *Fidelista* would surely cause . . . well, it just could not be done. We made up a story, which I told my aunt on the phone and which I have told everyone since. Now there is no reason to hide the truth.

I am here today in the United States because I need to be free. I don't like controls. But my heart is still in Cuba with the men and women, the children, the old people, *el relajo* [the fun and games]. I am a *señora* [a married woman] now and have been for a long time. It is a form of slavery, but you are most of the time in control of the master. [She smiles conspiratorially.]

Shortly after the *Fidelistas* took over, my family left for our house in Key Biscayne. I stayed behind with my grandfather, who would not go because he was too sick. My older brother—a *Fidelista* like me—stayed too. We tried to be part of the change, but there was no room for us. Pablo [her kidnapper] became a member of Camilo Cienfuegos' staff. Then he died in an accident similar to the one which took Camilo's life. Pablo was the oracle of my personal conversion to Fidel. To everyone else I was a society *señorita* who wanted to play at being a revolutionary. For Pablo I was a capable woman and a committed friend.

With the death of Pablo, my world became very small. Everyone I had grown up with had left. Finally it hit me. I was in the house that used to belong to Mr. Du Pont up on the point [the northernmost point of the island of Cuba]. The place was worth about a million dollars. He had abandoned it intact, and it was now the property of the people. I had walked through this place when the Du Ponts were there. I remembered the servants and the famous daiquiris, which were served by a bartender hired expressly to make them. I remembered the Du Pont family, with their epicurean French phonology, which I could imitate so well. Then I looked around me and saw about two dozen young people from a school, in bathing suits, running around and jumping into the swimming pool where there had seldom been a ripple before. I thought of the days when the Du Ponts had been there. I fit better in that past.

At that moment I decided I did not belong to the revolution. I had belonged to Pablo and his vision of the revolution, but I would never keep to the ideology all by myself. There was nothing left there, so I came here to Key Biscayne. I often sit here, looking south at the ocean and trying to feel what lies beyond the horizon: that thriving, convulsing, rejuvenating mass of 10 million people now, down and over a bit, on my precious island, green like a crocodile. I stand here and, if I don't feel anything, I cry.

Crashing Upon the Shores of Liberty

A sociologist studying Cuba in the early twentieth century once observed that society there was bipolar: one half white, refined, and sweet like sugar, and the other half dark, raw, and pungent like cigars. He called the polarity "the Cuban counterpoint." This is how he described the counterpoint: "Tobacco is dark," he said, "ranging from black to mulatto; sugar is light ranging from mulatto to white. Tobacco does not change its color; it is born dark and dies the color of its race. Sugar changes its coloring; it is born brown and whitens itself; at first it is a syrupy mulatto and in this state pleases the common taste; then it is bleached and refined until it can pass for white, travel all over the world, reach all mouths, and bring a better price, climbing to the top of the social ladder."

Those Cubans who arrived in the First Wave were definitely from the "white, refined" half. That was fortunate, because when they landed in the United States, the people they met were similar to themselves. It was a marriage of sugar and sugar. The few social problems associated with the early Cuban arrivals were overcome by an overwhelming American outpouring of affection and support for the brave refugees. The United States, a country forged by countless migrations, understood and extended an open hand, an act the Cuban-Americans remember fondly and struggle to pay back.

ive in this mutual acceptance and welcome,
ɔsence of value conflict, and the similarities in
:kground between the refugees and their hosts
issive encounter of Cubans and North Ameri-
successful immigration. There was plenty of
ɪ̴ɔɔɪɪɪ ɪ̴ɔ̴ ̴̴̴ s in Miami. In fact tourism was so poor during
the years of the First Wave that many hotels were only too
pleased to offer the new arrivals rooms at $4 to $9 a night until
they could find other quarters.

It was very difficult for a Cuban to find a job that paid well
in Miami in the early 1960s, and many members of the First
Wave were forced to start their own businesses. A former lawyer who had saved a few dollars bought a bankrupt restaurant
on Second Avenue. It was the best he could do—low capital
investment, a good location, a good business for his large family. He put the whole family to work.

The previous [Chinese] owners had called it Restaurant
Hunan, but the sign that said "Restaurant" was out of order
and needed to be replaced. It cost $81 to buy a new, gleaming
red "Restaurant" sign and $20 to buy an artistic, green "Café"
sign, so Restaurant Hunan became Café Hunan. Café Hunan
watched the continuing migration of Cubans into the United
States and showed them a human face.

Martha Losada was nineteen years old when she arrived in Miami
in 1962. She is a writer and reporter who has travelled the world in
free lance assignments for nearly all national magazines. I asked her
to remember back to her first day in Miami as a Cuban refugee, and
she told me her story as only a gifted observer and reporter can. Ig-
noring the twenty years that dim memories she volunteered clear details which made me feel as if I was there beside her, at the Teresa
Hotel, on the first day of her new life.

Martha Losada: I remember sitting at the counter of the Café
Hunan on Second Avenue in Miami. We had walked there
from the Hotel Teresa, five blocks back, where we had spent
our first night in exile. What a night! I tossed and turned
between the barely white sheets of the "Family Hotel" that
a Cuban had bought with the dollars he had taken out,
when such things could still be done. What foresight!

The price is right [$8 a night], and those who can pay the price are fortunate. When you have just arrived, $8 is just that. Later on it will be a whole week's grocery bill.

Flagler Street seems like the vital artery of downtown Miami. Kress, Woolworth, Burdine's, Baker's, Walgreen, and the White Castles line up on both sides of the straight and narrow street, which this April morning is covered with brilliant sunshine and heat. We walk down the street to the smells we first encountered as tourists years ago. Hamburgers, popcorn, hot dogs, air conditioning, the persistent smell of chemical disinfectants, which from now on will always be part of our lives. But there is something different which did not greet us when we were here before. What is it? The perception arrives first as a sound, then as movement, and finally as a concrete event. I hear the voice of a man, rough and loud, saying to a waiter, *"Oye, vate, ponme un coffee ahí!"* [Hey, Brother, get me a coffee!]

I smile in recognition of the familiar dialect, the smell of his cigar, and the thick, well-trimmed mustache. About the neatly pressed *guayabera* [a traditional shirt] that covers his torso, he says, "I packed it along with the three changes of clothes they let me take." A few steps beyond I am shocked to encounter a typically Cuban store and then another and another. A Cuban couple is walking down the street—she in a skirt one size too small, he with an air of feigned disdain for the shopping trip. Burdine's is nothing like El Encanto, but it will do. I buy a package of gum and begin to chew it. I hate gum, but I chew it thinking that the rhythmic movement of my jaws might help me Americanize faster.

A short distance from the street Martha Losada describes, on Biscayne Boulevard, were the newly opened offices of the Cuban Refugee Emergency Center, funded by the Cuban Refugee Emergency Act, and quickly dubbed by the American press as the Tower of Liberty. This organization was opened after the U.S. government took over the task of settling the refugees from the churches and other institutional groups. She begins to talk about the center.

Martha Losada: I remember the incessant murmur of the crowd. Cubans just arrived, like me, are lined up three deep, waiting to be checked in. Nearby an enterprising Cuban has established a coffee shop on wheels, selling Cuban coffee, *pastelitos de carne* [meat pastries], and *papas rellenas* [stuffed potatoes]. My first impulse is to leave, but the task at hand is both necessary and urgent. A refugee must seek refuge, and this is where it is done. The bureaucratic umbilical cord must be attached if one is to survive: the check for $60 for each single person and $100 per family, immutable sums known as the "60/100"; the card that identifies you as a "parolee" [on your word]; the address of a family that has volunteered to sponsor you.

I take my place at the end of the long line in the April sun. The line moves slowly toward a Cuban dressed in a white shirt and red trousers. He wears proudly the insignia of officialdom—a button with the legend, "Cuban Refugee Emergency Center Staff." I'll always remember his look of disdain. The people in the line are a microcosm of Cuban society. A poet composes a rhyme which I have forgotten, but one line I still remember: *"Ayer te vi en el Refugio hablando mal de Fidel."* [Yesterday I saw you at the Refugee Center saying bad things about Fidel.] I intercept quiet, nervous looks. "He worked with the government," says one man as he points an accusing finger at another in the crowd. An argument ensues and is ended by a tall man in a panama hat, who says, *"Cuba es muy chiquita mi negro. Cuidado que aquí el que mas o el que menos tiene tejao de vidrio."* [Cuba is very small, my friend. Be careful. Everyone here lives in a house with a glass roof.]

The murmur returns as the shouting stops. I remember that I am hungry but also broke. I am very uncomfortable. I think everyone around me is too. Who didn't collaborate with Fidel? Who didn't march on the street or go to a meeting or work for the government? I am bothered by the thought of possibly being accused in public by people who got here two months before me, who now have the authority to label me, to put me on a list or to circulate a rumor. My paranoia knows no bounds. Standing near the line is a group of men with oddly familiar faces. One in particular seems familiar. He leans casually against the wall, his hat resting on the back of his head. I know him, but from where? An older man behind me sees my anxiety and clears my doubt, *"Chivatos, mi hijita,"* [Spies, my daughter.] "It doesn't matter whether they work for Fidel, Batista, or Kennedy. Watch out." I remember where I have seen their faces. It was in a newspaper, or perhaps *Bohemia* magazine, in January of 1959. It showed the faces of some of Batista's secret police, wanted in Cuba. Now one of them is leaning against a wall in Miami, making me sweat more than the afternoon sun. Another of them looks at me intently for a few moments and moves along to study someone else. I want to run away from the heat, the noise, the children pulling and crying, the smell of cigars that have gone out, the sound of English, which no one understands, over the loudspeaker. I am now inside and I find a chair in which to collapse.

The numbers are called in English over the loudspeaker by a polite lady, and yelled out in Spanish by every bilingual person in the crowd. They call my number, and I see a thumb pointing to a desk, which I approach in anticipation. I am now in another line, waiting for the polio vaccine, the interview card, the chest X rays. From room to room I wander in a daze. Someone stops me and asks, "Have you been given your Red Cross kit yet?" I shake my head and am handed a paper bag with a red cross painted on the outside. Inside are a razor, two blades, two Band-Aids, and a bottle of aspirins. I get a card that entitles me to free lunch and dinner at a local restaurant for seven days.

Behind me a man whispers suggestively, "Did they check you out yet, pretty one?" I move to the other side of the room. At the end of the adventure I am, officially, here. I have a parolee card, an application for permanent status, a food card, $60, and the Red Cross package. I am a new American immigrant. I sit on the bench in the air-conditioned building, pondering my fate. I say out loud, *"Gracias, Fidel!"*

Shortly after the U.S. took over the task of caring for the refugees, both U.S. policy, and the city fathers of Miami, who hosted the First Wave, began to put pressure on the group to move to other parts of the country—to New York, perhaps, or

Boston or Philadelphia—anywhere but Miami. The message was clear: the Cubans were less welcome in Miami than in other cities. For a while no business licenses were issued north of 8th Street "to people who did not speak English" and maybe that is why Little Havana developed just south and west of there.

A new federal program pushed relocation by providing funds to move people to the Northeast. First 30,000 refugees were moved, then 100,000. But the worsening economic conditions in the Northeast brought half of them back to Miami within a year. Miami was a magnet for other reasons. It was the symbol for any hope of returning to Cuba, and the hope of returning to Cuba was all many exiles of the First Wave had.

Sergio Espinosa was a child of great intellectual and artistic promise. He could read and write at the age of three. He spoke Latin at four, and when he was eight he gave a piano recital at the Teatro José Martí in Havana. He also wanted to be a soldier.

Sergio Espinosa: Fidel and my father were enemies—personal enemies from the time when Fidel was at the university with my father. I was sent to the United States, and a month later my father was taken prisoner in Cuba and shot, without a trial, because he had said publicly that Fidel was engaging in Stalinist-type purges. My father was a man who would give his life for his country and Fidel knew it, so he killed him.

My mother came to the United States in January [1960]. We were relocated to New York, where we lived in the lower west side of Manhattan, in the garment district. Everything there was grey or black or rusted. There were newspapers all over the floor of the first apartment we found and a smell like no other smell I know of. We tore away the newspaper and found carcasses of dead rats underneath and hundreds of insects of every type and description. My mother screamed every time we turned over another wad of newspapers and found what was buried underneath. Being in New York we qualified for a $180 check from Welfare. The rent was $65 a month. The first day we bought an electric heater, but we had no electricity.

We spent all night in darkness. It was very cold. The apartment was alive with roaches and rats. We huddled together in a cot. The next day I went downtown to have the electricity turned on. That first subway trip—what an experience! I didn't know about the rush hour and went early in the morning. There were a thousand people rushing into the car at once. I missed my exit and wound up in Brooklyn. When I got back, it was late and my mother had been crying.

I enrolled in a public high school and flunked the first term. My mother cried in desperation. I couldn't understand it either. The high school was full of drugs and petty crime. The teachers didn't know how to teach; the material they presented was too easy. Nonetheless, I couldn't compete with the other kids who knew English and had been there longer. It was sink or swim, and I sank. I couldn't understand what was happening to me.

I left school after one year and went to work at a shoe factory. We were very poor, and I couldn't see what good it would do to continue to fail in school. My mother lowered her expectations for me; I could see it happening. I said to myself that this was what was meant by growing up—learning that your dreams of childhood are just dreams and that you are no longer a child. I lied about my age to get a better job, then I lied about having a diploma. I met a lovely girl at the factory where I worked. We fell in love and got married in 1964. I was seventeen.

Neither Sergio nor his mother could understand the full impact of the change that had taken place in their lives. The transplantation of their truncated family, from a safe and congruent cultural environment to a dependency upon the state in the hostile environment of the urban poor in New York, was much more than they could take. Cut off from the support of family and friends who had been able to stay in Miami, they found themselves adrift in the belly of the New York melting pot.

Sergio Espinosa: Manhattan is a terrible place, you know, though it is probably a good place for some people. As far as I am concerned, I can rest in peace if I never see New York again. And you know, I am a product of New York. I can see it in many things I do now. Manhattan is a rock. I mean the whole island is one big rock sitting in the middle of the Hudson River, with thousands of man-made rocks on top of it, the Empire State rock, the Chrysler Building rock. You know what I mean? It is a hard place, New York. Like me.

I spent five years with *mamá* in New York before we moved back to Miami. She aged a great deal during those five years. She was very disappointed and bitter. She found refuge in religion, but the distance between her and me kept on widening. That year in Manhattan was a nightmare for all of us. I still had not felt the full impact of my father's loss. I thought, in the back of my mind, that my father was still alive, that he had a plan and was in hiding in Cuba, carrying it out. I spent all of the first year having nightmares about returning secretly to Cuba to rescue my father. My father was still alive, I kept on telling myself. With my mother I had to pretend he was dead. I thought that was how my father would have wanted it.

I hadn't told my mother that I had left school and was working full time. But one day she heard about it and cried all night. I remember that night very well. I was laying in my bed in the living room and she was in her bedroom, sobbing uncontrollably. I was crying too. I went to the kitchen and got a knife and cut my veins. [He pulls back his long-sleeved shirt and shows me the healed cuts in his forearms and wrists. Slowly he rolls back his sleeves and buttons them up.]

I was delirious for a long time. Then I saw my father inside my room. He talked about my life in the future and he told me I was going to live. They discovered me and took me to the hospital. My mother couldn't cope with it. She forced me to take psychiatric tests. I was almost committed to a mental hospital, but my uncle [her brother] stepped in and brought us to Miami to live with his family.

My mother died a few years ago, after a long and painful illness. She was not very strong, and she suffered a great deal in her life. With her savings of $5,000, I eventually bought a shoe factory. I cannot understand how she saved the money. Things are going very well for us economically now, and we follow the advice she always gave me. She said, "Sergio, *aprende a hacer una cosa mejor que cualquier otro y tendrás abundancia.*" ["Learn to do one thing better than anyone else and you will have abundance."] And here it is [he holds up his feet to show me a pair of cowboy boots], the best boot in Miami.

It was a good American idea which had never worked. To take the refugees and disperse them around the country in order to avoid the political flak that comes from "Port-of-Entry" communities after a massive immigration of people seeking refuge. The policy simply called for resettlement of the new arrivals wherever sponsors could be found. There was no cultural perspective which was cognizant of the serious detrimental effects brought about by the separation from family and other supportive environments. The official aim was to ease the burden in Miami, and spread the refugees around.

Jesús María Laserie was an expert in the gambling business. He wanted to be resettled in Las Vegas. Instead he was sent [with his family of six] to Queens, New York, where the Immigration service had found a sponsor.

Jesús María Laserie: Without any doubt, the worst thing that can happen is to find yourself in a strange place with no money and seven mouths to feed. You do not know where to go or to whom to turn. I spoke the language; that was not my problem. My problem was how to get myself and my family from New York to Las Vegas on $30, which is all I had when I finished paying the taxi that brought us from the airport to the home of an Irish family that had agreed to help us out.

The family that greeted us was really fine. They are still our closest friends. There were ten people in this family, and we were seven. They still have the same big house in Queens. I told the kids to stay out of the house as much as possible so that it would not be too crowded inside. I found a job the day after I arrived, packing grocery bags at the A&P Supermarket. At the end of the first week I spent all but $10 of my paycheck in groceries. I could see that it was going to take me a while to save enough money to rent a place. Winter was coming and we had no warm clothes.

I looked for more work. There was a fellow at the supermarket who took bets on horses—numbers, you know. He offered to put me in touch with the man who ran the numbers, the "bank," so that I could make a little more on the side. It was illegal but it was only gaming, not drugs or anything like that. I mean I had to survive somehow.

After a few weeks I was taking $500–$750 a week in bets. I got a 20 percent commission, so I was doing pretty well. A man who doesn't have $5 to his name puts 50¢ on a number in the hope of making $300 by nightfall. For the day he walks tall. It's as if he's already gotten his number. Just thinking about the bet helps things go easier.

We found a house near our friends, and the children began school in the fall. We had money for clothes and other essentials. The day before Thanksgiving I placed a bet myself, on number 787, and it came in. I will never forget it for as long as I live. I won $3,000 and spent some of it on a trip to Las Vegas. I ended up in Reno. There I looked up a friend, an American who used to work in the Sans Souci in Havana. He was a pit boss at a top spot in Reno. He offered to put me to work that same day.

Eventually we all moved to Reno. It was the middle of the winter, and in New York we were all freezing our butts. It was warmer in Reno, so everyone was happy. First I worked the tables, then security, and then the front office. I had twenty years' experience with gaming and tourists. The company made use of that but still paid me like a dealer. One day I went to see my boss to ask for more money. He said that if I wanted to make more I could help him with his other business, which was importing. I told him yes. He doubled my salary.

I was sent to Miami and discovered what we were importing—illegal gambling equipment, contraband liquor and cigars, and anything you like. Whatever had to have duty paid or could not be brought in legally we brought in illegally or duty-free. There were payoffs, sometimes, to high government officials. I was in charge of security, which included making the payoffs. I know every crooked cop and customs official in south Florida and their price.

I turned state's evidence last year. I found out they were importing drugs—heroin, cocaine, marijuana. I had never had anything to do with drugs, so I went to the police. It was not a very smart thing to do, but I just had to do it. I could not help some young kid get hooked, but I could not get out either, so I had to go to the police. The guys have not gone to court yet. They say that if they go to jail I am a dead man.

You don't decide one day that you are going to be a criminal. I think you just try to survive the best way you know how. Morality is not so clear-cut when your survival is threatened. What's the morality of taking a person's hard-earned property away, like they did to us in Cuba? What moral code can justify that? No moral code. None. The state didn't need my house or my car in order to survive. My family and I came here looking for another way of life. I end up as a criminal in order to have my family survive. Were there better ways for me to do it? I don't know.

In Havana a big part of my job at Sans Souci was to catch the cheaters—card counters, team players, and others—who came from the United States primarily to play no-limit blackjack. They can break the house in one sitting. But I could spot them a mile off, and as soon as they began to set up the house I would ask them to leave. I thought life was like that. If you got caught you had to leave, but meanwhile you could play the best odds you had. I don't want to sound as if all I have is excuses about this thing I did, in which I got caught. It was wrong to do that—to bring drugs in for the children in the streets of Miami and New York. There's no way of justifying it. That's why I spoke to the FBI about it, the whole importation business, run from Reno and Vegas.

Gaming is not a clean environment. It is not like a doctor's office or another office. You deal with all kinds of people in the gaming business, and the circumstances in which you often find yourself are part of the business. People who make easy money like to gamble, and the house sees to it that they lose. It isn't the cleanest of business environments, but it doesn't have to be involved in drugs or sex or anything else; it can just be gaming. As a matter of fact, it is not gaming to me unless it is free of drugs and sex; they have no place in a gaming house. I couldn't be a part of all that was going on. That's why I was forced to go to the FBI.

Jesús María Laserie is a hunted man. He lives on a borrowed identity in a Miami suburb under constant surveillance by the authorities who have guaranteed his safety.

Jesús María Laserie: I had to talk. It was the only way to protect my family from my life of crime. Now I have a job that allows us to survive, but I live in fear of retribution. I have to admit that I feel unsafe no matter where we are. I will always have to lie about our life or run the risk of being discovered. I am very sorry for what happened. I hope God gives us a chance to start a new life. You won't see me around a gaming house again. *Es el ambiente,* [It is the environment,] *ese desgraciado ambiente* [that wretched environment].

Amparito Sanchez vda. de Mensa is typical of the group of Society people from Cuba who came to the United States with most of their assets but no usable skills. She refused every invitation to be interviewed as did all of her peers. She told me her reasons for refusing over the telephone.

Amparito Sanchez vda. de Mensa: I am afraid that my life now is very dull, so I no longer grant interviews. At one time I would grant an interview if it was for a good social cause. That was when I lived in Cuba, where I had something to say about what I thought and did. Now I have nothing to say, because I think and do nothing every day. Now I do not grant interviews. No. Thank you, but no.

In Cuba Amparito Sanchez vda. de Mensa was a rich and genteel matron. Since she would not speak to me about her experiences, I interviewed a friend who knew her well in Cuba. Martha Estrada's portrait of Amparito Sanchez vda. de Mensa may depart from objectivity. It is, however, subjectively faithful as a portrait of the antecedents and American life of one member of the First Wave.

Martha Estrada: Her story is almost typical of the people of the *Sociedad* in Cuba—the pedigreed. Amparito Sanchez vda. de Mensa lived in the Vedado section of Havana, in a gorgeous mansion with enough servants so as not to feel the loneliness of widowhood. Every afternoon she and her friends—I was one of them—played poker and canasta, and the betting got quite heavy. Amparito liked to gamble. Sometimes she lost and sometimes she won, but whichever she did, she always did it on purpose. Those were memorable afternoons. The bejeweled fingers of her perfumed hands shuffled the cards as expertly as she served the bridge cakes from *El Carmelo de Calzada* [a fashionable bakery] and poured the Johnny Walker Black Label all of us shared, but which was ostensibly for Father Calvo, who often joined the group. The servants, whom she had "color coordinated" from blonde to black, went back and forth to the kitchen bringing the endless stream of food and beverage.

Amparito's property in Cuba was taken away and with it went her income. Several weeks later she arrived in Miami replete with jewels but more lost than she had ever been. As the months went on, Amparito's jewels began to change ownership. Carolina [Amparito's sister] traded them, so she said, for a few dollars from a buyer no one but Carolina ever saw. Amparito divided her time between her son's and her sister's house, but in neither place was she truly welcome. Her son was having marital problems and her sister was stealing her blind. She could only find solace in her poker playing, which was now a penny ante sort of game that she played with some of her old friends. Her conversation began to take on the characteristics of the typical refugee; that is, she talked about Cuba, food, and cooking. Finally, her jewelry was all gone, and she was forced to take a room in a hotel for senior citizens in Miami Beach. No one wanted her except her old friend Clara, who had lived a similar life. Together they now share the $98 a month rent for one room.

Several months ago I was walking down Collins Avenue when I saw her familiar face, her hair now white, her weight over 200 pounds. She was quite animated, talking with her friends and playing poker. Her poker playing is her last source of happiness. And she was very positive. "I am just fine, my dear. I go and visit my jewelry at the pawn shop once in a while," she said with a twinkle in her eye. "Who knows, maybe someday I will make enough in this game to buy some of it back." As I was leaving she pulled me aside to tell me of her latest technique for "staying alive while eating less." "Every fifteenth of the month they have a special on Coca-Cola at the market. I buy them and day-old doughnuts. A few of those and you are filled *hasta el topete* [up to there]. That's all you need." Amparito is a victim but she is also a survivor. There are many like her. They are victims of their own inability to adapt, but they survive just as they are.

Cuca Plata is a handsome woman with glistening white hair neatly arranged in two *trensas* [braids] on the top of her head. Her hands are soft, her fingernails well manicured. She is in her son's house in Tampa, visiting from her home in Boston. I joke that she may be turning into a Yankee from living too long in New England. She laughs at the idea, and before she sets out to disprove it, she lights a thin, crooked cigar which smells like jasmine and rum.

Cuca Plata: Look, my son, I am *cubana*. I am an American citizen, but I am *cubana*. Do you know, I almost didn't get to be an American citizen? You want to hear this?

I went to the judge, and I had learned all the questions. He asked me the first question: where was the White House? You don't have to believe me if you don't want to, but I couldn't remember where the house was. [She pauses.] I think I've forgotten again. [She turns to her teenaged granddaughter, who is sitting near her.] Where's the house, *Princesita*? Oh, yes, Washington. I always get it mixed up with New York. No, New York is the woman, the Statue of Liberty. Washington is the house. So anyway, son, the judge, very serious, asks another question: Who is the president of the United States? I don't care if you believe me or not. I couldn't remember the name of the man. It was just after an election, you see, and there were several men running for president. For me English names are difficult to remember; I didn't know who won. The judge swore me in anyway, because he said I had done a good job in raising my children. I have nineteen children, thirty grandchildren, and three great-grandchildren. What do you think of that? [Laughter.]

Cuca Plata is ninety-four years old and in full possession of her senses. She was born in Cuba in 1886, the third daughter of Bonifacio Plata, general of the Imperial Spanish Army. As a consequence of Cuba's liberation from Spain in 1905, at the age of twelve she left Cuba with her seven sisters and two brothers, her father, her mother, two aunts, and her grandmother to live in political exile in La Coruña, Spain. She lived there for ten years. In Spain she met and married Julian Porras Trujillo, a young Cuban lieutenant of the Rural Guard attached to the Cuban diplomatic delegation. They returned to Cuba in 1932. I asked her why.

Cuca Plata: The Spanish Civil War and the Depression all rolled into one. Julian said, "Let's go to Cuba," and I followed. I followed my husband wherever he went. Maybe that is why I had nineteen children [she smiles suggestively].

Her husband had died the year before, and her sons had already left for the United States. In 1961 she was forced out of Cuba for the second time. All of Cuca Plata's efforts went toward keeping the family together in exile.

Cuca Plata: I am *cubana*. Sometimes I think of dusk in the field in back of the house in Cuba, and I want to cry. We lived in a small valley between the hills planted with coffee. I can see it as if I were there now. *Yo soy de allá.* [I am from there.] But my only regret is that I came here too old to enjoy this place. This place is for young people. Old people just sit around and get moldy, like cheese. They stink too. I am not talking about myself. I am very fortunate. I have my *Princesita* [she hugs her granddaughter] and my daughter. Actually, she is not my daughter but my son's wife, but I have never had a daughter like her.

My father used to say [after World War II] that the next war would be fought between communists and capitalists. Then he would point at the pasture where the cows were grazing and say, "Those cows are called capital and we are capitalists; therefore know your enemy." We knew Fidel was communist because of the Russians.

Things did not go very well for us here [immediately after arriving in the United States]. We all came together, you know, early on, except for Mario [Bolaños], my oldest grandson. He stayed behind because he had to finish school. What an intelligent boy he is. We went to Boston because we couldn't find work in Miami. My sons are all hard workers. This son here, where I'm staying, was a rancher in Cuba; *terratenientes, nos decían* [landlords they called us], but for him, here in Miami, there was no job. We lived on the checks from the *Refugio* [the Cuban Refugee Emergency Center] until they stopped paying us. [To her daughter] Tell him the story of the *hijo de marica* [Her own swear word which she says more or less means "bastard."] Forgive me, you look like a decent fellow but you know the word. I want to make sure everybody who reads this book knows what happened.

Esther Bolaños is a delicately beautiful woman in her fifties. While Cuca and I talk she is in the kitchen preparing our lunch. She comes out of the kitchen drying her hands on a towel which hangs from her belt. Her face, clear and without makeup, becomes thoughtful and serious as she sits beside us to tell us the story of their first encounter with American bureaucracy.

Esther Bolaños: We had been in the United States three months, and my husband couldn't find work. We lived in Miami on a $189 monthly check from the *Refugio*. Early one Sunday morning a social worker came over. We all thought it was a cable from Cuba, but it wasn't. He had a form he wanted my husband to sign. I didn't understand very much of it, but it was some sort of authorization to have them check our bank accounts. We had just obtained official custody of an account with $260 in it that my husband's father had started in a Miami bank twenty-five years earlier, just in case. We were saving the money for the fare of my oldest son, Mario, who had remained behind to attend school. We didn't have anything else. We didn't dare touch the money in the bank. All we had was this check from the *Refugio* and the old account. We had been warned not to tell the *Refugio* anything, but we thought we had nothing to hide. The account had been opened in 1935.

At the end of the month, instead of the check, we got a notice from the *Refugio* that our aid was discontinued [Cuca Plata interrupts, saying, *"Hijo de marica"*], and it was a few days before the rent was due. We called everybody we knew. We went to the *Refugio,* we did everything we could, all in vain. At the end of the month we told the landlord we couldn't pay our rent. He told us to get out. We packed everything in a supermarket cart we had "recycled" from the dump, and we moved out. It was raining that day. All eight of us were walking down the street, soaking wet, holes in our shoes, the clothes in the shopping cart growing heavier as they soaked up the rainwater. Finally, we reached a friend's house. We needed to raise $50 to check into the cheapest hotel in Miami. We used the phone to call everyone we knew. Finally a man came to visit our friends. They told him of our plight. He wasn't even a Cuban. He put his hand in his pocket and he loaned us $75. We checked into the motel and paid a month's rent in advance. No extra charge for the cockroaches or for Cheesey, the kitchen mouse.

Cuca Plata: That is the way it was. But God helps those who help themselves. The next day the motel owner offered Carmen a job as a maid. It was only two days a week, but *algo es algo* [anything is something]. We rented a cot for the girl with the extra money.

Esther Bolaños: We solved the problem of shelter, but the problem of food persisted. We had a new refrigerator in the room, which was empty except for the last of the canned meat we had brought with us. It was our only source of protein. We ate it a teaspoon at a time, with beans and cornmeal. I would go to sleep at night thinking of food and

would wake up and begin to plan the meals of the day.
One day, cleaning one of the rooms, I found a salami and
some cheese. We had a banquet that night. My husband
spent the days walking from hotel to restaurant to factory,
looking for a job, he found nothing. He said he ate outside,
but I knew better. He lost twenty pounds that month, but
he would eat only half of what I gave him each night. I
lived in fear of an illness or some other catastrophe on top
of what we were going through. People left cigarette packs
in the rooms, and these were my husband's only luxury.
When we were invited to someone's house for dinner, our
stomachs would only accept a few bites, and we were too
proud to take any of it home. It is easy to accept food when
you don't need it and nearly impossible to accept it when
the hunger you feel turns it into a shameful thing.

I was curious about why they didn't use the $260 in the bank to
buy food. Surely priorities had to be adjusted by the misfortune.

Cuca Plata: I told you, that was for Mario to come here. I didn't
dare touch that, no matter how much hunger there was.
We trusted our *destino* [fate]. Do you know what I mean by
that? You have a fate and I have a fate. It is our fate to be
here together talking like this. But suppose that what is
happening is not good and pleasant, like our talk. Suppose
it's something bad, like living on charity. Is that also your
fate? Of course you don't want to admit it, but that is also
your *destino*. When the War of Independence in Cuba sent
me and my family to Spain in exile, the times were much
worse and then they got better. That was our *destino*. Your
destino is what you can think up and can make happen.

We found work in Boston. My son became a teller at a
bank. Carmen found a job at the insurance company. Mario
came here and *mi Princesita* was born. All of my children
who are still living are here [in the United States] now. At
Nochebuena this year, Carlos Antonio, who works for the
phone company, called everybody on the phone at once.
Soon everybody was talking at the same time and it was a
lot of fun. It makes me cry with happiness that our fate is
good and our life in this beautiful country . . . America
the beautiful . . . [she is stopped by her emotions].

The Entrepreneurs

Much has been written about the success of Cuban-Americans in the free enterprise arena. During the early days of the First Wave, national magazines, the New York *Times,* and the broadcast media featured the stories of Cubans who had been forced out of their homelands, penniless and defeated, and, in just a few years, had risen to positions of power in American industry. This story, widely labeled among the Cubans themselves as "the Cuban success story," was repeated so often by the media that it became a stereotype.

There is a certain American quality in the story of people who go from rags to riches, from adversity to success and the stereotype was helpful to Cubans, who were carried by the positive momentum it helped create.

When the stereotype first began to take shape it was probably not true for most Cubans. All stereotypes are true sometimes; they are just not true in all cases. For most Cubans of the First Wave, life in the United States during the first decade was full of unemployment, underemployment and failure in the business arena. But eventually the strong entrepreneurial class that immigrated made the stereotype more widely applicable.

Claudio Sanchez was fired as manager of the Havana branch of an American bank when it was nationalized by the revolutionary government. He decided to leave Cuba. He found a job in Miami as a shoe salesman, door to door, and he worked at it until he got a job as a night teller for a Miami bank. There he worked his way up to assistant manager in three years, began to take night courses in business, and five years later had the equivalent of an MBA. Today, twelve years later, he is president of that same bank where he began as a teller.

When I talked to him, in the winter of 1980, voters had just approved a referendum repealing a county ordinance which had labeled Dade County as bilingual. Claudio Sanchez backed the idea of bilingualism. He believed it could help reduce language prejudices against Cuban-Americans in Miami. The referendum, he felt, had destroyed his efforts to build a bridge between the Cuban-American community and the rest of Dade County. He was angry at his fellow Americans. "Sour grapes," he said. "Just sour grapes."

Claudio Sanchez: We didn't take Southwest 8th Street by force, you know. We bought it. Some of the people we bought it from are living in Coral Gables or Miami Beach, retired on their profits but unhappy that they didn't make a better deal. People tried to keep us out of the business section of Miami through ordinances and zoning. It's nothing new; it happens to everyone without political pull. It's not racial or anything like that.

But this opposition to bilingualism in Dade County is different. The county ordinance which these "former Americans" around here voted for says [he reads], "The county shall appropriate no funds for activities that promote another language and culture other than the American culture." Whose American culture? You know what will happen? There will be no money for the St. Patrick's Day Parade or the Hanukkah festival or German-American Week. The activities that promote the Spanish language and Hispanic culture are not funded by the county. I pay for some of them when I insist that all bank personnel dealing with Latin Americans be bilingual.

I'm afraid my neighbors are crying sour grapes. We haven't done anything other immigrants haven't done. On the contrary, we have done exactly what the Europeans did at the turn of the century, except that we have done it under more adverse economic conditions.

Claudio Sanchez arrived in the middle of the First Wave. His struggle to regain professional status is very typical of a class of men who exemplify the spirit of free enterprise, a willingness to work beyond what's expected, confidence in the face of risk, and aggressiveness in the face of competition. I asked him about the business climate in Miami around the time of his arrival.

Claudio Sanchez: It was bleak, no question about it. Most of us were too busy trying to get back to Cuba. We didn't see many opportunities.

One man, Nicasio Lopez-Puerta, did the plowing [opened the doors] for all of us. I mean all. He helped not only business people but also institutions, and he was very effective in Washington, speaking for the Cuban cause. He wasn't one of the crazy *Batistianos*, but he hated Fidel and his politics were very conservative. Nonetheless, he lobbied hard for money for bilingual education and the Cuban Refugee Emergency Act. And now with the *Marielitos* [the Third Wave] he has gone all out. People don't know this. He would not tell anybody himself, but people tell me he has pressed them for certain things for the Cuban refugees; he always denies it.

Nicasio is not a very wealthy man. He has a profitable business, but the big money is passed on to the investors. If you want him to manage your money here, you have to wait in line. He is very shrewd, but he is always giving his money away. Go to see him. Tell him I told you that. If you want to get him to talk to you about important things, begin talking about Cuba.

Nicasio Lopez-Puerta likes to be home in Coral Gables on Saturdays, so he can catch the college football games on television. He immigrated to the United States as a little boy in 1933, but as an adult he owned a home in Cuba and returned often. He was a prominent member of the Cuban business community and an able financier, well known as a source of American capital in Cuba. One evening in Havana, in December of 1959, there was an attempt on his life, which nearly succeeded. He left Cuba immediately after and has never gone back. Since then he has devoted his life and most of his free time to helping those who want to leave Cuba.

Nicasio Lopez-Puerta: I nearly died from the bullet wounds. I
was in Havana on a real estate deal. This was before the
Urban Reform Act took everybody's property away. I was
there to invest the capital of my friends. You must think of
people who have given you their life savings to invest as
friends, not clients, or you won't stay in business long. I
took their capital out after the attempt on my life, and I also
took my friends out. We all lost money, but I didn't lose
any of my friends. We took out about $20 million and we
left behind about the same amount. It doesn't sound like
very much now, but in 1959, $20 million could buy you
downtown Miami if you wanted it, which no one did back
then.

   We tried to put the money to work here instead. There
were thousands of Cubans coming every month who
needed work, but the economy couldn't provide for them
and the forecast was bad through 1960. People began to
blame the "refugee problem." The Miami *Herald* showed
us up as a bunch of . . . well, you know, like the extra
relative, the one who has stayed too long and has no place
to go. The *Herald* didn't give us an even break. They blamed
us for the recession. We had to do something.

   A bunch of us got together and went to see President
Eisenhower. We had given money to his campaign, and we
wanted to petition him. We went and told him about the
bad press and asked him to make a statement of support
for the Cuban refugees. At that time, people who came and
had no relatives here—and I am talking about 1959 when
there were only 20,000 Cubans in Miami—didn't have anywhere to stay or work, and most of them had no money.
There was no welfare, except from the county, which was
all for the black people. There was really only private
assistance for the refugees. But we didn't ask President
Eisenhower for money. We went to ask for verbal support.
He was a compassionate man and a great president, and he
declared into law the Emergency Assistance Act, which
Kennedy later formalized into the Cuban Refugee Emergency Act. This was a system within a system. It was a
model program in many ways, because it helped Cubans
get on their feet and do something. *Invéntala* [create it] is
what we do here; we do new things. My uncle always said

that people should do new things in order to prosper. I say also, do old things in new ways. [He looks at me seriously.]

Cubans have done very well here in Miami. I am surprised myself. People have made too much of it though. It is no bed of roses. Things have a way of getting very tight once in a while. People survive the best they can. You are always shooting from behind the end zone. The real story in Miami, and among Cubans everywhere in the United States, is the middle- to lower middle-class guy, trying to raise a family and doing a damn good job of it. But everyone focuses on the big success stories. They are not the real story. They are what everyone thinks should be the real story.

Of all the members of the First Wave, the Cuban-American entrepreneurial class is the most visible. This segment lives to the limit of its reputation. There were at last count 20 bank presidents, 220 bank vice-presidents, and 19,000 businesses run by Cuban-Americans, with combined assets in the billions of dollars. Not all of them are members of the First Wave, but before 1959 only two vice-presidents in all the banks in the United States could claim Cuban ancestry, and they were both in Tampa.

Tampa, Florida, was the first American city to put the Cuban-American talent for enterprise to a test. The American cigar industry was born a dozen blocks from the downtown area, in a small community called Ybor City. Ybor City is really not a city. Two years after its birth a century ago, it was taken over by Tampa. Yet the passing of the years has failed to erase the original flavor given to it by its Cuban founders. There, in October of 1885, workers of the Sanchez y Haya Company rolled the first "Havana" cigar. A year later the factory was producing, by hand, 500,000 cigars a month.

In 1891 José Martí sat in an Ybor City restaurant called Las Novedades and planned Cuba's war of independence from Spain. The restaurant also served as political headquarters for Roosevelt's Rough Riders. Today the heirs of Martí and Roosevelt meet in the same place, now called the Columbia Restaurant. Their strategy is mostly financial and political, but their aims are the same as those of Martí: "the overthrow of the foreign occupation and freedom for the Cuban people."

I am sitting at a corner table in the airy back room of the restaurant. Maximiliano Pons, a fifty-six-year-old businessman who runs a multinational manufacturing firm is playing dominoes with his three friends, Sergio Espinosa, Porfirio Sanchez, and Nicasio Lopez-Puerta. Maxi, (as he is called by the others) is a dark, handsome man with a powerful domino strategy. I ask him about his hopes for Cuba.

Maximiliano Pons: Our aim is to restore a set of values to Cuba, not the least of which is freedom. [He takes his turn at dominoes, manages to block his opponents, and then continues his answer.] Our aim is to bring economic order to the Caribbean, which can only be done with a capitalist Cuba. [He takes another turn and keeps his opponents blocked. They grind their teeth and each taps the table as he gives up another turn. Maxi stabs the air with his cigar.] Then our aim is to show the capitalist world that there can be democracy in Latin America without starving people or shooting the opposition. As you can see, I have neutralized these three very able domino players for two whole moves without shooting them, through sheer superior ability. What do you say, fellows? [He places his last domino and ends the game. The group dissolves into loud protests. Maximiliano Pons moves along to the bar, and I follow him.]

I came to the United States in 1960. After Fidel nationalized the American company I was working for, I decided to leave. My family left with me. The company's U.S. base offered me a job in New Orleans. I took it, and after a short while I was moved to Caracas. I have never worked for anyone else in my life except when I worked for my father. I went to work for the company right after school and moved along from job to job as I saw things that needed to be done and other people showed confidence in me.

Being a successful businessman and moving up the corporate ladder are one and the same thing. You accept responsibility and devote yourself to it entirely. You take risks and challenge the assumptions. You must be honest with yourself about your own abilities. And you should not be open. You must be essentially closed to outside scrutiny, including the people who compete against you inside your own company. Generally, I follow the axiom, "Never complain, never explain," and it works for me. I've noticed some of my Cuban colleagues follow the same rules.

He paused to acknowledge the greetings from several patrons of the establishment and to relight his cigar, a handmade product of a Tampa factory of which he was a part owner. I used the pause to ask him about the "Cuban rules" he talked about.

Maximiliano Pons: The rules are actually not Cuban but came to Cuba from Spain, from the Catalan traders who were my ancestors. My father was a Catalan from Barcelona. He owned a trading business in Barcelona that had been his father's. He left Spain during the Civil War and landed in Cuba very nearly a poor man. In Cuba he would buy empty sugar sacks, trade them for finished rope, and sell the rope to shipbuilders. With the profits he would buy a shipload of oranges from Málaga, Spain, trade it for steel in Pittsburgh, and import the steel into Cuba for use in the railroad.

I worked for him after school in the afternoons and during the summers. By the time I was born, he had a lot of money but we had to work for our allowances and save for vacations, which often consisted of trips to Florida. I worked for him as a counter. I literally counted the items he bought, sold, or traded. This was a great honor for me. The relationship between trader and counter is recognized in Catalan history as a privileged relationship. But he was not a father in Cuban or even Spanish terms. The Catalan way calls for the son to suffer at the hand of the father, so that the son grows stronger than the father.

I finally broke with my father when I went to college. I elected to go to Yale and not to Salamanca, where my father wanted me to go. I wanted to be an American very badly. I became an American aspirant. The United States had just emerged victorious from World War II. I was away at Yale then. Four years later I returned to Cuba, went to work for a leading American company, bought a house in the Marianao suburbs—the whole thing.

Fidel turned me back into a Cuban. I resented being driven from my homeland. I hated the exile's feeling of rootlessness. I could see that in my father and I do not want it for me. Returning to Cuba is my goal and regaining my Cuban background was the product of my exile.

The other players join us at the bar and Maximiliano Pons changes the subject immediately. The conversation turns to business.

Sergio Espinosa: Being in the shoe business is a very difficult thing today. Imports have always been a chief factor in the shoe business. I didn't know a thing about shoes when I first went to work at a shoe factory. I liked the work. Some people think this is crazy, but I'm in the shoe business because I like the work—the buying and trimming of the leather, the style changes, even the sales aspects. I love going to rodeos all over the Southeast and giving boots away on promotionals to sell more boots. To remain alive in the shoe business, you have to specialize, like I do. I make cowboy boots and snow boots for another label. But when you specialize like that, things can go wrong overnight. You may lose 50 to 60 percent of your market if one retailer switches to Corfam or some other gimmick. When the kids decided they wanted high heels, I sold twice as many boots in a year. Then not one single high-heeled boot could be sold, given away, or turned into a funny-looking baseball mitt. I tell you, my business went out the door.

Perhaps it is typical of the entrepreneurial class in the United States, or perhaps it is just typical of the Cuban entrepreneurs I have met, but one observable characteristic of their entrepreneurship is that it is attributed by them to a need to succeed for the benefit of others, rather than for personal or financial gain.

Sergio Espinosa: We run a family operation. If I lay off 10 people of the 150 who work for me, chances are I'm laying off a relative, who may also own some stock. Layoffs can hurt a bunch of friends. So there's a great deal of pressure on me to keep the ship steady and on course.

I have four sons now, and one of them is ready for college this year. He was turned down by several universities he wants to go to. He is very disappointed. But he has me as an example, since I didn't go to a university and still managed to do well. I think he may come into the business full time. He is no problem—works hard, no drugs, and very conservative. He has a girl who wants to get married. I wish he would play the field a little bit more. I married too soon and never had an opportunity to enjoy being young. I want him to experience his youth. I got a good deal on a Ferrari, and I gave it to him for his eighteenth birthday, but I'm afraid he is more the Chevrolet type.

The laughter dissolves and Sergio says he is very worried about Miami's recent turn to violence. When I interviewed him earlier and he told me about his attempted suicide in New York, he said the daily violence he saw on the streets of his ghetto home impressed him greatly. He seems to be reliving some of that in Miami.

Sergio Espinosa: Since the riots [in Liberty City] and Mariel, Miami has become a very hostile place. It was kind of lawless before, too. I remember hearing of problems between the blacks and the whites. Of course there was Civil Rights violence in 1968 and problems during the 1974–75 recession. But this year, I had to close for several weeks because my factory was on the other side of town, across from Liberty City, which is where the trouble started.

The police department is in shambles, and criminals in Miami know it. The only way to go anywhere around there is with a gun. It is difficult to raise children in that place. I suppose things are bad all over. I remember the high school I went to in Manhattan—Charles Evans Hughes—on 18th Street. It had tall bars on the windows and armed guards and the feel of a prison. I hope my children are able to face the problems that will be theirs in the future: keeping the business alive and providing security for themselves and their families. It is not going to be easy in the future. It isn't easy now.

Porfirio Sanchez is sixty-four years old. He is a real estate developer in Miami and Maximiliano Pons' father-in-law. I ask him about the business climate in Miami.

Porfirio Sanchez: Some markets are better than others, and the American market is the biggest in the world for nearly everything. You can sell anything for which a market exists; all you have to do is introduce a new twist. You make it cost less or look better, deliver it to the door, or sell it on time. But you need something for which a market exists and then you make it better. Only people with large capital can create new markets, especially national markets, but once established, they are like cash cows, if you know how to milk them.

In that sense I learned everything from Nicasio [points to him]. He and I were partners in Cuba. He owned the building in which my warehouse was located. I owned the land. We were in agricultural products, primarily pesticides and herbicides. I waited too long to leave the country. I wouldn't let Nicasio sell, and he couldn't do it without me. I thought I had no place to go. I was a man of forty-five who knew no English, only hard work. What would life be like in the United States? At least in Cuba I knew I could always survive. My family could survive. I told myself it couldn't get much worse than it was in 1960—food shortages, repression, and *paredón* [firing squads]. But it did get worse. We lost everything.

Nicasio called and said to come to the United States. He told me I had to make some money and pay him back for all the money we lost due to my thick head. Our first venture in the United States was a shopping center. I think we opened the first in-town shopping center. Now they are all over Miami, and I have seen them in other states. But before then you only had two choices: go downtown without your car or look for a parking space for two hours. We had a parking lot and the "under-one-roof" publicity, and it worked out very well. I was the contractor and builder, Nicasio the mortgage broker and manager.

We didn't do anything right the first time. I couldn't control cost. I was being cheated right and left and Nicasio aged ten years. We almost said, "The hell with it, let's go bankrupt." It was the middle of the recession of 1960 and no one, least of all retailers, was putting up money. We had no renters, no income, and no capital. Nicasio had the idea of opening up our own stores on the vacant property.

The idea worked, and we did good business despite the recession. We sold and built other shopping centers. We are doing other things now, but the idea is still the same. Find a market and improve on the competition. It is the healthiest of free enterprises, because the one who benefits is the consumer. The important thing is to keep on moving, improving your products, entering new markets, acquiring new assets which produce new growth. You cannot stop centrifugal force. If you try, everything comes crashing down. "No growth" is idiocy. There is nothing but growth, nothing but expansion, ever since the Big Bang. You grow, you die, and someone else is born. You just have to keep on going.

Nicasio Lopez-Puerta seems disturbed by what Porfirio Sanchez has said.

Nicasio Lopez-Puerta: I don't really share the Cuban's existential view of the world. I mean there are many Cubans and many views, but the essential Cuban philosophy of life and work is what I don't share. In this respect I exclude myself as a Cuban. Life to them is built around more—more cars, more houses, more of everything. Even spirituality. Nothing is enough. There are Cubans who spend $50,000 a year on their religion alone—gold statues, First Communion, and baptismal parties—it doesn't matter whether it's pagan or Christian. This excess is good, according to the Cuban philosophy. I think it is a result of being exiled; they're afraid it isn't going to last.

I came here at the age of eight. My father was a businessman but not a megalomaniac, you know, wanting to be into everything. I went to Coral Gables High School one year. They kicked me out because of behavior problems, so I was sent to military school and there met other Cubans and found them very much like me. But now that I am older I can see the differences, so I can tell you what I see in the Cubans, because I don't speak about myself. You know, in the movie *Love Story* there's a famous line: "Love means never having to say you are sorry." Well I say: "Being (a) Cuban means never having to say you are beat." Let me illustrate that for you.

Back in 1973 something happened here. If it had happened any place else it would have spelled disaster. The economy had taken off after 1961 and made a small dip in 1968. We [the Cuban-American business community] did well during the dip. We thought it was working to our benefit, and we bet all we had. We could see the trade potential, and we were afraid someone else would come in and buy it out from under us.

In a sense, racial discrimination helped, because there were no outside bets on Cuban-run Miami businesses. Discrimination helped us, in other words, to keep the investment to ourselves. But we could borrow money, because by 1964 we had some pretty good balance sheets among solid businesses. And then when 1968 came and we didn't do too badly, we thought we would take off. We opened banks and went into manufacturing and consumer goods in the Caribbean market as well. Someone could open a bank, and buy the stock with a loan from another bank, guaranteed on real estate bought with the promise of new income. We had control of real estate and owned the bank. We were meeting the notes and growing like mad.

Then came 1973. Bankers started looking for their money. It was like a run, a big recession, lasting almost three years. We almost lost it all again, but nobody could say we were beat. Our business community survived.

Porfirio Sanchez asked Nicasio for permission to tell me the "Arabian Nights Story" and the men erupted into a roar of laughter which brought the attention of everyone in the restaurant to our corner of the bar. Maxi said no, he shouldn't tell me, but Sergio said that it was too good to keep. Finally Maxi agreed, providing that no names were mentioned, and I agreed to say that it happened in Saudi Arabia when in fact it had happened in another Persian Gulf country.

Porfirio Sanchez: Nicasio and I had acquired control of a financial institution with capital from a Saudi businessman who asked his banker for a reference in Miami and was given my name. I managed the assets of several Europeans in the United States, but the Arab's share was double what I was managing. In order to make the investment safe, I bought, with Nicasio, controlling interest in a real estate company. The stock was then pledged as collateral for a loan from a bank, which I used to finance the construction of apartment buildings. This was, of course, legal here but not in Saudi Arabia.

To make a long story short, the bottom fell out of the market in 1973. I either had to sell the real estate at an unbearable loss in order to cover my losses in the other business or borrow from the real estate company. The Saudi Arabian investor informed us that he wanted out. The Miami economy was not doing well, and he had other places, like California, that he wanted to try. It was like a house of cards when you take out the bottom floor. I went to Saudi Arabia to explain to him that I couldn't liquidate in the middle of a recession. I explained to him what I had done with his money. He went crazy. He had me jailed.

I was charged with theft, for which the penalty is the severing of both hands, but blind luck prevented that from happening. Nicasio went to Washington and got me released a day later. By 1975 the Arab had his money out and wanted back into another deal. I told him, "you promise not to give me any money to invest, and I promise not to develop my oil reserves in Palm Beach." *Que vá.* [Never again.] I only take investments from Americans and Latins from now on.

The evening with these four friends continued through dinner, a succulent *paella* as the main course, and the stories of long "runs" with stocks in the market and absolute financial disasters coming one after the other.

Nicasio Lopez-Puerta considers my question about which one factor was most responsible for their business success. As his companions sip their coffee he says. *"Sí, hay que estar en la onda."* [Yes, you must be tuned in to the wave.]

Nicasio Lopez-Puerta: I am talking about the sound wave. Communications and business are one. If you are not a part of the wave, you don't do any business. When you come from the outside and everyone thinks you are scum or a pitiful person, they don't offer you anything to buy. When you are part of the sound wave, you get all the deals you want and some you don't want, too. Who the hell cares that some man who used to be an engineer in Cuba now makes plastics and needs $30,000 to buy a machine? That man is not a part of the sound wave. He is some poor slob with a dream. Well, suppose that poor slob doesn't get his loan. Instead he makes his own machine at home, and one Christmas he cooks up 3,000 happy, jowly, plastic Santa Claus faces, working seven days a week in a rented garage with the whole family. You think any person would do that today? How about an old man who left his country and refuses to let go of it? Would you work twelve hours a day, seven days a week, making Santa Claus faces? Of course you wouldn't. But they do, the refugees. He sold the faces for fifty cents each and made a profit. But who the hell cares?

I had friends here, friends going back to my childhood and people who had become prominent. I also had access to investment capital. *Yo estaba en onda.* [I was tuned in to the wave.] I tuned several people in. [He looks at Maximiliano Pons with a feigned air of disdain.]

Maximiliano Pons: Would you listen to this man? He'd have you believe that he is responsible for every Cuban's success. What sound wave is that, Nicasio? Monday night football. That's what it is. That is the sound wave you got us hooked into!

The men laugh and rib each other until the conversation turns to Cuba and Fidel.

Porfirio Sanchez: Sometimes I wonder about why we were put here. In the early years in the United States, before the Bay of Pigs, I thought we were here for one reason only: to go back, to liberate Cuba from the worst plague it has ever suffered from. Today, I see us more in the context of other Hispanics in the United States and Latin America, sharing . . . I don't know what. Certainly more than a language, more than nationhood. Broadly defined, maybe a race, a sense of our own peoplehood. I think that is why we were put here. To be a part—the southeastern part or the northern part, depending on where you are—of the race that seeks human justice, the Hispanic race which struggles so hard to find a place. [A long silence follows.]

The men look at their watches, say goodbye, and give each other the traditional *abrazo* [hugs]. Maximiliano Pons offers to give me a lift back to my hotel in his car, a chauffeur-driven Mercedes limousine. Reclining behind the anonymity of dark grey tinted windows, he speaks more seriously than before.

Maximiliano Pons: Don't make a mistake about it. Providing Fidel lives and Cuba is enslaved, none of us can live here and be happy or feel we can go home again. Until we liberate the land from Russian ownership and dispose of Fidel and his gang of hyenas, you and I will never be free. Make no mistake about that.

Maxi is saying this to me in 1980, twenty years after he immigrated. His position is not rhetorical. It may be exaggerated and a bit dogmatic, but it is fully believed and sincerely felt. Twenty years later, the goal remains the same. Back in 1960 the only subject worth talking about in the Cuban community in Miami, New York, and elsewhere was how we were going to spend the next year in Cuba. Like the old Jewish pledge, "Next year, in Jerusalem," the Cuban rallying cry was *"Año Nuevo en Cuba."* [New Year in Cuba.] The one objective was to return to Cuba.

Cochinos

Between 1959 and 1961 conditions in Cuba worsened. Food shortages became commonplace. The Cuban currency lost so much value that it stopped being traded internationally. Sugar markets, controlled by the United States, became unprofitable. Tourism stopped. Fidel was having a tough time hanging on to his power, and for the first time seemed vulnerable to attack.

Fidel had become convinced by mid-1961 that only a strong dictatorship would ensure his survival as leader of the country. The anti-Castro ranks had expanded to include members of Fidel's cabinet and the revolutionary forces. It was rumored that he had engineered the accident that had killed his comrade from the Sierra Maestra, Camilo Cienfuegos, for advocating a return to constitutional guarantees, and that he had demoted and jailed several of his own supporters in the 26th of July Movement. The "Dictatorship of the Proletariat"—as Fidel's reign was beginning to be called—set out to put everyone under surveillance. Neighborhood committees were appointed by the revolutionary government and given license to observe, report, and punish the "antirevolutionary" activities of the people who lived under its domain.

The exodus from Cuba continued at an increasing pace. Several airlines started daily direct flights to the United States.

Visa waivers were being issued by the U.S. Embassy for all Cubans who had relatives in the United States, but American policy was neither clearly articulated nor effective. After Cuban expropriation of American-owned business, a limited-interest strategy was formulated by the U.S. government. The seizure of U.S. businesses helped revive the old imperialistic instincts. Cuba was viewed with paternalistic anxiety by the U.S. State Department. Its policy was cautiously optimistic, opportunistic, and reflective of its wounded pride. It was not a policy consistent with its position of leadership.

The CIA was authorized by the White House to step up its covert activities against Fidel. By January 1961, Fidel had used CIA involvement as an excuse to imprison 40,000 people and order the death of 10,000 more. Fidel was aware of recruitment activity among Cuban refugees in the United States backed by the CIA for the purpose of launching an invasion of Cuba. It became impossible to keep the planned Cuban invasion a secret. *U.S. News and World Report* had printed articles about it, the Miami *Herald* publicized it, and 2,000 Cuban households in Miami knew about it through family members. It is safe to assume that Fidel also knew. His watchful eye misses little of what goes on in Miami.

The anguish of the Cuban community in Miami is echoed in the actions of those days. Thousands enlisted to receive training and return to Cuba. One of them was a professional military man who had survived three Cuban presidents.

Manolo Llerena had been promoted to colonel during the Batista regime and this marked him for destruction by Castro's revolutionary army. He left for Miami the day after Batista was overthrown.

Manolo Llerena: Shortly after I arrived in Miami from Cuba, I met another former Batista army officer walking down Southwest 8th Street. He had heard that I was dead, and someone had told me he had been sent to jail. And here we were hugging and kissing each other like a couple of fags in the middle of the street. He told me that the CIA was organizing a group to go back to Cuba and offered to put me in touch with the head man. I signed up the next

day and began to recruit others. We had a small base camp
in the Everglades. The real training was conducted in Guatemala. I worked out the training exercises and was in
charge of recruitment.

The Everglades base camp was the first to be established
by the CIA to train Cuban expatriates in military tactics. Manolo
was one of the first to arrive at this camp. The camp was not
well run and the assortment of men who gathered there shared
nothing more than the dream of returning to Cuba. They thought
[as did Nixon's "plumbers" sixteen years later] that they were
serving the legitimate interests of the free world by going to war
against Castro. They had CIA backing, unofficial government
endorsement, and sharing the American belief that Cuba was
on the path toward communism, they were ready to die in order
to save their country from oppression.

Manolo Llerena: By the spring of 1960 we had 2,000 to 3,000
people—not all in training but signed up. They were mostly
former soldiers, but we also had many patriotic young men
who wanted to see their country free again—people who
had lost family members to the "justice" of Fidel. We
weren't a bunch of mercenaries. We had a solemn purpose
and the backing of the U.S. government. We didn't want
Marines in Cuba. We wanted our own *soldados* [soldiers]
returning to claim their freedom in glory and for the good
of the people. There were no politicians in this group, but
when we ran a successful raid on army installations in
Cuba, the politicians took all the credit. We took orders
from military people and we had a military purpose.

It was difficult to keep morale up and there were many
security leaks. Some of us spent eighteen months in camp
without much to do except train. Some went AWOL and
were seen with their families in Miami. This was bad.
Miami was filled with rumors.

I went back to Miami in late 1960 and read a story in
the Miami *Herald* that described everything we were doing

in detail. Every time the news leaked, the CIA would post-
pone the plans. Kennedy was indecisive and never wanted
this operation at all. At least that is what I think. Every
delay brought new anxieties and more dissensions. When
we finally left Guatemala, the camp was about to explode.

My conversation with Manolo was raising more questions than
it was answering. As he spoke of the widespread knowledge of the
invasion I wondered what persuaded the CIA that an "announced"
invasion had the possibility of success. Did they think that they could
bluff Fidel by pretending they had more military force than they actually did? Were these tactical questions considered? Did they expect
Fidel to give up?

Manolo Llerena: You have to understand the mood of the Cuban people. First of all there were a lot of people in Cuba
ready to join an armed invasion. Then you have to con-
sider that we were talking about our homeland. José Martí
and Antonio Maceo had suffered for it and died. It didn't
matter that the odds were so long. We were lucky to have
U.S. help and the backing of Guatemala and Nicaragua.
But we would have gone it alone. Anastasio Somoza risked
becoming a target of Fidel Castro when he allowed the invasion forces to assemble there. Let me show you something. [He goes to his bedroom and returns with a worn
piece of paper in a plastic cover.] I got this from a friend
before we both left, and I kept it in my shoe, in between
my toes, until we got back to Miami.

It is a poem, cut from a printed page. Only the last three stanzas
can be read. The title is "Call to Arms."

> Cubano, take up arms,
> your Country calls you on to immortal war,
> the last shell to be fired in this war
> will usher in Freedom.
>
> Cubano
> The Trenches await you,
> like a furrow looking for its seed.
> The trench is in Cuba, Cubano,
> Men on their knees, call you home.

Only by showing your principles,
will its shout awaken the sleeping consciousness,
there is need for you, Cubano,
to fire the rifle of justice.

Manolo Llerena: We had to go, no matter what the odds; we had to liberate Cuba at all costs.

Ramon Puerto was a sergeant in Batista's army and a friend of Manolo Llerena: He discussed freely the details of the invasion in which he participated and his part in it.

Ramon Puerto: The exile was a very difficult experience for me. I didn't have a steady job for several months, and when we got here in 1959, there wasn't any welfare or Cuban Refugee Center or anything like that. We lived hand to mouth, in a trailer in Hollywood [Florida], for which I paid $150 a month—an outrageous amount of money at the time. There was nothing my wife, Rosario, and our two small children could do. I couldn't hold on to a job. [He pauses to wipe a tear away.] I didn't know what was going to happen to us. I was a military man. I joined the army when I was seventeen because I wanted to learn how to read and write, and one day when we were picking tobacco, a man from the Guardia Rural [the Cuban rural army] came to us and said that the army would teach us how to read. I joined up.

I went through hell the first few months after we came here. I got a job in a company that made refrigerators. I did the loading and unloading of trucks. They paid me under the table—you know, off the books. My back was sore one afternoon and I was resting by the side of the building. The foreman came down on me for being lazy or something. I let him have it [he punches his palm with his fist], and he fired me. It was very difficult to keep a job.

Finally in July of 1960 I joined up with some of the other fellows from the Cuban army days. We met with a man from the CIA. Do you want his name? No, I better not tell you; he's still around here. Anyway, he said that the

MRR [Movement of Revolutionary Recovery] was in on it and that we were going to Cuba. There were lots of people there that were good soldiers. I knew them all. The man from the CIA said we would all get paid, even if we got caught, and the money would go to our families. Rosario and the children needed it. I joined. They gave us a name—Brigada 2506. We were sent to Useppa, an island near Florida in the Gulf of Mexico, to train. There were about twenty or twenty-five of us in the first group. We all had military experience. I was in the light infantry; Carlos, Artime, and Orlando [Former Batista Army Personnel] were all trained in artillery and weaponry.

We got too big for the island and moved to a farm in Guatemala. The name was Helvetia, I think. It's been so many years. There were barracks and plenty of food. By November or December there were about 400 of us. We were trained and ready to go in a month. Before we went, we intervened as a brigade in an uprising in Guatemala, in the city of Puerto Barrios. *Fidelistas* there wanting to start a revolution had infiltrated the peasants who worked the bananas. We didn't get to fire a shot in Puerto Barrios. By the time we got there, the B-26 that the CIA brought had bombed the place and the peasants had surrendered. We were told that was the way it would be in Cuba.

By March of 1961 things were beginning to heat up. My wife wrote that there were rumors in Miami about our whereabouts. Fidel was accusing the United States of planning an armed offensive to the island, you know. We were found out, and I think this is why we moved fast, even before we had a chance to do full exercises with the troops. Everybody was afraid that American public opinion might stop the action. On the 9th of April [1961] Colonel Frank came to see us and told us of the plan. We had 1,500 men—seven battalions and the command and the light artillery. The next day, at dawn, we left Puerto Cabezas, in northern Nicaragua on the Gulf of Mexico. The ships were already there. The ships belonged to the García Line. There were other ships coming from Vieques in Puerto Rico, but we weren't told very much about that.

On the 13th of April we were briefed by Colonel Frank again. The troops had already boarded ship. I remember the trees on the side of the pier. It was a very hot morning and the trees were cool. The entire command was there, including the medics and the priests who gave us the benediction. Colonel Frank did an excellent job. He told us the plan. There were to be three separate landings around the Bay of Pigs. The operation was called Pluto. There was Playa Azul, which is also called Playa Girón, Playa Roja—I don't know about that one. Playa Larga was where my battalion would land, and Playa Verde was about 10 kilometers east of Girón. Girón would be the command post. My troops would be the first advance. I had requested that from Artime. I didn't want to go back to Miami alive. I had had enough of exile. I wanted either to stay in a free Cuba or die. Paratroopers would land in Yaguaramas just ahead of us, between Playa Larga and the "Australia"—a sugar factory which my men were supposed to take. We had to hold on for seventy-two hours. We got the intelligence report from a tall blonde fellow called Bill. He said that Fidel was totally unaware of these plans and had no troops in the area. The closest troops were in Santa Clara, which this man Bill said was seven hours away.

Now I had gone from Santa Clara to Girón many times, and it never took seven hours unless I went by horse. It was more like two hours, but anyway I wasn't in any mood to argue with the CIA. San Román, who was our military leader, asked about the conditions of the Cuban armed forces. Bill said that Fidel would have little artillery and no air power. The air power he had would have been destroyed by the air raids of our own B-26s, which I had seen in action in Puerto Barrios in Guatemala. Artime asked about the people already in Cuba, in the mountains, and the people the CIA had found to join us. Colonel Frank said that there were over 700 guerrillas in Escambray, near Girón. As soon as word got to them of the invasion, they would join the group in Playa Verde. He said that the ships carried armaments for over 6,000 men. They calculated that within 72 hours over 5,000 people would join the Brigade 2506. They would be called to arms by CIA operatives, radio broadcasts, leaflets, and guns dropped from airplanes.

San Román asked Frank whether he should take and hold the positions or forge ahead if he could. Frank said,

"You will be so strong militarily that you will want to forge ahead. You, San Román, will take a jeep and move to the head of your troops on the main road, and when you get to the *Carretera Central* [Central Highway], just stick out your hand as if to make a left turn, and head on out to Havana." We all laughed. We were all self-confident. We were such a bunch of idiots.

Teresa Martinez's brother was one of those the CIA expected to oppose Fidel from inside Cuba. He had offered to store guns and explosives at his family's dairy farm. They would be used during the invasion to blow up a Cuban military installation nearby. Fidel's G-2 knew about it several months before the invasion.

Teresa Martinez: I remember ever since I was a little girl how often people said I was to be tested by adversity many times before I died. It [the invasion] was for me a fulfillment of their predictions: When the communists found the explosives my brother had stored in the house out back, they took away my husband and shot him for something he did not do. He was an honest man, a businessman, and was never involved in politics.

When I was born the doctor gave one chance in twenty of my surviving the week. I spent my first eight years in hospitals and sickrooms fighting disease. Now I have spent nearly twenty years fighting those who took over my homeland and the man who killed my husband. Fidel Castro killed my husband. He pronounced his sentence in a speech, a few days before they executed my husband. Do you know what happened? No? I will tell you then.

My husband and my father were partners in a dairy farm outside of Havana. We were farmers and property owners. From the beginning, the agrarian reform pointed us out as targets for nationalization. Our farm included my father's house, *La Casa Grande* [The Big House], our own house to the left, some farm buildings, and a house for my brother, who did not live there but came on weekends.

It was not a big operation by American standards, but our cows supplied the milk for 400 families. We were well known in the area, and perhaps we were an obvious target during changing political tides. A fence marked the boundary between our property and government-owned land where the army was building antiaircraft installations. We did not know what they were doing there until after the invasion. My brother was persuaded by some friends to let them use his house on our property to store some boxes. My brother told us they were chemical supplies and equipment, but they were actually guns, dynamite, and . . . gelatin explosives, I think they called them. Enough to blow up the military installation. This was only a few months before the Bay of Pigs. It was probably connected with that.

One of the people who helped my brother put the boxes in his house was a spy for the G-2. A few hours after the boxes were delivered, we saw two cars full of armed men come into the farm. It was a quiet, moonlit night. I remember my aunt yelling, "It's the G-2! Oh my God." The sound of her voice carried in the night's silence, and we heard it at our house. So did my brother, who was at his house behind *La Casa Grande.*

My brother took off on foot. He knew the terrain and he knew why the G-2 were there, but the rest of us had no idea why they were there. They said they were looking for my brother and some guns. They searched my house, my father's house, and the other buildings, but since my brother's house was not visible from where we were, they did not see it until daybreak. That is when they found the explosives and took my husband away.

The newspapers and public opinion pointed to my husband's innocence. He was respected in the community. The press referred to him as the "wrongly incarcerated father of five." Pleading his case, I got as high as Raul Castro's secretary. I could get no higher than that. When I saw her, she told me that Fidel Castro had said, "Neither a distinguished name nor a father of five will prevent me from punishing the counterrevolutionaries." And that was that.

The charges were brought up before a "popular court," as they called those lynching mobs. They pronounced the sentence Fidel wanted: *paredón* [the firing squad]. My husband was executed on January 20, 1961.

The episode of the Bay of Pigs, *Cochinos,* as it is known to us Cubans, has been described in numerous journalistic and fictional accounts. The events are almost familiar to the American public. But to understand what really happened in *Cochinos,* events must be seen from the perspective of the participants. The Cuban-Americans had promised on their honor to return to their homeland. The United States, as the most powerful hemispheric influence, had a strategic interest and was party to the promise. Everyone knew an American-backed invasion would be launched in Cuba, because everyone knew the United States was committed to it. The only questions were when, where, and with what force.

Cochinos was an "announced war," which, in the words of the Spanish proverb, *Guerra anunciada no mata solado* [kills no soldiers]. If a large-scale, prolonged armed conflict had followed the invasion, the death toll would have been enormous. There were 120 deaths in *Cochinos,* and had it not been so well publicized, there could have been thousands more. In the middle of the invasion the American promise of military support vanished in a cold foreign policy calculation. With it, any hope of success for the armed conflict disappeared. Nonetheless, the invasion proceeded as planned and announced. Fidel's Cuban Revolutionary Army went on alert on April 15, 1961. This is how the witnesses remember *Cochinos.*

Fidel Castro (*In a speech given on April 23, 1961*): During the early hours of the 15th, because of certain news received from the Province of Oriente, we did not sleep. All the signals from one moment to another pointed to an invasion. We were on alert.

Manolo Llerena: Our B-26s began to fly over Air Force headquarters at about 6 AM to release their cargo of bombs. The bombers were under the command of Captain Villafana, who had been with Fidel before. There were seven B-26s to bomb four airports, but we found no aircraft. We only destroyed airports. The attack had been anticipated by Fidel. Strategically, it had taken place too early. It took the troops two more days to reach *Cochinos.* The air attack should have waited. Fidel still had a full air force when it was over.

Fidel Castro (*In a speech given on April 23, 1961*): We had taken certain precautions against air attack, particularly against our attack aircraft. They could not be seen from the air. We had also temporarily controlled the movements of certain people, we know them, counterrevolutionary scum and enemies of the Revolution.

Ramon Puerto: The Cancer [Fidel] moved against us very swiftly and decisively. Between the air attacks of the 15th and the landing on the 17th [April 1961], there were over 100,000 arrests in Cuba. Only when we [Brigade 2506] were behind bars were these people let go. We heard strategic reports that we were surrounded by about 20,000 troops, with artillery and tanks already at the edge of the forest beyond the swamp.

  We were awaiting the promised air cover from the United States in order to proceed with the invasion. The reports about the number of troops did not faze us. They could be true; they could be false. We could hold out for seventy-two hours if we could knock out the artillery. We needed U.S. air cover; we couldn't do anything without it. Fidel's antiaircraft guns were knocking out our B-26s as if they were flies.

  Rafael Fernandez was one of those arrested in Cuba before the invasion. He had no plans to join the invasion force when he was detained. He now owns a jewelry store in New York City.

Rafael Fernandez: The G-2 came to the house on April 12 [1961]. We were away celebrating a niece's birthday. When we got back, the neighbors told us that they had come looking for me. I had no reason to hide from the G-2, except that, as a jeweler, I knew a lot of *Batistianos*. But they had interrogated me once before and let me go. Nonetheless, something inside me told me to get out of the house. I went to my friend's house in Caibarién and stayed out of sight for a couple of days. The G-2 men came back the next day, and when they found I'd gone, they took my father-in-law. My wife called me in tears. I went back to Cienfuegos and turned myself in on the 14th so that they would let my father-in-law go. The invasion was the next day.

They put me in a theater, Luisita, with 3,000 other people. We stayed there a week. We ate only what people would bring. The place smelled of urine and sweat. Several people collapsed, and an old man died.

Sylvia Gonzalez was also a party to the invasion from her command post far away from the front in *Cochinos*. When I interviewed her in her home in Key Biscayne she walked me through the Spanish-style twin living rooms. Like the rest of her home, the rooms were very large and decorated with expensive art. Among them is a large painting of José Martí, falling to his death in Dos Rios, during the first days of the Spanish-American War.

Sylvia Gonzalez: This house became a Cuban army field office in exile. My brothers set up radio equipment over in that corner, and this living room was full of people anxious to know what was going on. Nicasio Lopez-Puerta and Maxi Pons sat on that couch, shouting instructions. "Tune in to Nicaragua!" "Tune in Havana!" "Call Washington!" It was all very surreal. It was our own mock war, fought in a living room with *Cubalibres, mojitos y saladitos* [rum and coke and hors d'oeuvres].

The invasion force was fully neutralized in forty-eight hours. The CIA's B-26s left Fidel's air force intact. The Cuban Revolutionary Army was ready for action. There was no massive uprising. No armed men came from the mountains. Boats carrying precious supplies and armaments were sunk before they could unload their cargo. Brigade 2506 anticipated imminent defeat as they made their way through the mud of *Bahía de Cochinos* toward the waiting armies of Fidel. We could hear them on the short-wave radio. It was a profound loss for all involved.

Manolo Llerena: I could see that they were going to beat us, and I was angry at the lies we had been told. I saw a young man, without his stomach, still alive after being hit by an artillery shell, convulsing on the ground, terror in his eyes. But even then I believed we were right.

Maximiliano Pons: Some of us asked Washington for a meeting with the CIA in Miami [April 17]. We met with two of Kennedy's people instead. I told them we were ready to jump into our own boats and go to Cuba if our demands were not met. We insisted that they keep their promise and help us get rid of Fidel. A couple of hours into our meeting with the Kennedy people, I got the feeling that we were being taken for a ride. The conversation was interrupted while the men called the White House. I took Nicasio Lopez-Puerta aside and told him I thought we were wasting our time. We had to talk to Kennedy. At that time none of us could vote except Nicasio, but he had been giving money for Joe Kennedy's kids' elections for a long time.

   We realized later that Kennedy had sent us his European elitist, who knew nothing of American interests in Latin America and who wasn't about to commit American resources, and maybe even some blood, to save a bunch of Cubans and kill communism in America. [I asked if it was McGeorge Bundy, who was then National Security Advisor to Kennedy. Maxi waved my question away with his hand and continued.] If we had been talking about supporting a group of West Germans who had crashed in the Berlin Wall in order to liberate East Germany from the Russians, if that had been the case, there is no question in my mind but that he would have recommended massive nuclear attack. This man, whose name I will never give you, would come to me a few months after *Cochinos*, when they found the Russian missiles, and ask me what I thought the Cubans were up to. I could have played him a recording of what I had already said during *Cochinos*, and he would have had his answer.

   Even then we had a chance to win this badly-planned and well-publicized secret invasion. Remember Fidel had over 100,000 people put away. He couldn't survive that for too long. We could have held out at the front. There were tons of explosives all over the island. I know—I paid for most of those myself. Kennedy's man laughed when I told him how many rifles and submachine guns I had bought and smuggled into Cuba. They had no idea that their own inflated claims were actually true. They miscalculated every event. They actually didn't think that Fidel would always be a thorn in their sides. "Russia's window in America" was the Kennedy rhetoric about Cuba, but they didn't believe it themselves. They thought Fidel would be toppled by his military in due time. It was a prejudiced and unempirical view, but it was all they had.

Russia was all over Cuba, and American intelligence knew it. Allen Dulles knew it. I knew it. But the *comemierda* [shit face] they sent me was only worried about the political popularity of their man [Kennedy]. He hated Dulles and thought that Cuba was expendable. Look at the cost of losing *Cochinos.* It almost caused a nuclear war. It cost the Democrats my vote; I became a Republican right then and there. Only the people who own a place ever care enough about it to keep the lawn well trimmed.

The Bay of Pigs episode was a failure but not a complete failure. Fidel won a military victory, but the Cubans won a moral victory. They kept their promise of going back to rescue all that had been lost and restore freedom.

Claudio Sanchez was a shoe salesman in Miami at the time of the Bay of Pigs invasion. Since that time he has risen to the presidency of a Miami-based bank. In the years following *Cochinos* he worked actively to keep the plight of the captured men in the public's eye, putting pressure on the Kennedy and Johnson administrations to obtain release of the prisoners.

Claudio Sanchez: After *Cochinos* there wasn't anything to do but keep a low profile and put your nose to the grindstone. Fidel had 1,500 of our people captured, humiliated, facing death or life imprisonment. That was over 1 percent of the Cubans in the United States at that time. About half the Cubans in Miami had relatives who had been captured.

The Kennedy apology made us feel even worse, frankly, because up to that time we weren't sure who to blame. It is easy to blame people you don't like. Now we had to cast blame upon someone like President Kennedy—a man we were beginning to like.

In this community [Miami] there were many months when we feared for the well-being of our captured men. There was, I think, a feeling of unity among the Cubans, and also between the Cubans and the rest of the community. We came together like we never had before. It was not until the last immigration [the Third Wave], during the spring of 1980, that the Cubans have been that united. After *Cochinos* we became one people—not Cubans anymore and not American enough to commit U.S. armed forces in the conflict. It was then that I think we began to see each other as members of a group, a social group. Our rose-colored glasses came off. Since then we've put them on only from time to time.

Miriam Llerena is the wife of Manolo Llerena, a member of Brigade 2506. She is one of the thousands of wives, children, and relatives of those captured at *Cochinos*.

Miriam Llerena: That period of time, while Manolo was in jail in Cuba, is not easy to recall. There was too much pain to continue life as it needs to continue, so everything stopped while we took account of our loss. Manolo was alive, but Fidel had killed hundreds of people, and none of them had participated in the invasion against him. I was sure Manolo would not live out the year.

People brought food and sat watching television. In Key West, where sometimes you can get Cuban television stations, people in hotels watched the trials. I couldn't bear to see any of it because I was afraid—afraid I would see Manolo and have a heart attack. My heart is not very strong. Manolo is the head of this family. What was to become of us?

The men in Brigade 2506 were captured three days after the invasion began. They were taken, partly on foot, halfway across the island to Havana. The crowds greeted them with Fidel's cry to the American government, *"Cuba es tu Waterloo"* [Cuba is your Waterloo] and became abusive of the men covered with mud and shame. Fidel selected this moment to announce that he was "a Communist . . . a Marxist-Leninist and I have always been." He referred to Cuba as a socialist republic. The crowds responded to the victorious leader with adulation and renewed support. *"Si Fidel es communista yo lo soy tambien."* ["If Fidel is a communist, so am I."]

Nicasio Lopez-Puerta: Like many Latin American neighbors, we always maintained here in the Cuban community of Miami that from the beginning Fidel, his brother Raul, and Ché Guevara intended to become communist when Fidel took power in 1959. He never changed. It was just a matter of bringing the people along. He removed private incentives and substituted patriotic slogans for them. He lost control of Cuba to the Russians even before the missiles. We told the Kennedy people first that we thought Fidel was going to bring in Soviet troops and aircraft. We knew soon after Raul Castro's trip to Russia that large-scale support would follow.

I reasoned with the President's men after *Cochinos* that we needed a plan, an approach to Cuba that would keep the country open. Instead, there were doubts about Fidel and fear of the political repercussions if such a policy failed. Right after *Cochinos* some people in the White House still thought Fidel was a nationalist. I told them what my professor at Columbia had said to me: "Well, if it walks like a duck and swims like a duck and quacks like a duck, I'd say it's a duck." They smiled politely. They should have done something. But the next move, they felt, was not up to them. It was up to Fidel.

From *Cochinos* to the Missile Crisis

A very significant set of events was put in motion by *Cochinos*, which nearly resulted in a nuclear confrontation between Russia and the United States.

Carlos Mendez, who came to the U.S. during the Third Wave in 1980, was an uncommitted collaborator of Fidel's and at times he held high offices in Cuba's Ministry of the Exterior. He also worked as a spy for the U.S. during part of the time he was a Cuban foreign officer. We met at an address he phoned into my hotel room, an hour before the meeting was to take place. It was the house of a friend in suburban Washington, D.C. Throughout the meeting he wore dark glasses and drank orange juice. As he spoke of events that took place over 20 years ago, his secretive manner revealed how little things have changed for some of us since the days of Soviet-American strategy and intrigue which led to the Missile Crisis.

Carlos Mendez: I worked for the Ministry of the Exterior during that time and until 1976, when they purged me. The minister was Raul Roa, a very competent senior diplomat. The intelligence came directly to Raul Castro. I was the conduit of that information for almost a year. We had reports that the CIA was distraught with the failure of *Cochinos* and that there would be another offensive before the American elections. Fidel is a politician on an international scale, and he decided to raise the stakes a little bit for the United States. He and Raul made high-level contacts with the Soviets, which went over the head of Soviet Ambassador Kudryatsev. There were also high-level contacts with Peking, but only Russia could provide what was needed in order to raise the stakes. We needed economic independence from the Western hemisphere—and weapons. I think even Raul Castro was surprised to hear the Russians wanted to put nuclear missiles in Cuba.

The Cuban economy was going into a deep recession in mid-1962. We needed to stabilize it, and we needed a few more MIGs. Nuclear missiles were a bit much for us, but not for Fidel. Khrushchev, the argument goes, wanted the missiles in Cuba to use as a bargaining chip in his alleged dream of obtaining West Berlin. Fidel knew it would get him an American promise of nonintervention.

After *Cochinos,* Fidel began to move unabashedly toward fuller membership in the Russian alliance. After a brief and empathetic flirtation with China, Fidel returned to the Russian camp with the knowledge that ultimately only Russia could be helpful to Cuba. China was the agricultural example of heroic rebellion, but Russia had money and arms to pay for the sugar. The revolution in Latin America could not be fought without Russian arms, technical aid, and supplies. The country could not be adequately defended against the continuing deterioration of the economy or the threat of new internal and external revolution without an alliance with Russia. After declaring himself a communist, Fidel moved to occupy the role of communist party secretary.

Some of the people who before *Cochinos* might have become part of the underground fight against Fidel gave up and joined him in his new public stance as a communist. There was little or no open dissent.

There was, however, some apprehension on the part of the Russians. The Russian-run Communist Party of Cuba, under the leadership of Blas Roca, had not welcomed Fidel as its leader. In spite of public remarks made by Roca and others supporting Fidel as secretary-general of the party, Russia, on the advice of Kudryatsev (their Ambassador to Cuba), was not offering support to Fidel. The Soviets were impassive and unconvinced by his political declarations. Outside of Cuba only the Cuban-Americans believed Fidel. They had always suspected that he was moving toward alignment with Russia, and now they had his confession.

Maximiliano Pons: Following Punta del Este [where the Organization of American States suspended Cuba's membership], Fidel began an undeclared war on Latin America. He gave full rein to Ché Guevara, whose dream had been to be a second Bolivar, hoping that, beyond Bolivar's accomplishment of liberating the South America of the nineteenth century, he would also succeed in uniting the independent states under the rule of Havana. Ché had made a mess of his technocratic assignment as head of the INRA [Agrarian Reform Institute]. INRA took land away from active production and put it under government control. People had "ownership" of the collective farms, supposedly, but no control. Ché assumed control from Havana. The effect was no control at all. The first year, replantings of cane, for example, fell behind by 20 percent. Rice production went down 20 to 30 percent in one year. I knew some people who owned a very beautiful piece of land in the mountains of Pinar del Rio [in western Cuba]. They had worked those eroded hills without tractors or irrigation for several decades, and the farm had always been productive. When INRA took over, it introduced equipment worth thousands of dollars and brought water from 1,000 feet below the mountain fields. Eventually INRA had to abandon the land as unproductive. Ché was not an economist or industrialist, but he was in charge. When he failed, Fidel named Carlos Rafael Rodriguez (currently Cuba's president) as head of INRA and let Ché pursue his real interests, which were murder and extortion in Latin America. Rodriguez, as it turned out, was an equally poor choice, but he had been schooled in Russia and had sound communist credentials, which Fidel needed at that time. This was when he was trying to prove to Russia that he was redder than they. Russia of course wanted a foothold in Cuba but preferred its own leadership—Roca, Rodriguez, Escalante. Fidel was too independent. He had what seemed to be dangerous ideas about international governance. Fidel kept on talking about "collective leadership," "a Cuban member in the Russian Politburo," "Russian missiles in Cuba," and his troops in Southeast Asia. Khrushchev seemed unmoved by the revolutionary thinker in Fidel. Russia accepted without enthusiasm the fate of the old Communist party and, fearing the potential success of a new China-Cuba relationship, began to collaborate fully with Fidel.

Carlos Mendez: These things are done both symbolically and practically. The first sign we had that Russia had promoted us, so to speak, was when we were placed just behind China at the May Day festivities in Moscow. That was a place of honor, and it led to a series of events, concluding with a mid-May Economic Cooperation Treaty involving about 3 million tons of sugar. But the most important gesture was the withdrawal of Ambassador Kudryatsev, who had been committed to the old guard, and his replacement with Alexayev, a man we knew and trusted and who had the ear of Khrushchev. We were certain that Fidel had won when Blas Roca said in a public address that Fidel was "the best and most productive Marxist-Leninist in Cuba."

Nicasio Lopez-Puerta: What happened in Cuba, after *Cochinos* and before the Missile Crisis [1962], was that Fidel restructured his power base. He had already exhausted the goodwill of the farmers and the middle class and the professionals. His only hope now was to retain the army on his side and try to control the Communist Worker Movement. In order to do this, he needed arms and supplies for the army, and the endorsement of Khrushchev for the communists. He succeeded in both areas, but not without severe tests.

Claudio Sanchez: Leaders of the exile community in Miami went to see Kennedy after *Cochinos*. When they left, they felt they had gotten a commitment from him to begin new invasion plans. Alpha 66 [an underground Cuban organization] stepped up its recruitment, and the raids on Cuban positions on the coast increased. Miró Cardona [former prime minister] and others around Miami were publicly saying that Kennedy thought six divisions would do the job. And then we had the Caribbean maneuvers. The U.S. naval maneuvers were advertised mainly to dissuade Russian initiatives, but they had a great impact on Fidel Castro. He was sure that they were preparing for a second *Cochinos*. Fidel had our people [Brigade 2506] in jail, you will remember, and it was only reasonable to expect that if we here in the United States had help from the American government, we would organize a new invasion. I was afraid of the effect all this was having on Fidel. I was afraid for the men of 2506. I was sure Fidel would execute them at the first sign of trouble. I went to see the assistant secretary of state for Latin American affairs. We spoke about giving Fidel a signal that if he executed our soldiers he would get it between the eyes. A few weeks later the message came back. Fidel had been told by Brazilian President Goulant that if the invaders were shot, public opinion in the United States would make an invasion inevitable. I think Fidel got the message. That's when he decided that no matter how hot it was, he wanted to hug the furry Russian bear. We in turn exchanged an invasion—which was already being planned—for a threat of an invasion, but our men had to be protected.

On July 1, 1961, Raul Castro left for Russia to seek more protection. His discussion yielded the promise of an increased Russian military presence, more equipment, and the use of a few short-range surface-to-air missiles [SAMs] to defend a few medium-range ballistic missiles [MRBMs] capable of reaching targets in the United States.

Carlos Mendez: The conflict—in diplomatic terms—arises out of a commitment to conflicting public statements. It is possible to say that diplomatic conflict would not arise from opposite positions taken privately. But once the opposing positions are known, conflict ensues.

The public positions of Cuba and Russia were known. The bilateral agreement between the two nations included the introduction into Cuba of Russian MRBMs. The public position of the United States was expressed in a speech by Kennedy who, responding to a charge issued by Senator [Kenneth] Keating, said that the United States had photographs of SAMs in Cuba. He added that the United States would have to act if MRBMs were introduced. This was the point of diplomatic conflict. There was only one thing for Russia to do: lie. Khrushchev sent a message to Kennedy, and a copy to us, saying that Russia would not introduce MRBMs into Cuba. But by that time we had already received the first one, and about seven more were on ships heading for Cuba.

Maximiliano Pons: The U.S. government was caught in a credibility crisis of its own. Ever since 1959, one or another senator had accused the Cuban government of having Russian missiles. The Russian missile file at the State Department must have taken up a whole drawer. The State Department also had a theory, the "Theory of the Fourth Floor" which said it was against all known previous Russian behavior to send missiles out of Russia. This theory died the same way most diplomatic theories are sacrificed—at the altar of reality.

Between the 16th and the 21st of October, six months after *Cochinos,* the United States was able to confirm photographically the presence of MRBMs in Cuba. Using this information, the State Department developed another theory. It reasoned that Khrushchev introduced missiles into Cuba to create a temporary strategic advantage over the United States—an advantage he would later negotiate away in return for Berlin. There was much public competition among diplomats and official spokesmen of the Kennedy Administration for scenarios of American-Cuban-Russian strategic intentions. The one scenario confirmed by

Khrushchev's autobiography was that he felt safe in introducing the missiles because, in his view, no American president would gamble on an offensive warlike posture so close to an election. But more U-2 flights revealed new MRBM sites under construction, guarded and operated by Russians. And Kennedy was feeling pressure from international political circles to act decisively against Russia. He acted decisively.

In a speech broadcast on the 22nd of October, Kennedy announced that the United States would impose a "quarantine" on Cuba to prevent further shipments of offensive materials. He invited Khrushchev to withdraw the offensive material already in Cuba and abandon construction of new sites.

Porfirio Sanchez: We were listening to the speech in Sylvia's [Sylvia Gonzalez'] house. At that point, we all gave a sigh of relief, because we were expecting an announcement of an armed invasion, and we knew what an armed invasion would do in terms of casualties. Instead we had been given a firm stance against Russia, without blaming Cuba. There was at that time the outside chance that the missiles were being forced upon Fidel. No one wanted him to go on a killing rampage inside Cuba, like it was rumored he did during *Cochinos*.

Carlos Mendez: The details of the American actions were known to us [the Cuban Foreign Ministry] a few hours after Kennedy's speech. As had always been apparent to us before, we were able to confirm once again that the blockade was intended against Cuba, not Russia. Sixteen destroyers, three cruisers, an antisubmarine aircraft carrier, and six utility ships were deployed in a semi-circle from Florida to the southeasternmost point off Puerto Rico. They had orders to [he quotes from a document] "inspect, stop, and, if necessary, disable [rather than sink] those Russian vessels *en route* for Cuba which were capable of carrying nuclear warheads, air-to-surface or surface-to-air missiles, bombers, or any equipment to support that material." This last item was meant to include staples, metals, fuels, and everything else Russian ships were carrying to Cuba. At that point, we in Cuba felt we were at war with the United States. Unknown to the United States, we had nuclear weapons ready to direct to the United States. Two of our medium-range missiles were ready to be fired. We had also deployed 20,000 Russian troops at strategically defensive posts throughout the island.

On the 23rd of October, 1962, Raul Castro moved to Santiago to take command of the armed forces. War posters were all over the island and the militia was called. Over half a million people were called that day. By the way, that was also the day that we cancelled the Pan Am flights from Cuba to Miami. Over 300,000 Cubans had left by that time; no more left until 1965.

The American blockade prevented Khrushchev from putting any more missiles in Cuba and led to an agreement between Russia and the United States which guaranteed nonintervention on the part of the United States in the internal affairs of Cuba in exchange for the removal of all Russian missiles from Cuba. But the combined events of the Bay of Pigs and the Missile Crisis resulted in a cancellation of all flights between the two countries. Over 100,000 people were now separated from their husbands, wives, children, or parents.

Cuca Plata: I remember where I was when I heard the news that the exits were closed [in 1962]. I was washing dishes, and the news was announced on the radio. We were all here [in the United States], except Mario [Bolaños]. He had been planning to leave but kept running into trouble with Immigration in Cuba. Now he couldn't leave at all. I feared for his life. We tried very hard to get him out and finally did—through Spain, in 1965. He almost didn't make it.

Martha Losada: My father and grandfather were left behind in Cuba. We thought we would never see them again. I had nightmares. My mother was hospitalized with a nervous breakdown. She was afraid father would get into trouble with the government and my grandfather would die without getting out. My mother and I spent our days writing letters to Spain and Mexico, trying to get visas. We even considered paying someone to go pick them up by boat.

Nicasio Lopez-Puerta: At the end of the First Wave we had a very productive core of people here in Miami and forming elsewhere. The focus was still on Cuba, no doubt about it. Most of us had relatives back there, and we knew that they were suffering political harassment or worse if they didn't behave. We began to lobby in Washington to reopen negotiations with Cuba so that political refugees could come to the United States. The U.S. government was very reluctant to approach Cuba so soon after the missile incident. I bided my time. We backed both Johnson and Goldwater and told them what we wanted—a family reunification program of some sort. It was not easy to accomplish. Eventually the United States established the *Puente de la Libertad* [the Freedom Bridge], and the Second Wave began.

Love is Repaid by Love
Amor con amor se paga

Nada mejor puede dar
quien, sin patria en que vivir,
ni mujer por quien morir,
ni soberbia que tentar,
sufre y vacila y se halaga
imaginando que, al menos
entre los publicos buenos
amor con amor se paga

Nothing better can he give,
who, with no country where to
   live,
nor a woman for whom to die,
and no pride left to hide,
suffers, vacillates, and rejoices,
thinking that,
at least among the good folk,
love is repaid by love.

José Marti, 1871

Love is Repaid by Love

The pursuit of freedom. It's the pursuit of something very complex and difficult to define. It is an abstract idea and full of symbolism. Hugh Thomas says freedom has been our dream since the first decade of Spanish rule, 400 years ago. Some of us are still pursuing it.

Some good things—health care, education, and a better distributed standard of living—came with the Cuban Revolution of 1959, but not freedom. The revolution says about freedom that it must enslave in order to liberate, that the people are the tyrants.

To admire the Cuban society created by the revolution one has to ignore its brutality and its tedium. The revolution's cultural impact was enormous; it made individuality and eccentricity as punishable as murder or theft, reaching deeply into the Cuban character. Revolution began to impose upon Cuban society, as Segundo Cazalis puts it, "the sad coloring of submission."

Yet those who challenged the tyranny of the revolution in the early 1960's have trouble coping with the integrity of some of its principles—universal education, health services, and a livable minimum wage. These programs did not exist before 1959, but they had no reason not to—no reason except the greed of previous tyrants. The Cuban Revolution has never brought about the utopia that Fidel Castro first described in his 1952 speech, "*La historia me absolverá*" [History will absolve me], when he said of the pre-Batista era, "Once upon a time there was a Republic. It had its Constitution, its laws, its Civil Rights, its President, a Congress, and Law Courts. Everyone could assemble, associate, speak, and write with complete freedom. . . . There existed a public opinion both respected and heeded."

Fidel implied that he was fighting to restore that earlier and better time, but he changed course and instead became one of the most repressive of all tyrants. Personal liberties suffered under Fidel. Even Marx had envisioned a society in which human beings were not regarded as government property, and the multitudes in uniform were surely supposed to be marching to a spot where they would disband. Under Fidel, disarmament would never come and neither would personal freedom, human rights, or economic abundance. These, Fidel reminded Cubans, were things of the past.

Empty shelves in stores symbolized the sacrifice each had to make for the revolution, a virtue to be widely praised. Fidel was in control. He abolished Christmas in a country that had celebrated it for nearly 500 years, and persuaded the people that a year's harvest was 18 months long, thereby getting them to work longer and account for the yields more generously. Just as in the past eloquent slaveholders had been able to explain why there should be a Sunday only once every ten days and still retain the love of their slaves, Fidel explained away his economic chaos as an ideological quest and succeeded.

The revolutionary reforms in health and education were very popular, and so was the opening of the exclusive clubs and private beaches to public access. There was great pride in Cuba at having faced the United States and freed itself of American influence. Still, in spite of greater equality in the economic and social system, the basic needs of some Cubans were not being met. Like those before them who had suffered while trying to survive, these Cubans sought to leave the country. They felt the need to rejoin their families in exile abroad. For them, in the words of Bertrand Russell, "If a more just economic system is only attainable by closing men's minds against free thought . . . the price is too high." The pressure for another exodus began to build inside Cuba.

Mario Bolaños is Cuca Plata's grandson. Oblivious to the plight of his family in the United States and their hopes that he might join them (for which they had endured hunger and misery) Mario attempted to stay as long as he could in order to observe and study the transformation of Cuban society under Fidel.

Mario Bolaños: I left relatively late by most accounts, and certainly by your measure of the First Wave. I left in 1965, between the First and Second Waves—in the middle of the trickle, one could say. I was one of the hundred or so Cubans who arrived during that year. I stayed behind for two reasons. First, I had immense curiosity about the profound social change that was coming over Cuba. Second, being both a little foolish and interested in the science of political change, I stayed behind ostensibly to go to school. But the university was closed for most of the time, so we formed a small study group instead. We used to meet at the Miami Cafeteria in El Vedado. The day they changed the sign to Heladería [Ice Cream Store] we were there, painfully mourning the Yankee loss and reluctantly welcoming the Marxist functionalism. Cuba was for our group the subject of intense study. We participated in as many political things as we had to in order to avoid government harassment.

A member of the group had obtained military rank in the militia, thereby giving us the instant credibility of a uniform. But we were spies—spies of the best sort, spies for academic disciplines. Some of the members of our study group had official jobs and were responsible for drafting policy action. We sat around at night in the café and debated the relative wisdom of the various options. But by late 1963 all had been settled between Russia and the United States with regard to Cuba. The United States had promised not to invade in return for Soviet missiles being taken out. After that there was very little change that could not be predicted. Fidel was in total control.

The university opened. I taught English and history on the Havana campus and continued my own studies. It was very difficult to survive. Compared to Byzantine academic politics elsewhere, the University of Havana, as run by the Cuban Communist party, was a moving panorama of Stalinist plots and counterplots. It was dishonest in terms of academic principles and what you knew to be truth and science and the proper role of politics in the academic process.

It was difficult to survive. People were jailed and tried for things unknown accusers had said about them. You couldn't say anything critical about the people in power or levy the mildest criticisms against the Russians. Protesters were sent off to Cuba's version of the Gulag Archipelago—El Principe—in Havana. They were left there without anyone knowing about them for months, even years.

One man, a very powerful thinker who wrote poetry, was sent to El Principe on charges that he was doing counterrevolution, the catchall label they used when they had no specific charges. They did this to him ostensibly to persuade him of the error of his philosophy in a proletarian state with no philosophy except that of the leader. But the fact is that they sent him to El Principe because he was able to persuade others. There is a Marxist principle that says that unless you figure in the official act, you get no speaking parts. They killed the man—I won't say his name. They killed him because he had become a counterforce. You know how they did it? They let him out of El Principe and told him to leave the country. At first he couldn't believe it. He took his family, filled out an application to leave, and was accepted. Although at the airport there were some relatively minor personal insults, he left for the United States and settled in Miami. Then one day, several months later, they planted a bomb in his car in Miami. He was getting to be a force in political matters in Miami affecting Fidel. Fidel knew about it through his intelligence network in the United States. He ordered the man sentenced for his previous crimes and executed him in the United States. Fidel can do that today.

Antonio Chacón sent his children to the United States in the First Wave but he was unable to join them until the Second Wave. As I interview him he sits on a stool in his study at home, in front of his drawing table, absentmindedly doodling. Several minutes of silence follow my question about his situation in Cuba prior to leaving for the U.S., and his decision to separate from his family. Before he answered he showed me his doodle. It was a picture of a bearded bald man (presumably me) holding a microphone, while a fat man with an exaggerated overbite (presumably him) attempts to bite through the microphone cable. We both laughed at his doodle and he began to answer.

Antonio Chacón: I make a living drawing cartoons, which at one time had political captions. Today [in the Miami *Herald*] they have a different orientation. That was an outcome of having to stay in Cuba after the end of the First Wave. When the revolution came, the editors of my newspaper were told to go back to censorship. In other words, they had to publish propaganda for the public. I am an artist— a creator. I can't create and also lie. I can't. What I create is always fiction, but it is what I want to say. I can't say what others want me to say.

I began to draw a comic strip about a man who went to work every day and came home to a jealous wife and two of her relatives. But there was nothing I could say about that which wasn't political. All the lines I could write that rang true had to be those dealing with the topic of the day. There were food shortages, and hundreds of thousands of Cubans wanting to leave. Everybody knew someone who was leaving [Cuba] or had left, and that's all they talked about. How could I do a comic strip on a family living in Cuba and not talk about the massive emigration or the food lines? If I talked about these things, my work would be censored or I would lose my job, but not to talk about them was to lie. So I did a comic strip about a Martian man; "El Marciano" I used to call him. He worked every day and came home to a jealous wife and two of her relatives. I didn't have to talk about Cuban politics.

I applied to leave the country in 1962, before the exits closed, but it was too late. Right after that the first nuclear confrontation between the U.S. and Russia [the October Missile Crisis] occurred. I just wanted to get out and paint pictures and feed my family. Here we were, caught in the middle. We had applied for an exit permit. This meant that I would lose my job at the newspaper. We had planned for a few months of unemployment. It was unavoidable. But back then everybody who had someone in the United States who could sponsor them would get out eventually. The United States would issue a visa, the Cuban government would issue an exit permit, and after some red tape and bribes and the like, you could get out in three or four months, a year at the most. Then, slam. The door closed and I was inside. Unemployed. We finally left in 1966. Can you imagine that? Four years knocking around doing "volunteer work" on weekends in order to get the food allowance. We lost our belongings. Everything we owned was sold or traded for food. We ended up living with my friend Jacobo, who took us in at great risk. I lost eighty pounds in those four years. It was so horrible I can't bear to think about how it was. I have tried to forget by pretending it was better than it was. But it was horrible. My friend's children had nothing to wear, except pants made from discarded sugar sacks. I watched my beautiful wife die of pneumonia in front of my eyes the year before we left. She was too weak to fight the illness, and medical attention in Cuba, like everything else, had deteriorated.

The day after I arrived in Miami, I went to see my old doctor, who was working in a clinic downtown. He remembered all of my illnesses and ordered some tests. But he had seen enough refugees to know without making tests what was wrong with me: malnutrition, diabetes, and high blood pressure. He was right. I'm fine now. These Cuban exiled doctors have developed a whole specialty like tropical medicine; these guys do "refugee medicine." I do a comic strip now in which a Cuban doctor says to his nurse: "Don't take his temperature. I know what it is. It is about 103°." She takes the patient's temperature anyway, and to her surprise she finds it is 103°. "How did you know?", she asks. "Simple," says the doctor. "Refugee medicine. He just found out he is getting resettled in Minnesota and his body is practicing getting warm." [He laughs at his own joke.]

After the Missile Crisis, Cuba turned inward, to the needs of its rural people. The cities were abandoned to decay. The scarce materials and those who knew how to work with them were sent to build schools in Oriente and clinics in Tope-collante. Food was strictly rationed—eight ounces of meat, ten ounces of rice, and a pound of beans per person per month. Children and old people got a ration of milk and one egg per day. In order to get food, people had to stand in line for hours—in the morning for bread and at night for whatever there was.

When Ernesto Cardenal, the Nicaraguan writer and poet, visited Cuba in 1970, he met a young man José Yanes of whom he wrote the following:

> "The poet José Yanes, one of the best of the young poets of Cuba, learned to read through the literacy campaign (of Fidel Castro). Before that he was a worker in a sausage factory. He is now a member of the Cuban Literary Guild."

In 1965 José Yanes had written a poem which he titled *"La Habana es una ciudad que espera"* [Havana is a city that waits.] His political attitudes are hard to discern. He sees the emptiness of the political slogans in the face of the realities of everyday life—trying to survive amidst the shortages and the social expectations. Yet he understands the reasons for the decay and abandonment of his city to the more pressing needs of the rural areas, and he waits for the men who are gone to return "one day to reconstruct her." His view of Havana in 1965 is as objective as any we are likely to see.

Havana Is a City that Waits

Every morning
returning above ground after the bombardment
men in this City resume their lives
as they can.
With militant faith,
their pessimism reaffirmed.
They go into the dirty street.
The buildings with no paint or plaster,
which the men cannot see by the dawn's early light
but which they know, unseen are there decaying.
The holes covered with op art nouveau.
demanding

EVERYONE AN AGRICULTURAL WORKER:
WHAT ARE YOU DOING TO ACHIEVE THE TEN
MILLION

GIVE EVERYTHING IN THIS DECISIVE YEAR

FULFILL THE RURAL NEEDS;
MORE AGRICULTURAL STRENGTH

TO THE PARTY: EVERY WORKER
A WORKER FOR THE OFFENSIVE

THE ORDER TO FIRE HAS ALREADY BEEN GIVEN
        OUR COUNTRY OR DEATH
        WE SHALL OVERCOME

The garbage cans, the lines at the stores, the cats, the militiamen standing guard at the corner, these are the things that welcome our men in the morning. That young man who walks fast belongs to *El Partido* [the Communist Party]. He knows that the city crumbles, but his vision is in the country; he sees new roads and hospitals. He goes into a corner store where an old sign moves back and forth in the wind with a rusty whine.

OQUENDO—CAFE AL MINUTO

He thinks of old times, but there is no return. He turns to look at people behind him loading up another *art nouveau* sign onto a truck.

NOW, WITH MORE DECISIVENESS
THAN EVER, WE SET FORTH TO REVERSE
THE DECLINE AND MOVE TO VICTORY

There is an old man with a black suitcase who hasn't seen the dreams. He has only seen the City each day looking worse. This daily view of urban life kills him. A boulevard remains lit one night. It looks to him like the city no longer waits for attack. He lives in his mind, in a time that is not now. In a city long dead. He cannot see progress. Each day his life is gray, and he gets lost in the ash.

And the lady who runs so fast down the street. She runs in vain. She arrives too late for the bread line. Now she can't think straight. Now she simply hates.

And the young man with the army fatigues. He used to go to school. Now he will cut cane in the fields. He hasn't slept all night. His mother cries at home.

Havana is a city that waits for light, for food, for buildings and for cars, for the men who will come one day to reconstruct her, and who are now in other countries, or in the depths of their own country, in dirty barracks, trying to lift up the whole island from its horror.

Faith, hate, love and the hint of hopelessness, dreaming. . . . Neon lights seem sweet in the early evening, and even mercury lights seem pallid.

The sun comes up over the buildings. I can now see the sign across the street, that shows us the only path:

HASTA LA VICTORIA SIEMPRE
[TOWARD VICTORY ALWAYS]

Once More Upon the Shores of Liberty

The deal Maxi and Nicasio had worked out for a new family reunification airlift of Cubans after the election of Lyndon Johnson was made a reality by mutual gestures on the part of Cuba and the United States. Brigade 2506 was exchanged for 10 million dollars in medical supplies, and an agreement for a family reunification migration of Cubans to the U.S. was signed. The flights from Camarioca, Cuba to Miami, Florida started in late 1965. Thus began the flow of the Second Wave.

The First Wave was homogeneous in character; the Second Wave was heterogeneous. The exiles were still white in the majority, but 24 percent were black, Oriental, or mulatto. Though educated people continued to predominate, there were many more tradesmen, carpenters, plumbers, farmers, and other members of the working class. These refugees brought no money or jewels with them. They did bring cultural assets in large quantities, among them an aggressive instinct for self-determination and their own definition of *libertad* [freedom]. They shared these cultural assets with the First Wave. Like those who had come to the United States earlier, they had earned their freedom.

Many who had declared their intention to leave the country before the exits were closed at the height of the October Missile

Crisis were caught inside. They had survived slave labor with little food and reduced social circumstances. Also, they had suffered the anxiety of waiting for an opportunity to leave the country.

The Second Wave brought most of Cuba's active academic and scholarly community to the United States. The climate in Cuba had shifted from support for academic pursuits, to toleration of them, and finally to complete disapproval. The government's posture was purely anti-intellectual. The introduction of political officers at the University of Havana and reduced support of students and faculty rendered the university inhospitable. The intellectuals were very positive about exile and expressed no desire to return to Cuba. They wanted to side with the United States against Cuba on the issue of *libertad*.

The U.S. Immigration and Naturalization Service used the same strategy of relocation that had failed during the First Wave. But because the Second Wave exiles had psychologically severed the umbilical cord to Cuba and were ready to start new lives in the United States, the strategy of relocation partially succeeded this time. Some of the exiles stayed in Miami and gave impetus to the now respectably active Cuban-American economy.

The Second Wave brought to the city of Miami over 18,000 lawyers; 2,500 doctors; 1,600 teachers; and 4,600 carpenters, masons, and bricklayers, all willing to work at minimum wage or below. Out of the need to employ their own, and in response to the favorable business climate which the entrepreneurs of the First Wave had already created in the United States and in the Caribbean, the Cuban-American economy was forced to grow and expand. Within five years of the start of the Second Wave, the trade emanating from Miami and reaching most parts of Latin America had doubled. Five years later it doubled again.

Members of the Second Wave were welcomed to the shores of the United States and helped in every way possible to survive and thrive. The Bilingual Education Act was passed with the Cubans' educational needs as a priority. Special tuition assistance was offered to those who wanted to attend American universities. Small business loans, educational development grants, and special services helped make the adjustment of these people more successful than that of the members of any other episodic migration to the United States. Recent economic studies estimate that the cost of the special help given the Cubans was recovered only seven to nine years later from taxes paid by these same individuals. But from 1966 to 1968 the United States was not thinking of that; it was simply being generous, like someone who feels guilty about a friend's predicament. The United States gave aid not as an investment in human development, but simply as a way to clear its own conscience.

The Second Wave had a strong economic view of itself. Many had learned the lessons of free enterprise by observing the deterioration of the Cuban economic system. They understood the need for skills and for individual incentives, which the Cuban system had ignored at its own peril. Members of the Second Wave had known deprivation, repression, and submission in Cuba. They were in the United States now, where they sought and found abundance, tolerance, and *libertad.*

In the following pages members of the Second Wave tell how they adapted to life in the United States. Instead of weaving their words into a chronicle of events, I will present them to you whole, as stories of acculturation and cultural re-creation. The paths of our cultural evolution in the United States are among the most diverse of all factors we can measure among the Cuban-Americans. Part of this diversity is in us as a people, but to a great extent it is due to our acculturation to a complex new society.

All of us in the United States, Cubans as well as others, live within a regionally varied but nationally consistent system of symbolic interaction labelled "American culture." Since this culture is different from the one in which we Cubans were born and raised, we are engaged in a constant search for referents which enable us to interact successfully with other people living here. These referents sometimes take the form of attitudes we adopt in order to belong to a given social group, or values we accept to gain recognition in our jobs or achieve peace within our families. When we first find ourselves in conflict, we reject American attitudes and values because they were forged by people with a different history—people of a different space and time. But slowly, almost imperceptibly, we incorporate the symbols we are learning here and get rid of those not in use. Acculturation results.

Whether or not we experience a shift in our cultural view (and if we do, the extent to which this shift is reinforced by the environment we inhabit) determines what we look like to each other and what we feel about each other, about America, and a host of other things.

What follows is a set of snapshots—word pictures of the lives and thought of members of the Second Wave.

Luisa Gil (her real name) was born in Camaguey, Cuba in 1951. She is a writer living in Miami and very active in the young generation of Cuban writers in exile. I translated and adapted her poetic short story "Recuerdo Vital" [The Vital Memory] because it articulates the deeply sublimated memories of the events leading to her national replantation and the tragedy which so often accompanies these events. In the story she tells us of the day she saw a butterfly over the waters of the Atlantic and thinking that it was lost and disoriented, miles from the scented flowers, suddenly recalled the suppressed memories of her childhood, which up to that time she had been unable to remember.

Luisa Gil: Today at the beach I remember clearly the happy child of seven who turned in empty bottles for a piece of candy brittle, and had already noted that the heat from the sun made chocolate soft. I remember the happy child who would walk across the street to the corner by herself [her mother watched from the window] to go to her friend Teresita's house. I believe Teresita is now dead, but I don't know for sure. I would always be thankful for the breakfasts my mother fixed for us to eat outdoors in the backyard in the chilly-warm early morning, when the adults were sleeping. Those who know only the nightfall have never been chilly-warm.

It was the same happy, clumsy child, student of piano and guitar, who dreamt things I no longer remember. Except perhaps being terrified of seeing *el loco* [the crazy man] who lived in my neighborhood. I don't remember whether I actually saw him or just thought I saw him. In any event, you had to pass by the window of his house with care, because the crazy man might pull your hair, and he almost always did it if you came too close to the window. I thought that he pulled the girls' hair because, though he had a ball, he had no one to play ball with.

Every day I used to go by the street where *el loco* lived, careful not to be pulled in, until one day when there was a big hullabaloo. I thought it was because the new year, which we were all waiting for, had arrived making such noise. But instead what had come was a new time. Fidel's revolution had triumphed. I didn't understand anything— only that my family began to fall apart bit by bit. My uncles no longer came around and not everybody was my friend. My father cried; I had never seen him cry before.

Nothing which belonged to us was ours, and I didn't even know what we had. After the immediate terror and the shouted slogans of my antirevolutionary sister had died down, we ate paper notes before each house search, and I helped. I began to understand. Then there was the bomb, the one they placed when I was doing my arithmetic homework. I never finished, having a good excuse for not doing it. The glass shattered in front of me and I almost lost consciousness, but they gave me *tilo* [linden-tree leaves] and I calmed down.

I don't remember enjoying the carnival after the bomb. I used to love carnivals, waiting for the last *conga,* when it was made up entirely of black people. All you could see from the street were the drums singing songs to saints I didn't know then, but I know them now.

It was all very complicated, the process of change. I don't know why I began to want to leave the country, even if I had to go alone. I don't know how I could have accepted the money Teresita gave me—she who told me she would never see me again. And how could I have turned my back on my whole family and not even seen my mother's tears and mine, which were to come? I had no awareness of the meaning of leaving everything behind. I had no idea what a looking glass called "exile" would come to mean. It's like not knowing what is on the other side of a playing card, not knowing where to stand.

It was a sad little girl who missed . . . what? She did not know. But she knew there was something missing at the orphanage where she could not make herself understood. She was at that time a very frightened little girl, far too overweight for her eleven years. And she had to grow in order to withstand all that cargo of ideas, politics, aggression, and loneliness. But everything comes to pass, and this remembrance passed too, to be replaced by youthful dreams of Disney World. "Everything passes, everything stays." She found words one day. Maybe they came from a previous life. She could have turned them into a neoromantic story, like the one I almost told here, but which I shall not continue.

I must get to the main point. This memory I have comes from another vital memory, that of trailing my hand along the wall next to the street, along the fences and the glass windows of stores. My other hand was nestled comfortably in my mother's, as she shopped or looked into store windows. She always said, "Don't run your hands along those dirty walls; you'll pick up germs." And I silently thought about which types of germs might live in dirty walls or what a germ was and whether I could risk his presence on my hand. I still run my imaginary hand along the sides of parked cars while I go in my own car until I become AWARE. And that's when I stop and get hold of myself, lest someone in a white jacket come along and put me away so I will never again see that magnificent butterfly fluttering over the Atlantic Ocean.

It's a shame I don't recall details. I don't remember whether she was white or green, this butterfly who, because she could fly, thought of herself as a seagull. All these things come to mind, when I think I am seven all over again, and could eat an *anoncillo* [a tropical fruit] or a *pirulí* [lollipop] from the *chino* [Chinese man] in Varadero [Cuba], where I became aware of some things and confirmed others I always knew. I know now why I bite my nails and why I need to be free and think of myself almost as a poet . . . *y soy cubana.* [and I am Cuban.]

Antonio Wong was born in Cuba of Chinese parents. He now owns a flower shop in Miami where we talked. He is a slight man, nearly thirty-three years old with a big toothy grin. As is typical of the Chinese in Cuba, he lived and worked around other Chinese, and was somewhat isolated from the balance of the people. Today, as a Cuban refugee, he is strongly identified with and aware of his Chinese roots, which he is endeavoring to pass along to his children. His life style and business are typical of other Cuban merchants on 8th Street, but he is not one of them. To the Cubans who visit his store daily he goes by his nickname, "El Chino."

Antonio Wong: I was about twelve years old when Fidel took over. I had two smaller brothers and two older sisters, and we lived on a farm outside of Camaguey. My father had a vegetable and fruit stand in the city. We all worked. I transported or grew the vegetables he needed for his business. My father came to Cuba when Lord T. Lee, the man he worked for in China, lost out to Mao Tse-Tung during the Long March in China. The lord boarded a ship with all the people who worked for him and their families. I think there were 1,500 of them in all on the one ship. First they came to the West Coast of the United States, but the final destination was Cuba. He had figured it all out.

There have been Chinese in Cuba since the Spanish occupation, and some of the families in Cuba had worked in China for Lord T. Lee, the protector of a sector of land, my father says, richer than he has ever seen. My people have been agricultural people for many centuries. Lord T. Lee was the fifteenth ruler of his line, and there were members of his family in Cuba. When my father arrived, he was given land to grow vegetables and fruit and a stand in the city to sell the produce from. Half the profits went to Lord T. Lee, who lived on a farm outside Havana. When I met him—I was about six then—he had a white moustache which reached almost to the floor. He had to hold it out of his way when he walked or sat down. He also always wore traditional Chinese clothes. He was a warlord in China, so his involvement in Cuban affairs was predictably military. He helped Fidel in the takeover.

When Fidel took over, both my father and I thought he would be good to Lord T. Lee's family. We had no idea the revolution would be communistic. We had run away from communism. Communism is not right for the Chinese; it is an imposed idea which one day the people shall shake off. Lord T. Lee died and Lord Ki Lee [Lord T. Lee's son] told us to come to Miami. Most of the family went to Mexico, but there are a few in Miami now. By choice, I am not a member of the family any more. Lord Ki Lee gave us our share of the money and let us stay here. We still hear of the family, but we no longer live in communion with them in the Chinese way. We are just friends.

It was pretty rough growing up Chinese in Cuba. There was much prejudice and open hostility. We had a reputation for turning the other cheek, and people abused us because of that. We could not speak Spanish perfectly or with a Cuban accent, and people made fun of that. Now I've learned English. I have attended college here, and I am an American citizen, but inside I am still a Chinese wanting to be a Cuban.

I have worked very hard here, and the rewards of my labor are very satisfying. I have this flower shop, and I'm happy with the way things are going. I worry about the future, though. I don't know what it will be like for my children. To be outside the protection of the Lord Lee family is to be exposed to circumstances, to have a cloudy future. My children's heritage is lost, or almost lost. What is a Chinese man without the knowledge and wisdom of the past?

I do the *I Ching* [the Chinese *Book of Changes*] with my young son as a game, and I make up philosophical problems for him. He is a very intelligent boy. Maybe he will have the knowledge of the past. When he is old enough, I'll take him to China. I have not told him anything about Cuba. He will be Chinese always but he does not need to know about Cuba. I am the one with Cuba inside. He will be another wandering Chinese who happens to like Cuban food. [He smiles.] Maybe someday I'll tell him.

Ismael Damasu is a psychiatrist living in California. When we met he was on duty at a Dade County mental health facility run by a colleague. Every Christmas when he visits his family in Miami, Ismael takes a busman's holiday, spending most of his time on call at the clinic. His large and deeply set eyes are quietly reassuring. He seems much older, like a father figure, not at all like a thirty-three year old. We spoke in between patients during the length of an entire day which included twelve appointments and me.

Ismael Damasu: I knocked around a great deal in the United States before I found a place where I could settle down. I worked for a while in Miami as a porter and went to New York and worked in the garment district. Finally, after two years of New York, I left for San Francisco in 1967. I was probably the first Cuban to become a San Francisco hippie. Fourteen years later, I feel very comfortable in the United States. But during those first few years, nothing seemed right. The years in San Francisco taught me about this country and the American people. I was isolated from other Cubans. I tried to be like everybody else around me, but no one around me was quite like me, not culturally or philosophically. I loved San Francisco anyway.

During this time [the late 1960s], thousands of young Americans left their middle-class American homes and ended up in San Francisco. They lived in the ghetto of blacks and refugees, like me. I lived on Cole Street, a block from Haight and Ashbury. They were, the press said, the flower children. They mistrusted American institutions and all manner of authority. To them there were no restraints upon the powerful in America. To them the entire system had lost its power to rule over their lives because of its own moral bankruptcy. The system must be overthrown, they said. These were revolutionaries from the middle class. Just like me at another time in Cuba. We sort of adopted each other for a while.

There were empty flats all the way up and down Haight Street. I lived in a four-bedroom, second floor apartment with no hot water, but with utilities and a very affordable rent. My belongings were a mattress, some pots, pans, and dishes, and a table I had found with four chairs, none of which matched. But I had more than the refugees from Duluth and Des Moines. The culture of the flower children set the rhythm of my life, and through them I saw what freedom was really like. My friends were strangers themselves to the world of the ghetto which they now inhabited. They wore flowers in their hair and walked barefoot and sang sad, soulful songs about momentous causes—peace, war, civil rights. The pimps tried to put the young girls to work for them, and often succeeded. But first they made them drug-dependent. That was the beginning of the hard drugs;

heroin paved the way for acid and the destruction of a whole generation of fine young minds.

Until I met the flower children and they became my friends, I was totally unaware of my own views on a wide range of issues, which these children discussed like every-day gossip. The nuclear issue, Vietnam, civil rights; they discussed these matters as some other people might dis-cuss the weather. They replaced the chitchat of life with the profound discussion of world matters. They were surprised when they found I had no well-developed opinions in these matters.

In the afternoons, coming home from work, I would walk past the pale-blue, pastel-orange, and natural-green Celestial Herbs store that had replaced the Seven-Eleven on the corner, and the smell of cinnamon extract, sandalwood incense, and *cannabis sativa* [marijuana] would announce that I was coming home.

Now I live in Los Angeles. I see many Cubans as clients in my private practice as well as at the hospital. There is much we can see in their mental processes and problems which is affected by the pressure and stresses of refugee life—either directly, like the man with the recur-ring nightmare about Cuba that won't let him sleep, or in-directly as repressed behavior that we understand to result from cultural conflict.

The people [Cubans] I see not as clients but as friends seem to be affected by many of these stresses, but are able to deal with them, either through an outlet or by hiding their discomfort. Cubans are very good at hiding discom-fort. It is culturally simpler to put up with it; but there are many people who cannot negotiate it. For example, I am treating a woman who has an unreasonable fear. Her mother, who died in Cuba, calls her every night, in her dreams, threatening to take her daughter's life for having left her behind in Cuba. She wakes up after that. This hap-pens every night. My patient is able to function but cannot go to sleep without pills. And every night she has the same dream. There are many people who suffer other recurring nightmares. A popular one is centered around a heroic act. An adolescent whose parents were left behind usually dreams of rescuing them. Sometimes he gets caught.

Sometimes there is violence and the parents die. Either way, there is stress. They cannot sleep. They are unable to accommodate their guilt.

The dislocations of life in exile are many and very important in terms of self-concept. The devaluation of things you know—how to speak the language, how to get from one place to another, who to call to get what action—is almost total. All these things have to be learned again from the start. Particularly when the individual comes to an environment where there are few others like him, the forced devaluation of knowledge is complicated by a decline in status, causing serious problems of self-image. Cuban lawyers and physicians who had to learn English to get a job selling shoes suffered a great onslaught upon their self-image. Those who regained their previous status were able to withstand the stress.

Here the family is the most important factor. No matter that the man had to wear a uniform, had holes in his shoes, and all, he was still king around the house. When some did not have that, their lives changed. They devalued themselves. Some still suffer from the stress.

The most profound change has occurred among the women. They are now not only homemakers, but also breadwinners. And very often, they are the only ones who speak English. The pressure of changed roles is intolerable for the men. The women sense this, so they assume a greater burden in the relationship. The traditional male-female roles are shattered. Yet cultural expectations remain. In the midst of it all, women find the strength to do battle. Their rate of death due to heart attack is twice that of women who have been able to retain the traditional role and stay home.

Cuban marriages dissolve at a rate which is 40 percent slower than that of Anglos, although the Cuban rate is going up. I don't have children as patients, but I see a good many of them in family sessions with their parents, who are my patients. The children assume the same burdens that afflict the parents. Some are even affected by the guilt behavior we discussed earlier, and have nightmares very similar to those of their parents. But even that is good because it reflects the strength of the bonds in Cuban family life.

When you lose a limb to an operation, let's say, the body adjusts to the loss gradually but certainly. The mind may never adjust. So it is with the refugee. The refugee is a "national amputee." He can work and function, procreate and swear allegiance to a new flag, but his mind may never adjust to the loss of the other life. To what it might have been. To what it can never be.

Pepe Ponce is a thirty-nine-year-old social scientist in New England. He arrived in New York in the middle of the Second Wave. A year later, using his research background, he learned that several counties in California were experiencing rapid economic growth and he reasoned this would lead to a good job, perhaps in his old profession. He left New York for California in a 1957 Rambler and several days later arrived in San Jose, California where he accepted the first job offered to him at the Dunkin Donut Central Kitchen. He tells how he reentered his profession after coming to the United States.

Pepe Ponce: The most vivid memory from my youth is the smell of frying foods. Most of my life, which I judge to be important because it is remembered, has a background of a kitchen and the smell of something frying. Maybe that's why I took the job at Donut Central—it just smelled right.

I remember one morning, after I finished my shift, I went out of the kitchen for a cup of coffee and a donut. Part of the pay was all you could eat. I sat at a table under a big umbrella. A fellow sat down at the same table and opened his bulky briefcase and began doing something I had done many times before—tallying survey forms. His name was José Campos, a Mexican born in California. Aside from the fellows who helped me load the garbage pails onto the garbage truck, I didn't know any other Mexicans, although you could see that they were everywhere in this county. José Campos had a nice-looking face, a generous smile, and a good suit, which he tried very hard not to get wrinkled.

After watching him tally his forms for a while, I noticed he had made a mistake and I pointed it out to him. *"Oiga amigo, se equivocó."* [Excuse me, you seem to have made a mistake.] He was very surprised, but when he realized I was speaking to him in Spanish, he was friendly and gracious. He corrected his error and asked me where I had learned to use survey instruments. I told him I had been a researcher in Cuba. He seemed even more surprised. He told me in his idiolect California Pachuco Spanish that his company was looking for other people to take surveys.

The table at which we were sitting was very close to the kitchen at Donut Central. I still remember the smell of fresh vegetable oil boiling around the nearly weightless dough, making the product that paid my wages and fed every Dunkin Donut shop in Santa Clara County. I asked him what the pay was. It was four times more than I was earning. We made an appointment to see his boss the next day. I could barely understand José's Spanish, but I could certainly understand his generous intentions. I invited him to have a donut on me.

For the first time in my period of exile I felt alive. José talked, half in English, half in Spanish, about the world he inhabited and the things he knew. He had never met a Cuban, and although he was very sympathetic toward the revolution, he thought the Cuban people were entitled to protest the political situation.

José went deeply into his soul and told me about his parents—migrant workers who settled out in Santa Clara, California, and became industrial workers. His eight brothers and sisters still lived at home. José was the oldest and the only one who had gone to school beyond the sixth grade. He was taking "soc-psy," he said, at the university. I didn't understand what that was all about. He didn't know how to say social psychology in Spanish, and I didn't know what it was in English, so he explained. The explanation led to my conclusion that it was some form of propaganda vehicle, and I knew about those. I asked him which branch of government he worked for. He seemed offended by the question. He was going to teach in a university, he said. That was what La Raza needed, people who could teach Chicanos about the society and make them better at politics and the like. I was in awe of José Campos.

When José suggested I try to get a job doing research,

I expressed my doubts. He assured me that I would have no problem. Surely he knew all about the job. I loved the idea of going back to doing research, even if it was just asking questions of people who spoke Spanish. I was not up to the task of doing it in English.

José introduced me to his boss, a gentle old man with polished manners and the settled air of a country banker. He regarded me suspiciously, no doubt because of my attire, an old gray sharkskin suit I had brought with me from Cuba. He ceremoniously handed me a typed page and asked me to read it: "Good afternoon, my name is ———. May I ask you a few questions? (If no answer proceed to. . . .)" He stopped me after I had unwittingly read the words that were meant to cue me. A long silence followed. The old man looked at José quizzically, and José looked at me the same way. They were surprised that my English pronunciation was so atrocious, that this articulate Spanish speaker would so laboriously grind out, with Spanish phonology, everything he read in English. Finally, José broke the silence. "*Pero*, he didn't even have an accent when I talked with him in Spanish; never thought he couldn't speak English." The old man looked in my direction. *"Dónde aprendiste a hacer encuestas?"* ["Where did you learn to do research?"], he asked. I must have done something right, because soon I was no longer baking donuts and living on the minimum wage. I was earning the immense sum of $4 an hour as a researcher!

My new job, in general, consisted of gathering information about the attitudes and behaviors of a randomly sampled group of people within a certain area, in order to estimate whether or not that area could support another branch of the Bank of America. Like me, the Bank of America had made the judgment that growth in California was inevitable. The only question remaining was, where is there going to be growth first? A branch bank is a very local institution serving a highly restricted geographic area. I didn't know much about the Bank of America, except that from the road I could see the severe-looking building with the massive Gothic lettering on the roof. Once it had been called the Bank of Italy, because it was founded by an Italian immigrant to serve other Italian immigrants, who must have saved a lot of money in order to make it the largest bank in the world.

I pounded the pavement with dedication. The hot July sun claimed casualties among my less committed and less needy colleagues. The young college men left for the beach, and those with other options exercised them. It almost ruined the company. We couldn't find enough survey takers, and those who applied did not have the right skills. It was the morning I drove to work with José, after we stopped by Donut Central to buy some breakfast for the girls in the office, that I was given the news. They needed me to do a new job. I was going to be a survey supervisor. But we had no people left and needed to deliver more work than we ever had before. José and I reviewed the situation and promptly panicked.

I remember only one thing. Many years earlier, as a boy in Cuba, I would sit at the kitchen table with my *abuelo* [grandfather]. We shared the fruit that he peeled and cut in small pieces, handing me every other piece. I remembered the smell of food frying in the kitchen behind us. I would tell him my nine-year-old troubles, and he would listen with a smile on his face, feeding me fruit. After I finished, he would speak to me about what was imagined and what was real and would conclude always with his own brand of hopeful irony. *"Sabes hijo, no te debes preocupar por nada, porque nunca nada te va a salir del todo bien."* ["Most important, son, don't worry about anything, because nothing will ever be all right."] I told José that, and he understood. He knew about enigmas.

Isaac Cohen is sixty-one years old. He is a former rabbi who owns an electronics business in Miami. I interviewed him in the second floor office of his company's warehouse, which looks down upon the row after row of assembly tables where electronic products are being prepared for market. The walls of the office are covered with pictures and other memorabilia from his days as a rabbi in Havana. There is a picture of him shaking hands with Carlos Prío Socarrás, Cuba's President in 1951, Fulgencio Batista, the dictator who took over in 1952, and Fidel Castro, while he was still without official rank in the Cuban government, this one dated February 1959. Inside a cabinet with glass doors I could see his rabbinical robes on a hanger covered with a yellowing plastic wrap.

Isaac Cohen: I am a "Jewban." I remember when we coined the word. I was a member of a group of American businessmen who went on a buying trip to Japan in 1967. We were all Jews. We stayed at the Tokyo Hilton. During the day we were all subjected to endless caucuses from our hosts in Japanese, and at night, the other two Cuban Jews and I would form our own caucus in Spanish. The American Jews felt excluded from both sides and called us Jewbans. [He laughs.] We are a very rare breed indeed.

There are about 500 Cuban Sephardic families in the greater Miami area today [1980]. There are more Ashkenazic families, about 1,200, mostly in Miami Beach. For the oldest among us, this was a journey which began in Greece or Turkey or Western Europe at the turn of the century and continued during the two world wars. The Cuban-Jewish community is rather close-knit, as are most Jewish communities during the first generation of immigration.

The Sephardic Jews were forced out of Spain by Queen Isabel in the fifteenth century. They immigrated to the Ottoman Empire in Turkey. The Ashkenazim came from Central and Eastern Europe. Our differences stem mostly from this migration pattern. The Sephardim eat Turkish food and dance to Greek music and speak in Spanish. The Ashkenazim from Cuba eat kosher food and dance to Yiddish music and speak in Yiddish and Spanish. When the Sephardim arrived from Cuba, mostly during the Second Wave, they found that the American Sephardim spoke Spanish also. The Cuban Ashkenazim found American Ashkenazim who spoke Yiddish as well. Wasn't that a practical thing to have happened? We are a community here in Miami. We have a Cuban Hebrew congregation, a Cuban Sephardic congregation, and a Cuban Hebrew Circle to which we all belong. We hold a convention here in Miami every year.

We are also very Cuban. A Jewban speaks Spanish at home and eats Cuban food and dances to Cuban music. We even play dominoes at the Hebrew Circle. I was born and bred a Cuban, raised on the streets of *Habana Vieja*

[Old Havana] near the docks. My wife is also Cuban. Our children are taught to be Cuban, Jewish, and American. These things are not mutually exclusive. To be a hyphenated American is in itself a good signpost for self-identity. To have two hyphens in your self-definition is to be specifically certain who you are.

Almost all of us who came from Cuba came in the Second Wave. The Jewish community in Cuba failed to act quickly enough during the First Wave, and when the exits were closed, the majority of us were still without an exit permit. We were finally allowed to leave after Camarioca. In a way the Second Wave made it possible for the Cuban community here in Miami to accumulate enough members to become largely self-sufficient. Right now [1980] there are thousands of people doing well, surviving and more than surviving, who wouldn't be able to make it outside of Miami because they don't know English. They have to remain in an area where knowledge of the English language is not a requisite for survival. This is largely a self-contained community within a community, and that is why it is so productive. It does not rely upon anyone else for answers or for handouts; it finds these things within itself.

That is one reason Cubans tolerate discrimination in the schools, for example. The Cubans feel that if the schools cannot or do not want to offer better quality education, they can take over at home or employ someone as a tutor or send the kid to one of hundreds of after-school programs. They'd rather do it themselves. This is probably something that will change with the young, and which is changing now. I like the Cuban community here in Miami. I want it to change; it should change. Life is change. I do not fear change.

Rosa Contreras is fifty-nine years old. She was a teacher in Cuba and recently retired from a teaching job in Miami. I interviewed her and her family while she was vacationing in New York.

Rosa Contreras: We arrived in 1966 and were relocated to Coldwater, Michigan, in the middle of the winter. I don't think I have to go into too many details to make you understand that the differences between Santiago, Cuba, and Coldwater, U.S.A., in the middle of winter are enough to dampen anyone's enthusiasm. But my husband Carlos is not just anyone, and thank God for that.

We had no relatives in the United States who could sponsor us, so we accepted the sponsorship of a church in Coldwater, Michigan. We had lived there three years when we moved to Miami. In Coldwater my husband was a gas station attendant and a grocery clerk. I taught Spanish at the church and waited on tables at a small restaurant. Everyone tried very hard to help us, and they made sure we had work and spiritual support. But the change was too severe for us. We could not adjust. We left as soon as we had saved enough money. Those three years in Coldwater are filled with happy memories. I remember the first Christmas: the gifts people brought for the children, the food, firewood, everyone sharing something with us. The second Christmas we had a Cuban *Nochebuena* and invited them all to our home.

The children became Americans right away. Carlos was very worried about them, but thank God they were never in trouble and are now good people, fathers and husbands. Carlitos—he is the oldest now at twenty-seven—was thirteen when we arrived. Miguel [she shows me a picture] would have been eleven then. He is now twenty-five. Carlitos is a farmer in Adrian, Michigan, and Miguel is an Air Force captain. I am very proud of them.

That first Christmas, after going through what we went through in Cuba, was a blessed event. We didn't have any money. Carlos had a dollar and I had sixty cents. We were not going to get paid for three days, and we had nowhere to borrow money. We talked to Carlitos and Miguel and told them the problem. Together we decided that instead of buying something for each other we would give the $1.60 to the church. We got dressed Christmas Day and went to church and contributed our total liquid assets and went home. A few minutes after we got home, people started to visit with gifts—sweet potato casseroles and turkey and eggnog, gloves and hats, and a jumper cable, the kind you can use to start a car with a dead battery, except we didn't have a car. The children remember this day very vividly. One of our church brothers bought them each a bike, and they still have them.

Carlos Contreras (Rosa's husband interrupts): I thought you were going to tell him about the eggnog. [He looks at Rosa, who is signaling him not to tell, but he continues.] We had never seen or tasted eggnog until that time. Manuel opened the first jar to try some, and it didn't taste good to him. He offered me some. I didn't care for it either. Rosa tried it, and she thought it would taste better if she warmed it up. Of course you know what happened. It turned into soft scrambled eggs and tasted even worse.

Carlitos Contreras (their oldest son): While this was going on, we were getting more and more jars of the stuff, and we couldn't understand how anyone would be so fond of something that tasted like that.

Carlos Contreras: We kept on experimenting with it. Rosa suggested we add sugar, which improved it. Then we took a bottle of anisette my brother had given us and added a touch. Now we had something. It might have tasted better with some rum, but anisette was all we had. We offered some to people who came later in the afternoon. They were very impressed and asked us for the recipe.

We really hated to leave these people who had welcomed us so generously. But we couldn't feel for that part of the United States what they felt, a sense that they belonged there. The anticipation of a rhythm of life—winter, spring, summer, fall—is difficult for us to have. We feel those same things for other parts of the United States. Carlitos stayed behind.

Carlitos Contreras: I found a summer job with a farmer, Mr. Dudley, which helped the family and taught me many things about land and crops and animals. Mr. Dudley was very old. His children had left and he had no help with the farm. He had 140 acres in Coldwater and another 84 acres in Adrian, near the Ohio border. After a year of working for him, Mr. Dudley told me that if I worked for him for another five years at no wages other than living expenses, he would give me the Adrian land and sell me his equipment there, the house too, on credit. This meant I could be in business. With the land I could get a production loan and grow winter wheat, because Adrian is far enough south so that most years you can get a pretty good crop out of it. I agreed to the deal after my father said yes, and I began to work full time after high school.

I like the farm and the people associated with farming. In farming every year there is a crisis. Too much rain or not enough rain. Snow too early, frost too late, the prices dropping or rising as a result of foreign policy made in Washington and New York. But every year I find a reason to say, "Thanks be to God," and mean it. Mr. Dudley was like a second father to me. He will never replace my real father, but I will always feel like his son. He taught me all I have learned about the United States, farming, and nature. My real father has taught me everything else. I didn't go to college, but I know more economics than those who did go. I'd like to see some freshly graduated MBA try to cope with my business for a year. He would go bankrupt. I learned all I know from experience.

Last year [1979] I went back to Cuba for a visit. I went to big "showplace" agricultural cooperatives and the like. I must confess to you that at one point I said to myself, "You belong here." Like everybody who goes back to Cuba after ten or twelve years, I thought about staying. What if I could stay and work these farms? But then I caught myself daydreaming. That is all it could ever be, a daydream, because I own land I would not be allowed to own in Cuba. And I promised Mr. Dudley that I would keep it until there was someone else to give it to, and Fidel is not the one he meant.

The Second Wave encountered a much different environment in the U.S. than did the first. This period is referred to by students of U.S. history as the loss of innocence of the American people. A period where the hopes and dreams of the fifties began to unravel, and America saw itself falling behind and losing ground steadily.

There was Sputnik and *Cochinos* to feed America's loss of pride, and the violent death of a President, a Civil Rights struggle, and a war it could not win. All this set the stage for a more profound look at the purposes of America. This was a period of great loss but there was great progress made.

The U.S. of the late sixties and early seventies was more willing to accept diversity in search of virtue and new pride. The Second Wave of Cuban immigrants was ready to remain here for a long time, maybe forever.

The thought of being American had not been widely shared by Cubans until the seventies. The first to think about themselves as a certain type of Americans—Cuban-Americans—were probably those who came in the Second Wave. Those before them were still committed to the maintenance and unification of a Cuban community for a return to Cuba. Meanwhile the second Wave was spreading all over the U.S., finding a home even where there did not appear to be any room.

Alejandro Mederos and his younger brother Rafael left for the U.S. alone. Their family had been granted permission to leave the country as a unit, but at the airport their mother and father were detained because they had been accused by the neighborhood committee of having illegally sold property that had been confiscated by the government when the exit permit was given. As a result, the children left alone in the plane that had intended to carry their entire family. Alejandro was seventeen and Rafael was twelve.

Alejandro Mederos: My brother and I were relocated to New Orleans to live with a family, but something happened; the family did not accept us. We ended up in an orphanage run by the Salvation Army. We left Cuba alone, because at the last moment, at the airport, the authorities grabbed my father and mother and told us to get into the plane without them. We had no relatives in the United States. My father knew someone in Miami but I didn't know who the person was. My parents are still in jail in Cuba. The U.S. newspapers gave the case a great deal of publicity, but no one offered to take us. We were too old. We stayed in the orphanage until I became eighteen, only a few months after we got there.

I already had a job, so I took my brother with me. We moved out of the orphanage and into an apartment I rented with my wages as a busboy. I cleaned tables at Café du Monde in the French Quarter of New Orleans. My brother was going to school. At the end of the school year, we moved to a mill town in South Carolina, close to Columbia. I found a job at the mill. My brother went to school and worked at night on piecework I brought home for him from the mill. This way I could be sure of what he was doing at night while I went to school at the University of South Carolina in Columbia. We lived in South Carolina until I graduated from school and was given a job as a management trainee for a company in Texas.

We had a very rough time. No one really cared for us. We had to make it on our own. But isn't that the way it is for most people? Who gets things handed to them? Very few people, and they are the unlucky ones.

My life in New Orleans is a very faint memory: going to work, cleaning tables, avoiding the muggers and the perverts on my way home at night, going to sleep, getting up again. Occasionally when I am in New Orleans, I go by the apartment we rented in the French Quarter, and some things come back. One night I had a toothache. I had lost a filling and had no money to replace it, so the cavity got infected. I was in excruciating pain. The apartment was on top of a restaurant. The owner knew me. He heard me moaning and came up to see me. I wouldn't let him call a dentist or take me to the hospital, so he went down to the restaurant and brought back a bottle of whisky. He told me it would take the pain away. Two swallows later I was feeling no pain. He waited until I fell asleep and carried me to the dentist. When I came to, I was on the dentist's couch with a new filling in my mouth. I remember that.

I remember discrimination. I was looking for a job in South Carolina, and a man told me to come back the next day. On my way out, I heard him say to his friend that the job should go to an American, "not some jiby-jiby Cuban turd." There were other jobs, but I was not the same from that point on.

Sergio Espinosa, who came to the U.S. during the First Wave and nearly died in a suicide attempt in New York during his first year of exile, recalls his first awareness of being a member of a minority immigrant group in American society, and of standing up for his rights as a Cuban-American.

Sergio Espinosa: I was so busy bowing to the United States that I looked like a Japanese. The United States was all good and powerful, according to the brainwashing given me by my uncle and mother, and even by the Cuban culture here in Miami. We should be grateful, forever grateful for having been granted a new life. *Amor con amor se paga.* [Love is repaid by love.] I heard that every time I got into trouble, and I believed it.

We Cubans were not from here, so we had to be twice as good, lest we be considered ungrateful guests. When I tried to borrow money to buy the shoe factory I now own, the American banker had a neat deal going on the side with people who wanted the shoe factory to close so that they could take over. I was turned down. I found the money. The banker told me I was crazy to buy into a failing business, without telling me that he was representing my competitors. I couldn't negotiate the deal without him. I was about to lose my life savings. Everybody told me to forget it, but I didn't. I accused the bank of conflict of interest and got a lawyer and the regulatory agency to intervene. They had to admit to the illegal practice, and I got my place.

People thought I shouldn't take people to court like that. It wasn't until Nixon that people here in Miami became politically active. There were always a few mavericks who had lived here a long time and knew the score from the inside. But for the most part we were more concerned with Cuban politics than with American politics. As a matter of fact, it was our concern over Cuban politics that brought us face to face with Nixon and made us decide to support him. Johnson, after the Camarioca Bridge ended, proved to be a weak enforcer of U.S. interests in Latin America. His State Department was preoccupied with

Southeast Asia [Vietnam]. He was not interested in worrying about a little island of 9 million people.

Meanwhile Fidel is having a field day, starting revolutions—or trying to—in Bolivia, Guatemala, Nicaragua; making great strides; still killing and imprisoning his opposition in Cuba; infiltrating the Cuban community in Miami. We were sure that Nixon would not forget Cuba. Nixon was more than a tried and true communist fighter. He was also a conservative. Many of us saw for the first time the differences between Johnson, the liberal who wanted to give everything away like Fidel had begun to do in Cuba, and Nixon, the conservative who wanted to make you earn it.

It may be a great simplification to say this, but it was Nixon who made us—at least here in Miami—aware of American politics. Many people in Miami were sworn in as citizens to vote for Nixon. Millions of dollars were collected here. People turned out to vote. That is when I first voted. Up to that time I was not really here.

Becoming Cuban-American

With our new awareness of ourselves as a social group, though a minority subgroup in the United States, our viewpoint began to broaden. We saw ourselves not simply as temporary guests who must behave well and who will someday go back to our home, glad to have been here. We are here to stay.

Our perspective on our own group is difficult to define. While my collaborators often speak with clarity and eloquence, they do not speak with one voice. The perspectives of the old and the young are affected by the chronology of their observations. The professional and the worker, the poor and the rich, the oppressor and the oppressed—each stands on different ground. Each tends to see the world only from his or her individual vantage point. That is not at all unusual. The philosopher Ortega y Gasset once said, *"Donde está colocada una retina, no hay otra."* ["Where one instrument of vision is located, there can be no other."]

But if one listens carefully to these different perspectives, one finds that they fall into two main categories, each as consistent within itself as it is different from the other. I cannot describe the categories as "liberal" or "conservative," since each category is a little bit of both. Nor can theories of social science dissect these points of view adequately. It is more a dichotomy of perspective.

Luis Losada and Omar Betancourt best express the two broadest perspectives of Cuban-Americans. I asked them to try to describe us, the Cuban-Americans, as a social group.

Luis Losada, a member of the First Wave, was educated in Cuba as a social scientist and lawyer. He is now on the faculty of a university in the Midwest.

He represents the perspective of one who had charted a professional course in Cuba, had abandoned it and successfully reestablished it in the United States. His perspective thus expands the full range of two societies. This perspective I call the bicultural perspective.

Luis Losada: I am afraid I am too biased to be objective. I happen to believe in what we are doing here in this country. We *Cubanos* have no reason to be ashamed. We have lived an exemplary life as an immigrant group and we will continue that way. Some of us have a talent for free enterprise. Some use that talent *para abrir surcos* [to plow straight furrows] and some *para abrir zanjas* [to open sewers] in this land.

We all more or less fit into the American cultural ecology. From it we have fashioned a creative subculture, more American than Cuban from a Cuban's perspective, but unmistakably a part of both. This subculture is dynamic. At first [during the early 1960s], it was very "revolutionary" in its focus on regaining freedom for Cuba. *Cochinos* changed all that. After *Cochinos* we put to rest the notion that we didn't have to build permanently here in Miami or New York, because we were going back to Cuba, where we would once again return to the lives we used to live.

The political conscience of the Cuban-Americans has never abandoned its concern for the bilateral politics of Cuban-American relations and the trilateral strategies of Russia, Cuba, and the United States. Cuban-Americans first read the international news in the paper and then move to national news or sports or comics. If you had asked a politically savvy Cuban-American about Martin Luther King in 1966, he would have said King was a communist, but he wouldn't have known who he was. Now ask about

Anastas Mikoyan. He will tell you more than you care to know. Some of us still are unable to refocus our attention on what I call internal matters—matters pertaining to being a Cuban-American, a permanent resident, a citizen with another transplanted national body; some of us will always remain Cubans in transit. But eventually most of us have had to face up to the reality of our own cultural group. After the fanfare was over and the open arms of 1965 turned into the closed pocketbook of 1969, we began to see that our concerns went far beyond the interests of Cuban-American relations and global East-West strategy. That was around the time Richard Nixon was coming back from defeat. Here was a man who could be trusted to deal firmly with Fidel and the Russians, and at the same time deal with new internal matters. Cubans were suffering from a sluggish economy, the loss of financial assistance to small business, and a drop in government interest in international sales by Miami businesses. Inflation was beginning to affect employment and erode savings, and awareness of discrimination was growing at the same time as the quest for civil rights. Miami was beginning to turn into a Cuban-American city, and we were taking responsibility for it. Getting Nixon elected was part of it.

For a Cuban who doesn't live in Miami, the city that houses over half a million of us is a distant but ever-present part of our life. It bears the same strange familiarity as a distant relative not often seen. It produces some of the same sounds and smells that Havana produced; it shares many of the same characteristics with which Cubans grew up—blue sky, palm trees, and Cuban business activity. Martha Losada noticed the familiarity of this environment when she arrived, early in the First Wave. Since then the cultural environment has continued to evolve to the point that a clearly distinctive new American culture—not quite Cuban, but Cuban-like—now inhabits every corner of the county of Dade. Luis Losada finds Miami fascinating; Omar Betancourt thinks it repulsive.

Omar Betancourt is a Cuban who doesn't live in Miami and never has. He was educated at an Ivy League college, and now, at the age of thirty-eight, lives in New York.

He arrived in the United States too young to have had exposure to the full range of Cuban culture as Losada has. Nonetheless he also was able to negotiate the change to a new environment and attain, in the U.S., the aspirations which had formed in Cuba—higher education, scholarship, and a role in the helping professions. He was brought here by his parents lacking sufficient understanding of the reasons for his emigration. Once here, he avoided the cultural bifurcation of Losada, assuming a more integrated perspective with his new environment.

Betancourt holds what I call the cross-cultural perspective.

Omar Betancourt: In one sense, I feel a certain cultural identification with *el exilio* [the community of Cuban exiles in Miami]. There is no doubt that I am similar. I enjoy walking down Southwest 8th Street when I go to Miami. I love to stop at a corner stand for some *café* [Cuban coffee], eat in a *fonda* [family restaurant], watch the Cubans in the fresh air of Maceo Park. This is what I have, in the sense of an immediate group, of which I feel a part. But really, at another level, I do not feel a part of this. I feel a part of *la sociedad Cubana* [Cuban society], and the Cuban exile community is just a bad imitation of it. I feel as if all my ideas and convictions go against the views of *el exilio,* and when I am outside of its environs I deny it.

If I had exotic words and pictures taken by Fellini of this place [Miami], I could perhaps describe to you what I see. *El exilio* is in itself a surrealistic *anarcónica* [anachronism], decaying. Still, it has some good things, which make me want to be a part of it. It is sad but true that if I had to choose between dealing with a Cuban reactionary and an American one, perhaps the Cuban reactionary and I at least have a common theme to discuss, at least we have that much in common. It is . . . something as surrealistic as what I have just said. Miami is of course the center. We all know someone who lives there or has lived there. If we have not lived there ourselves, we have passed through it at some time.

Little Havana is like every other immigrant enclave in the United States, except it is more economically alive than most enclaves. But that is all it is—an ethnic enclave. I don't know if it has an official geographic definition, but everyone would agree that its equator is 8th Street. Most Cubans

don't live in Little Havana; they live in Hialeah, West-
chester, Tamiami, Coral Gables. There is no pattern to
Cuban residences in Miami, except for class patterns. If you
can afford the place, you can usually buy it. But Little Havana is where the poor and the old live. It is also where
the lifeblood of the community—the business sector—is
situated.

As you walk down 8th Street, in a sense you have entered a time capsule that has transported you to the past.
In Miami Cubans live or try to live in *La Cuba de Ayer* [a
song entitled "The Cuba of Yesterday"]. It is a mythical
country we have fabricated, where nostalgia and myths
abound—myths we have created and have tried to materialize. In Little Havana nostalgia turns to nightmare as it
mixes with American kitsch.

If Havana of the 1950s sometimes looked like a copy of
Miami Beach, with its mafiosi hotels and rhinestone ele-
gance, the Miami we have built for ourselves has the un-
real appearance of a copy of a copy.

The cultural center of Little Havana is probably the
Restaurant Versalles, on the corner of 8th and 53rd Avenue
Southwest. It advertises itself as *El Palacio de los Espejos*
[The Mirrored Palace], and of course everywhere you look
there are garish mirrors. It is supposed to be the best example of *criollo* [creole] architecture in the area, but it must
actually be the result of the architect's imaginary impression of the French palace, Versailles.

Nevertheless, Restaurant Versalles is the place where
all kinds of people get together to do business, share gossip, and make political deals. Practically touching elbows
are members of the old Cuban society and the new *potentes*
[powerful] of *el exilio*—the Batista military men and the
Castro mercenaries. Everyone goes there—loan sharks and
"importers of scarce merchandise," business executives and
factory workers, even an occasional incognito CIA plant.
Since it is one of the very few places in Miami that stays
open late after midnight, Restaurant Versalles begins to
collect the party people who do not want to go home. It is
filled with politicians looking for votes or avoiding their
wives, *quinceañeras* [debutantes] getting out of their parties, and homosexuals from The Warehouse [a gay bar]

across the street. It was in the Versalles that someone crashed a chair over the head of Luciano Nieves [a news-paperman] because he advocated establishing diplomatic relations with the government of Cuba. This happened shortly before he was killed.

The Versalles is an amusing copy of those Havana night spots, like the Tropicana and the Sans Souci, which were once truly elegant. It doesn't come up to the originals, but it fits in with the rest of Little Havana.

Down 8th Street, on the corner of 27th Avenue, is the Royal Trust Tower, which houses the offices of *La Cubanísima* [the most Cuban] radio station, WQBA. *La Cubanísima* claims to have a more powerful transmitter than any other radio station in Miami. When it is not jammed by the Cuban government, WQBA reaches Cuba as clearly as it reaches Little Havana. Aware of its power, its objectivity compromised, this station serves as an unofficial Voice of America.

A block beyond *La Cubanísima,* there is a store that sells ancient potions for recalling saints and spirits—voo-doo and *santerismo* [idolatry] potions known for their miraculous qualities. For the customers' convenience, these magical mixtures come in aerosol cans. You might want a can of *Siete Potencias* [Seven Potions in One], or perhaps *Amansaguapos* [Make Aggressive Men Tender], or maybe you need *Amárrame El Hombre* [Tie My Man Down To Me]; push the button and the problem is solved.

Afro-Cuban religions are definitely on the rise. The *santeros* [the high priests of Afro-Cuban religions] have had a great deal of success attracting new clients, not just among the Cubans or the poor, but also among North American blacks. It is said that one is *haciendo santo* [doing a saint] when engaging in *santerismo.* It can cost a small fortune. Devotees buy gold statues and offerings and special cloth-ing, and the fees to the *santeros* can run into thousands of dollars. Apparently we have not lost our faith in the power of saints.

Turn right on 17th Avenue and you can walk to Miami Bay and a small chapel called *Ermita de la Caridad* [The Chapel of Mercy]. It looks like a tent, but it is made of granite and it points to Cuba. There, for 50 cents, plastic bottles can be purchased to carry Holy Water back to Union City or West New York. You take some of the water collected at the *Ermita del Cobre* in Miami and put it in a bowl before your own statue of *Virgen de la Caridad del Cobre*, placed in your living room but pointing toward Cuba. And then you pray. We have not lost our faith, so it must be working.

The newsstand on 8th Street carries some large-circulation dailies [*Diario de las Américas, Réplica,* the Miami *Herald*] and the underground press. The underground newspapers are usually free to the reader, their costs paid by some interest or another whose position the newspaper advocates. Here are some of their titles: *La Verdad* [The Truth], *La Nación* [The Nation], *El Expreso, Debate, El Matancero, El Ausente* [Absent], *Patria* [Country], *Espectáculo* [Spectacle] and *Girón* [the organ of Brigade 2506]. The community that reads these papers becomes offended easily and quickly suspects communist involvement. The provocations that are printed in these newspapers are intense and well aimed. Each faction represented thinks it knows the views of the others and disagrees with these views. Every group "proves" it is right. Thank God they use the papers to express their opinions, not fists.

In 1975 the corner of 8th Street and 18th Avenue was the place to go for marijuana and cocaine. It was called *La Esquina del Pase* [The Passing Corner]. Now the *pase* has moved elsewhere. Here there are Cuban-owned clothing stores and service establishments. Continuing to walk, one crosses the Eighth Street Park, where old men play dominoes and discuss times gone by. At 13th Avenue there is a monument honoring those who died in *Cochinos*. Rumor has it that at this monument E. Howard Hunt and *Macho* [Bernard] Barker had their talk about Watergate.

From there it is a short walk to the restaurant *La Esquina de Tejas.* It is known as the Pentagon, because it is said that this is where the big guns gather. In the same day, you can negotiate a Miami city ordinance with a local politician and help plan another Cuban invasion. It is also the place to watch some of our best street characters. On a good day one can see *El Hombre del Cuadro* [The Man with the Picture], who walks around with a large photograph of

Batista hung around his neck; *Kilo Prieto* [the Bronze Penny], who works at a local clothing store and often hands out cigars with a picture of Fidel on the band; and *El Loco de la Calle Ocho* [The Nut from 8th Street], who likes to organize minilectures about American politics on street corners. According to his scenario, the United States is under the control of Castro agents Jimmy Carter and George McGovern. He insists that Jimmy Carter was actually born in Santos Suarez [a suburb of Havana] and that George McGovern is really from Luyanó [another suburb]. He claims that he met both men in Havana, having a *café* in the original *La Esquina de Tejas,* and that Fidel is responsible for having placed one in the Senate and the other in the White House.

Luis Losada: Miami is really important to most Cubans as the base of their culture in the United States. The Cuban-American culture that began to be defined as the Miami version came into contact with other Cuban-American versions in New York, San Francisco, and Atlanta. Tentatively at first, the Miami community became more influential than the others. Miami is Mecca, and it is also Jerusalem. The culture emanating from Miami affects Cubans all over the United States. But it also reaches further, to Latin America, as it establishes strong and important ties with Puerto Rico and the Dominican Republic in one direction, and Panama and Mexico in another direction. Our viability is increasing. We are beginning to accept political responsibility as Americans.

Probably the first time Cuban-Americans consciously participated in American politics was when Nixon ran for president. They raised money and started citizenship drives to increase the number of voters in the 1972 presidential election. And it all paid off. Nixon noticed their impact and grew closer to them. Nixon had always felt comfortable around Cubans. His best friend—Bebe Rebozo—was a Cuban, and his personal valet and his household manager were also Cuban. He began to see Cubans as a source of political and financial support and his most loyal fifth column. This all ended with Watergate, but in the minds of many Cuban-Americans, Nixon never betrayed them. "Our

White House" [Nixon's Key Biscayne home] became a political symbol for our people. They tried to serve what they
thought were the legitimate interests of the American presidency. Cuban loyalty to the principles of the Republican
party and those which Nixon himself represented was
stronger than our awareness of the United States as a nation. That is why we became involved with Nixon's Watergate.

As an American, I am proud of the fact that we are
collectively offended by excessive acts of power on the part
of our leaders, and furthermore, I do understand that Nixon
had to be publicly chastised, which he has been. But as a
Cuban, I cannot understand the naiveté of these Americans, who in the first place bring a third-rate burglary to
such national and international consequence, and in the
second place fail to notice the evil which threatens the
United States around the world. To us Nixon is still an
honorable man. He got caught because he became involved
in trying to help the Cubans who broke into Watergate. He
paid for most of their defense expenses and gave the families money and support, directly and through his friends
in the Cuban community, so to us he is clean. He is guilty
of lying to investigators and the like, but not of leaving
people in the lurch, and since we are those people, he is
all right with us here in Miami.

After the momentary setback, we continued *abriendo
zurcos* [plowing furrows]. A very large middle-class group
with traditional Cuban values gave form to this endeavor
in the 1970s. The speed of the change was like a strong
wind on the sails of this middle class—almost too strong to
control. The fast pace made us fear family breakdown and
disaster. We reentered politics in self-defense. We assumed
social and economic leadership of our community. For the
first time, the future of Cuban-Americans, socially and economically, determines the social and economic health of
their principal environment—Miami. There will come a
time, I am sure, when Cuban-Americans will have such a
large impact on the economy of the United States that any
adversity which befalls them will be felt by the economy as
a whole.

Omar Betancourt: I think that's a mistaken perception. We tend
to overestimate our own effect upon this society. The pre-
cise opposite is true. When Uncle Sam catches a cold Cubans get pneumonia in Miami. Don't forget, we are still the
largest group of working poor left in the United States. The
average Cuban-American in 1979 had an income below the
poverty level. Those were the ones who were working!

During the years of the Second Wave, integration in
American society was possible only at the lowest levels.
Today we are integrated, but primarily in institutions that
need token "Hispanics" or places we own, our own businesses, banks, and so forth. Back in the 1960s people who
had been dentists in Cuba worked as hotel porters in Miami
and, of course, no one expected any more than that. It was
a means of keeping body and soul together. That was all
that mattered, for a while. Then came the struggle for credentials and licenses—going to night school for three years
so that you could get a license to enable you to do the thing
you had done for ten years in Cuba. The protectionism of
professions is still the most powerful barrier to complete
social integration.

The "Cuban success story" has hurt the Cuban community in some ways, and it has helped it in others. First
of all, let's be clear about this: Cuban economic success is
a myth. According to Dr. Lisandro Perez [a Cuban-born
sociologist doing economic research], Cubans earned less
per capita in 1975 than any other ethnic national group
which had immigrated to the United States during the
1960s. He also found fewer Cuban professionals working
in American institutions and a greater number of working
poor than any other immigrant group of the 1960s. There
is no doubt that many Cuban-Americans have done well in
the United States, but these numbers are smaller than the
myth indicates.

There is one good thing about the myth of Cuban success: it gets a good number of people trying to emulate it
and moves us closer to success. Like the matter of bilingual
education—that is, teaching children in their own language
and in English. Bilingual skills made it possible for Cubans
in Miami to develop business with Latin America and make
Miami the capital of Latin America. If not for our dual lan-

guage ability, we wouldn't have been able to build up the economy as we have. The unemployment of Cubans and everyone else, at least, would be twice as high as it is. Bilingual education is so successful here that they will soon do away with it. It is already the most powerful difference between success and failure for our kids.

Yet to be pro bilingual education among the monolingual English-speaking people in the U.S. is to be a traitor to the values of the United States. That is nonsense. We are doing just what every other American immigrant has done. We are working the land and sharing its fruits. The land around here [Miami] is very arid, but trade with Latin America is obviously very fertile. With a strong bilingual capability, our people will be able to earn for the United States its share of Latin American trade. That will undoubtedly lead to better relations with the southern part of the hemisphere and improve matters economically for Miami. So why are they opposed to bilingual education? I'll say it one more time: It is working to help our people who came here do better.

Then there are those who were born here. Chances are they don't even know Spanish and have forgotten how to be Cubans, except for the occasional plate of black beans. Culture conflict still afflicts these American-born Cubans, but it occurs when they come home to an antiquated set of values, a culture trapped in a mud hole living in the past, stuck in 1959, the official Cuban "end of time." At home and in this community, what we offer these young people are values which are not viable in the world today, an archaic identity against which all sane adolescents rebel.

Luis Losada: The children of the Cubans are in great peril and are saved only because they have discipline. Some were born in Cuba, others here. Some arrived speaking English, others did not but have learned it. Everyone watches television, the immigrant's acculturation encyclopedia. Everyone measures his own values against the values on television. We all develop attitudes about mother, family, religion, class that are influenced by the way television conveys these things. When I say television, I mean something tangible. But the cultural encounters of the children of the refugees can also be seen in their interactions with the cultural environment of this nation at work, in school, and at the supermarket. We have no choice in such encounters but to create a subculture—a piece of the old with a piece of the new, with a base in what is ours. This subculture needs to be widely emulated to be reinforced, and this happens when it begins to see its own effect upon the environment and the reflection of that effect in the media. The subculture is changed through its own self-expressions, but this is a dynamic and unstable process. We are not doing too badly, though.

The most surprising of all the achievements of Cuban-Americans—in my opinion anyway—is what happened at the University of Miami from 1963 to 1968. Cuban-American students consistently scored higher than any other group, including American-born whites of European extraction. They stopped the survey in 1968, but I bet you the story is the same today. These are not delinquents and drug addicts. These are hard-working people who make their own way, without harming anyone else, in the tradition of the immigrant to the United States. Education is very important to our culture. Do you know that even though only 30 percent of all Cuban exiles graduated from twelfth grade, over 70 percent of their sons and daughters finish high school, and 80 percent of those go on to college? This is as high a percentage as the first immigrant group of East European Jews. We are building cultural capital, as well as adding to the supply of trained human resources in the United States.

Omar Betancourt: When I worked with delinquent adolescents, Cuban and Puerto Rican [in New York], I learned that to do social work in this community is only to patch up one problem while other problems develop. It is very sad for me to have to admit that only 70 percent of our youth completes high school. What happens to the other 30 percent? Do they go away? Do they die? No. They stay.

Cuban youth are in a difficult spot. Like every other urban minority, when you decide to Americanize and move forward by the book, then you encounter prejudice and run back in search of cultural roots and community support.

But the community, at least here in Miami, is too narrow-minded to see that these youths are casualties from the acculturation war. The 30 percent do not go away.

Have you seen what the Cuban youths look like? The *zapatacones* [ultra-high-heeled shoes], the overly painted faces, the discotheques. This we can't blame them for if we understand what has fed it. There is a Cuban subculture, *Americocubana* [American-Cuban], with fashions vaguely like those of Cuba and the United States—the worst from both. This, of course, is assimilation. Having access only to the lower American social classes, the subculture imitates these classes and is immediately rejected by both Americans and Cubans. The Cuban home cannot tolerate this kind of assimilation, and the upwardly mobile Cuban-Americans fail to employ their less fortunate countrymen and bring them along. These marginal people are present in other cultures. For the Mexican-Americans, they are the "Pachucos" of California. They are a testament to our failure to build a just culture. The *Americocubanos,* the 30 percent, don't go away.

And so goes the discussion about whether the glass is half empty or half full. For me, there is no argument, the glass is both half empty and half full, or at least it was back then, in the final days of the Second Wave.

Those Left Behind

The Second Wave ended in 1973, having brought to the United States an additional quarter of a million Cubans. Diplomatic relations between Cuba and the United States were barely existing since the Missile Crisis totally disappeared. Over 350,000 Cubans who had applied to leave for the United States still remained in Cuba. About half of them had relatives in the United States. The Family Reunification Program brought together over 100,000 families, but another 200,000 families remained separated.

Those left behind in Cuba were the most heterogeneous group that had ever applied to leave. There were twice as many blacks and lower-class workers as in the First and Second Waves. This was politically significant. It took a great deal of courage for these people to express a desire to leave Cuba. It meant social isolation and economic deprivation. They concentrated all their energies on the day when things would change and they could reintegrate themselves within Cuban society or abandon it forever. For six years travel in and out of Cuba was impossible, except on official business. It was a miserable existence for those trapped inside.

Adela Cisneros suffered great personal hardship and eventual imprisonment in Cuba. She came to the United States in May 1980 as part of the Third Wave.

Adela Cisneros: I have never been with Fidel. Never. Ever. I lived twenty-one years of subjugation under that man, and each and every day I prayed to God to give me strength not to lick the boots of the *miserable bandido* [miserable bandit], the killer, the madman. My life for twenty-one years has been less than surviving, if that is possible. I was put in jail four times: first during *Cochinos,* then during the missiles, then after the purge of 1970, and the last time in 1975. All told, I have spent six of the last twenty-one years in jail, and the last five consecutive ones. I am not able to go along with the political line and keep my mouth shut. I must do what I must do.

This last time I was charged with planning, or participating in planning, an attempt to murder Raul Castro. I wish I'd done it, but I hadn't. It was all so that they could get back at me for refusing to sing their song.

I can't tell you how much I suffered under the boot of the *miserable bandido* Fidel. I've been in every prison in Cuba. I was a nun—a novitiate—then.

Estanislao Menendez is another of the recently arrived Cubans who was caught in the Cuban security apparatus. He had expressed a desire to leave the country but had not been able to do so before the Second Wave ended.

Estanislao Menendez: I was born in a town in Oriente [the easternmost province of Cuba]. I have been a farmer all my life. Look. [He shows me calloused, sunburned hands.] I learned to read and write during the revolution, in 1961, and I supported Fidel. Before the revolution, Fidel and his men used to hide around here. [He points outside to his backyard in Hialeah and catches himself in the error.] I mean, where I used to live in Oriente, up in the mountains of the Sierra Maestra. I gave them food and sometimes took messages to Santiago, since I also got along with the *Guardia Rural* [Batista's Rural Guard].

Fidel turned out to be an evil man. My family—a brother, two sisters—all left. They had to leave. Fidel took away their land. My brother used to own *120 caballerias* [40 acres]. When a law was passed that you could only keep the land if it was all being used, he bought a lot of cattle, about 500 head, I think. Then came the law that said that people could only own 5 acres apiece. He split the land among his 8 children, 5 acres each. He also split the herd of cattle. A meat shortage developed and suddenly he looked too good. They passed another law—that parents are not the legitimate guardians of children, the government is. They took away the land my brother passed along to 4 of his minor children, leaving him with 20 acres and 200 head of cattle. Then they took the rest and changed his farm into a cooperative. He lost the whole thing, and became an employee of the government.

Finally he left for the United States. He claimed me when he got here. I wanted to leave too by that time, though I didn't have as much reason as my brother. The only land I owned was a piece of a hill so steep only goats could climb it. No one wanted what I had, and I didn't want what someone else had.

In 1973 the exits were closed. I had a U.S. visa waiver, and a *núcleo* [a number corresponding to a place on the list of those waiting to leave Cuba], but I couldn't get out. Fidel's secret police came by one day [in 1974] to check on me. Why did I want to go? Why didn't I do volunteer work? I was forced to cut cane on weekends. I cut cane every season until *La Flotilla de la Libertad* [The Freedom Flotilla].

Until 1979, when it once again became possible to return to Cuba, the island was completely closed to the Cubans outside. Those inside [in Cuba] and those outside [in the United

States] had nothing but their memories of each other and the
hope that one day they would be together again.

> In my sleep I see the
> shoreline coming closer
> coming fast as I run
> across the blue waters and fly
> across the white city to the green
> land and the warm tender hand
> of *abuelita*. Grandma please
> don't die before I can come back to you.

Beatriz Arias, 1974

THIRD WAVE

Cuba No More

" . . . By nightfall on Holy Friday we had about 300 people. They were everywhere on the grounds, sleeping wherever, and we were waiting for instructions from Peru. On *Sábado Santo* [Holy Saturday] we began to feel the full impact of the exodus. Thousands of people came to the embassy. Some ran inside and stayed; others just came to see what was going on, then left. By nightfall, there was no space left inside. We had nearly 10,000 people on the grounds. I must say, there was no conflict. But it was impossible to take care of so many people for more than one or two days. Our toilets were backed up by Sunday. Someone painted a huge sign in English to show the foreign press helicopters flying over the embassy. It said "CUBA NO MORE."

Return to Cuba

When I asked my collaborators to think back to the years after the Second Wave and tell me what was foremost in their minds during that period, the great majority said, Cuba. To return to Cuba, as visitors perhaps, to see those they left behind, or as Martha Losada put it . . . *A oler tierra mojada* [to smell the wet soil]. These same people of the First and Second Wave who had fought so hard to adjust to life in the U.S. never for a moment abandoned the dream of going back to Cuba someday. In 1979, on the twentieth anniversary of the beginning of the First Wave, they got their wish. That year, over 100,000 Cubans living in the United States, returned to Cuba for personal visits of eight days' duration. They went in response to a special invitation from Fidel, who needed their dollars to meet the rising expectations of the Cuban people in the midst of continuing internal economic deterioration. Miami greeted the news of the restoration of flights to Cuba with an initial distrust of Fidel's intentions. The Cuban-American community became deeply divided between those who wanted to go and those who wanted everyone to stay.

Fidel had calculated that carefully controlled tourism might not create internal problems, and its income would alleviate internal pressures for consumer goods. He also knew that to improve trade relations with the United States he had to go through the Cuban-American community first. Every other way had failed. So he rolled out the red carpet for Cubans visiting from the United States. He refurbished two of Havana's largest hotels and arranged for transportation, meals, and sightseeing—all at the price of $850 per person.

Maximiliano Pons: After some people here in Miami had traveled to Cuba, I heard from Fidel Castro's secretary that Castro wanted to talk to me in person. I was called and so were six others. We were all opposed to trading with Fidel Castro and opening the door to the United States for him.

The U.S. government had already lifted travel restrictions, and Castro was permitting tourist traffic, but none of our group had gone there, and he wanted us to go. The whole purpose was to work with us. You understand that I can't give you too many details on this, don't you? [I nod.] Fine.

When we received Castro's invitation, we agreed to meet with him on another island, convenient to both parties, but he didn't show up. His secretary called later and said that Dr. Castro waited for us on the island on the 18th [two days after we had agreed to be there], but we had not come! I told her that I wanted to speak to him and that I would hold on. After a long pause, Castro took the phone. I suggested a new meeting place and asked him to be on time. He was on time.

His story was the same one we have all heard before: "Cuba is nothing like you say it is. Cuba is a place of freedom and duty and literacy." It sounded sweet, but he was not convincing. Thousands of people ended up going to Cuba. I wanted to go myself. There is someone there I want to see before he dies. I'm afraid I will never see him again. [His usually controlled face twists in pain at the thought. He recovers quickly.] But not until Fidel is gone.

Most Cubans in exile in the United States had dreamed for two decades about the opportunity to return to see their families; some had lost faith in the dream. When it became a reality, nearly every Cuban in the United States had or could get the fare. The slightly open door quickly burst wide open. In one month over 10,000 Cubans traveled back to Cuba. The visits and family reunions were more numerous than Fidel had predicted. From his point of view, this was good. His dollar holdings increased dramatically during 1979. In addition, since most of the services purchased with those dollars (hotel, meals, and so forth) were not used by the returning Cuban-Americans, who invariably stayed with their families, the net income was higher than anticipated.

What Fidel had not calculated was the impact of the communications between the returning exiles and their relatives and friends in Cuba. The carefully controlled expectations of the Cuban people under communist rule were dramatically raised by what they saw and heard from the arriving exiles. Suitcases were full of goods that were scarce or nonexistent in Cuba. For the first time those who had not left the island saw microelectronic marvels and programmable toys. They admired pictures of modern, well-maintained houses and listened to stories about how much money could be made in business in the United States. There were also stories about freedom and democracy, and about the anguish of separation.

Martha Losada: We needed to tell these people whom we hadn't seen for twenty years that the time we had spent in the United States had been good and that we had been successful. They had been told other stories. My aunt, for example, had read in *Hoy*, the official communist newspaper, that large numbers of Cubans in Miami were unemployed and that the Americans discriminated against them. We had to set the record straight. We probably exaggerated a bit—maybe more than a bit. We are proud of our accomplishments, and we told many people about them. When you see these young people, asking questions with their eyes, you want to say, "Yes, it is better there. It is free. You can say what you want. You can work and not starve." We probably said it too often. I went to Cuba twice in 1979. The second time, around December, I could feel that the pressure was on. People—my family—had developed expectations about coming to the United States. They were unrealistic expectations, like a child's dream. Come to think of it, they were like the dreams I had had about remaining in Cuba. Each was totally out of the question.

After our visit, *papá* suffered a stroke and was critically ill for several weeks. His will to live was gone. He was very old, but his father had lived to 100 and that was his goal. He used to call it his "goal of life." If not for his will he would not have lived as long as he did. He had been in World War I as part of the Allied Forces and had been shot in combat. He had also been wounded in an unsuccessful *coup d'etat* against President Prío. People say my father threw himself at the assassin and was shot. This was no common military man who babbled about law and order in order to put people in chains. This was a man who did not hesitate to give his own life to save the life of another. After we left, *papá* grew melancholy and began to talk about dying. No one told us anything about it. He had a convulsion and went into a coma and died several weeks later. If I had known that this would be the effect of the visit, I never would have gone.

Rafael Fernandez: My family stayed in the United States the first time I went back. I didn't know what to expect. I was alone on the first flight returning to Cuba. I didn't want my family around in case something went wrong. It was very tense at the airport in Havana, but there was a spirit of getting along, not making it hard for us to come back. The problem was that Cuba had been closed to the outside world for too long. There was so little freedom that there was bound to be trouble. At the airport the military people going through our bags tried to be polite to some of our loud-mouthed companions, but you could see there was going to be trouble sooner or later.

Cuca Plata: Me? Go to Cuba? Are you crazy or something? What would I do there? My whole family is here. I didn't lose anything back there. But I sent my grandchildren. I had a little money saved, and I sent them one by one. I wanted them to know firsthand, so that they wouldn't have to guess. They came back and told me all about it. They said, "*Abuelita,* they are so poor," or "*Abuelita,* socialism is very good." I tell them I don't care. I do care but I won't tell them. All I want is for them to take a look and make up their own minds, like I did.

Ramón Cisneros was a clinical psychologist assigned to a neighborhood committee, which meant that he was considered loyal to the government of Fidel. His job in Cuba was to advise the committee president on strategies for keeping the neighborhood "A la vanguardia de la Revolución," [at the vanguard of the revolution].

Ramón Cisneros: The day my cousin Mario returned to the United States I cried the whole day. We had been like brothers, and now that we had the opportunity to see each other again, I respected and loved him even more. Then suddenly we had to say good-bye again. [He shakes his head.] I couldn't make it happen in my mind. Before his visit, I could say to myself that I had a job to do in Cuba. I could see the reality of life in Cuba. The reality didn't bother me. Things *had* to be that way in order for Cuba to survive. Now I didn't know. My cousin knew so much more. How could I live in darkness for the rest of my life?

Of course our expectations were totally out of proportion after the visits, but that was only part of the problem. Fidel also reacted badly. Instead of proceeding as he had, liberalizing the consumer goods situation and financing it with tourist dollars, he seemed to reverse direction. No one really knew why he did it, but I could understand it psychologically. Things were not going well for him in his personal life. Celia Sanchez [Fidel's best friend] died, and then another loyal friend, I don't remember her name, committed suicide—all within a month. He stopped the liberalization program. Travel to Latin America was suspended. Fidel had never really liked that idea. I knew he was feeling the loss of Celia and his own mid-life crisis.

And so, one by one, person to person, the Cuban-Americans who visited Cuba and the Cubans who welcomed them home traded stories. Eight days with the brother whom one hadn't seen in ten years simply whetted the appetite for a longer visit. The sick and the old, left behind in Cuba, seemed to get older and sicker after the visit. The Third Wave of Cubans to the United States began as an undertow of the First Cuban-American Wave returning to Cuba. We, the visiting Cuban-Americans, brought it into being and enjoyed its cooling moisture. We also tasted the salt and paid most of the price of the sudden shock of its implacable humanity. It was worth the price.

The Mad Exodus

As tensions built inside Cuba, the Peruvian Embassy became a favorite target of would-be Cuban exiles. It began with Angel Galvez, a traffic policeman who in the summer of 1979 parked his motorcycle beside the embassy, climbed over the fence, and asked for political asylum. A dozen others followed, managing to slip inside in spite of tight security. A favorite way of getting inside, before boulders were placed on the driveway, was to acquire a large truck, crash through the gate, and drive up to the front door, all the while trying to avoid the curtain of bullets from the Cuban Army guards' automatic weapons.

The Peruvian ambassador had not been cooperative with those seeking asylum. After the first few incidents, he warned that in the future diplomatic immunity would not be offered. In a public address to the Cubans, Ambassador Habisch also threatened to return everyone who had already been given political asylum. The forced entries into the embassy stopped for a while. But on January 7, 1980, a station wagon carrying twelve people—four men, four women, and four children—ignored his warning and broke through the gate. Apparently acting with his government's permission, Ambassador Habisch returned these people to their homes and wrote a letter of apology to Fidel.

Castro published the letter in the front page of the government newspaper, *Granma*. He followed the action with a diplomatic offensive. Cuba's exterior minister, Isidoro Malmierca, called a meeting of foreign delegations in Havana. He suggested that they follow the example of Peru in handling Cubans seeking political asylum. The ambassadors were stunned. One by one, they announced that their governments would not go along with a change in the agreements governing political asylum. Finally, it was Ambassador Habisch's turn to speak. He stated that his government had "disauthorized" the measures he had taken with regard to exiles and had instructed him to look for them and bring them back to the embassy building. Habisch informed Malmierca that he had already done so. Shortly after this meeting, Habisch was replaced in his post as Peruvian ambassador to Cuba.

Malmierca reported to Fidel, and Fidel ordered him to get the Cubans out of the embassy. Negotiations at the highest levels began between the Peruvians and the Cubans. The Cubans wanted the exiles returned, but the Peruvians were determined to take them to Lima.

By Tuesday, April 1, the negotiations had reached a stalemate. On that day a bus carrying six people crashed through the embassy gates. After a heavy exchange of gunfire with Cuban forces guarding the embassy, the six were able to enter the building. There were now 31 Cubans in asylum in the building. Two of them were seriously wounded. The day before, an embassy guard had been killed.

Tensions between the governments of Cuba and Peru continued to grow. Additional Cuban Army guards were stationed outside the embassy, and people going in and out were subjected to a complete search. The Cuban government, publicly insisting on the return of the exiled Cubans, threatened to use force to go inside and get them.

Rustino Ferra was a Cuban employee of the Peruvian Embassy. He is a witness to what happened inside the embassy during the days of the Holy Week. Given a choice between staying in Cuba or exile in another country, Ferra became a refugee and was airlifted out of Cuba, first to Costa Rica and then to the United States.

Rustino Ferra: Relations were really bad between the embassy and the Ministry of the Exterior. There were intense communications and threats. We were denied permission to fly the refugees out of the country.

The chaos began on Friday, April 4, 1980—Holy Friday. In Cuba we don't celebrate religious holidays, so it was just another working day. It was a cool, sunny morning. I was working on the second floor, fixing a toilet, at about 8:00 AM, when three very large steamrollers, the big machines with steel wheels that are used to flatten roads, came up to the embassy. These machines smashed through the gates and proceeded to cart them away. We had placed boulders in the driveway and heavy iron gates to protect against someone crashing in with a car or a truck, but the three steamrollers flattened them in a matter of minutes, or even seconds. I remember falling down to my knees and praying to God that we would not be attacked. The embassy was giving political asylum to about 31 persons, who in the previous two months had crashed through the gates. That is why we had the rocks and the gates. Now they were gone, and I was sure things would not improve.

Before the steamrollers came, diplomatic tensions had been escalating between Peru and Cuba, but I thought it was because we were giving asylum to Cubans.

Suddenly, Fidel removed the guard and the boulders in the driveway. It didn't make sense, opening the embassy to Cubans who wanted to leave. We were puzzled and afraid. By noon, we had checked in a few people who had come to ask for asylum. We searched them and found no weapons, so we let them stroll through the grounds. It was a quiet group. There was a great deal of uncertainty, but there was order and consideration. In the afternoon a broadcast from Radio Havana made it clear that Fidel had a plan:

[Excerpt from the April 4th broadcast of Radio Havana, Cuba.]
The Revolutionary Government of Cuba has made the unilateral declaration that any person finding his way by force into the embassy of any country will not be allowed to leave the grounds except for jail. The embassy personnel are

warned that they accept exiles at the risk of loss of diplomatic immunity.

By nightfall on Holy Friday, we had about 300 people.
They were everywhere on the grounds, sleeping wherever,
and we were waiting for instructions from Peru. On *Sábado
Santo* [Holy Saturday] we began to feel the full impact of
the exodus. Thousands of people came to the embassy.
Some ran inside and stayed; others just came to see what
was going on, then left. By nightfall, there was no space
left inside. We had nearly 10,000 people on the grounds. I
must say, there was no conflict. But it was impossible to
take care of so many people for more than one or two days.
Our toilets were backed up by Sunday. Someone painted a
huge sign to show the foreign press helicopters flying over
the embassy. It said "CUBA NO MORE."

Rafael Fernandez, who lives in New York, was visiting Miami
during Holy Week. He quickly became part of the relief effort and did
not return to New York until July.

Rafael Fernandez: On Saturday night we heard about the
people breaking into the embassy. There had been rumors
the night before, but we didn't have any notion of how
many people were involved until Saturday evening, when we
learned about the numbers at the embassy. We were ready
here in Miami for any sort of emergency having to do with
Cuba. People rally fast. We had a meeting, which was the
best meeting we've ever had, on Sunday the 5th. This was
Resurrection Sunday, and most Cubans went to church and
from church to the radio station [WQBA, *"La Cubanísima"*]
on 8th Street. The idea was to help the people in the embassy by flying in food and other items in chartered planes
and getting the people out in the empty planes.

On Monday we began to collect money. By 8:00 PM we
had $100,000 and enough food pledged for 50,000 people.
We had contacted Fidel's government and asked for permission to land and safe conduct out of Cuba for those
in the embassy. We had no response. People were going
crazy around here. They wanted to go back to Cuba by

force. There were 400 teenagers gathered at a parking lot, demanding that Carter give them guns to go and liberate those at the embassy.

The old militants came out of the woodwork and advocated one or another military remedy for the situation. Some people began to train troops. Varona [Tony Varona, a former politician] said he had evidence that the people inside Cuba wanted to fight Fidel Castro. You could have put a sign-up office on 8th Street and had 10,000 soldiers in a day! There had never been anything like this in twenty years of exile. Everyone pulled together and helped each other, kept each other informed and in good spirits.

There was no panic—only concerted action. Even the military threats were part of the concerted action. The Cuban community in the United States made up its mind that what was going on in the embassy was proof that the people in Cuba had voted with their feet. They were challenging the proletariats' dictatorship, and they had to be rescued from the hands of Fidel at all costs. The Cuban community in Miami was together in a week. But we were getting ready for 10,000, not 100,000. No one could get ready for that. [He shakes his head and smiles.] Fidel's Machiavellian moves. How to take a massive failure and turn it into a massive success.

Rustino Ferra: The revolutionary government finally shut us down at nightfall on Palm Sunday, *Domingo de Resurección*. The soldiers returned, and so did the barricades and the artillery. The communists gathered a mob outside and had them throw stones at the people inside the embassy grounds. We threw the stones back at them. Fidel came to the embassy on Monday. After insulting the political exiles, he assured everyone that they would be allowed to leave the country. He called them *escoria* [scum], and no one said a word. There was much fear in the Cubans. Fidel announced that he would grant safe conduct to those who wanted to return home. Only a few took him up on the offer. I don't think anyone believed this man Fidel any more. The government brought chicken dinners and threw them over the fence at us. It was not nearly enough—food for only about 500 people. Only the children and the old ate. There was no room to stretch out on the floor. People were sleeping in shifts, and children—naked, dirty children—were lying in their own excrement.

Fidel kept his promise and gave Peru permission to transport the exiles out of Cuba. The government of Peru announced that it would take 1,000 of the refugees. Other nations were asked to do their share and offer refuge to the balance. Fidel refused to fly the 1,000 to Lima, claiming that the distance—2,500 miles—was too great for his planes to travel. He asked that he be allowed to begin flying the refugees to the United States for redistribution to other countries. The United States did not accept his offer, but Costa Rica did, and President Rodrigo Odio signed an agreement with the Cuban government to send the refugees to San José, Costa Rica, only 700 miles away.

The Costa Ricans were prepared for the Cubans. The exiles were housed and fed and offered work while they waited to be relocated. The international press had converged on San José. The flight of the refugees from Cuba was being publicized throughout the world and had given Fidel an international black eye. Fidel reacted by ordering a halt to the Costa Rican air bridge. From now on, people had to fly or sail directly to the country that would make them an offer of asylum; there would be no exits through San José. Meanwhile, Fidel faced a more serious situation. There were signs of wide support for the exiles, and he feared that if something were not done to control their flights, popular sentiment would lead to an uprising.

Fidel prepared to take control of the internal situation, which was rapidly getting out of hand. His offer of safe conduct out of Cuba for the Peruvian Embassy exiles raised hopes that he would allow others to leave as well. He chose the celebrations of the nineteenth anniversary of his victory at *Cochinos* [April 19] to hold a mass demonstration supporting his leadership and opposing those who had chosen to leave. But the demonstration failed to curb the flight from Cuba.

Estanislao Mendez: I decided to escape from Cuba when I got to Havana. I was picked up in Oriente and taken to Havana in order to participate in the April 19 rally celebrating *Cochinos*. It was my turn to volunteer to go, so I went, but when I got to Havana and saw what was going on, how people were packed at the embassies, I took off and went to the bay at Havana. There I found a boat and boarded it. We avoided the Cuban shore patrol by following them out of the bay—that's right; we were right behind them. Then we headed north to the United States.

Fidel tried a new tactic to gain control of the situation. Instead of preventing people from leaving, he would permit them to do so. But he would mix among them a few of his agents and all those people who had given him trouble. The plan called for political prisoners to constitute a third of the population he would let out. Among the prisoners would be people convicted of common criminal offenses, such as rape, robbery, and assault. A third would be composed of people he wanted to get rid of: homosexual men and women, mental hospital inmates, prostitutes and other people of the streets. The final third would be made up of those who wanted to leave and had risked their lives to do so.

Fidel put his plan in action as soon as it was conceived. He ordered the embassies once again secured, and he began to pull people out of jails and hospitals, and off the streets of Havana. It was then that he began to reveal his diabolical plan for exporting thousands of his political foes, jailed murderers and thieves, persecuted homosexuals—his "scum," parasites, and those he called *lumpen* [from the Marxist term *Lumpenproletariat*, modified in Cuba to mean "a man without manhood"].

Pepe Ponce: The truth of the matter is that if there is an opportunity to get my brother out, even if it's a hundred to one, and even when it involves danger and expense—I spent $60,000 on the boat alone—I would take such an opportunity. I owe it to my brother and my family, and I owe it to this country, which has made it safe for us and has welcomed us. I owe it to the United States to say, "Fidel,

we want everyone who wants to come here; they are too
good for your system of hatred and famine." The United
States said it welcomed the refugees with open arms and
an open heart. I owe it to the United States to carry out its
policy.

When I heard Fidel say that we should go and pick up
the *gusanos* [worms], I knew he was talking about my
brother. God love him, he's eaten out enough holes in
Fidel's rotten apple to deserve to be called a worm.

Pepe Ponce lost no time. He bought a lobster boat and got a crew
together in two days. His supplies were sufficient to accommodate a
long stay or bring back 100 exiles, and he was prepared for either
contingency.

It is hard to say when the Third Wave actually began—whether
it began with Angel Galvez, the traffic policeman who used his motorcycle as a stepladder to get over the fence at the Peruvian Embassy,
or whether it began with Pepe's boat. Pepe arrived in Key West on
April 21, 1980, two days after the mass demonstrations in Havana and
Fidel's offer to release those who wanted to leave. He returned with
forty-two Cubans. Only two of his passengers were related to him;
one was his brother Gonzalo Ponce. The other passengers he picked
up at the beach in Mariel. Several were former military people, and
two were brought to the beach by a friend of Fidel. These forty-two
Cubans can perhaps be considered the first members of the Third
Wave.

Gonzalo Ponce (Pepe Ponce's brother): We got the call from
my brother on April 20, as soon as he arrived in Cuba. We
didn't want to come at first. I was not a *Fidelista,* but I was
working, and I did what I had to do in order to keep my
job. You can't expect to keep a job like the one I had at the
National Institute of Science unless they think they can depend on you. I really did want to get out; I'd had enough.
But there were eleven of us—my four sons, my wife, my
grandchildren. I didn't want to leave them behind. [Tears
come to his eyes.] As fate had it, we left alone—my wife
and I—the children and grandchildren were left behind.

It was all because people have no rights in Cuba.
Maybe they never did. Fidel has been in power for so long,
even for someone as old as me, that sometimes I don't re-

member what it was like before. But as I was saying when you asked about how we got out, well, my brother called on April 20. He wanted me to go to Immigration and file the papers so I could leave. This was the first time I'd heard from him. He was calling from a hotel in Mariel, and he wanted me to leave.

I wanted to leave Cuba and so did my wife, but we didn't know what to expect. And my brother was saying, "Run, run." We did not know what to do. The children said, "Go," and we went. Immigration told us to go to Mariel. Pepe was there with his boat. No one else was there yet; it was too early. A couple of military people asked if they could come and gave us their guns. Then a government car arrived carrying two people in handcuffs. They talked to Pepe for a long time, and he eventually agreed to take them along. There were about thirty people standing around waiting for a boat. Pepe asked everyone to come with us, and they all did. It was not a bad trip, but we knew the two men who had come in the government car were being sent to the United States to spy, and we were all very afraid. Pepe was furious at us for being afraid of them.

Pepe Ponce: I remember as a child how my brother Gonzalo would always know what to do. When we were in trouble, because we were getting home too late or something like that, Gonzalo would tell me not to worry and would make up an excuse that got us out of trouble. Now, after twenty years of Fidel, my brother was not as sure of himself. I had to yell at him on the phone from Mariel, "*Mira carajo que yo no me gasté $60,000 para irme sin ustedes.*" [Look, you shit, I didn't spend $60,000 to come here and leave empty-handed.] I finally convinced him to go to Immigration and then straight to Mariel.

I had my ship, with its crew of three, anchored at about mid-bay. That way I could get away if someone tried to board us. The Cuban Marines were told to accommodate me, but to watch me, so someone was always following me wherever I went. I was carrying a black travel bag with $50,000 sewn into the lining, just in case. Mine was the first boat from the United States the guards had seen.

My brother and his wife showed up alone, instead of with the whole family, as I had told him to do. He said he had misunderstood. Can you imagine that? We had to wait to see if I could get the rest of the family to go. I called them and talked for over an hour, and finally they all agreed to come. I went back to the boat.

When I got back, I found that my brother had accepted two "prisoners," or that's what he called them. They were two of the police who wanted to go to the United States and had turned in their guns to my brother. We had taken two "prisoners" from the Cuban Armed Forces, inside of the Bay of Mariel, and my brother didn't seem to think there was anything wrong with that. I left for shore, but before that, I told the "prisoners" to stay out of sight until I got back. I figured it would take the family two hours at most to get to Mariel, and then we would go. Meanwhile other boats were coming in from Key West, and most of them were docking at the pier. It was a humid, very chilly night. There were red skies that dusk.

I waited eight hours. No one showed up. I couldn't reach anyone by phone. I didn't know what the hell was going on. Later we found out that they had a flat tire and no way to repair it and no other transportation available. They didn't arrive at Mariel until the next afternoon.

At 4:00 AM, after having waited eight hours, I was approached by an army captain, a friend of Fidel, very well known, who had come to the pier in a government car. He told me he had two sons he wanted to send to the United States with me. He offered me his handgun as a gesture of good will. Then he handed me two young men in their twenties, handcuffed and with their heads bowed. At first I told him I wouldn't do it, but I gave in when he spoke to me as a father. I felt for my sons what he felt for his.

I had to make a decision: leave now with my brother and his wife, or risk having people ask questions about all these "prisoners" we had taken—the two on the ship and the two on shore with me. I decided to go. In order to get permission to leave, you had to inform the harbor master. When I did that, I was told that I needed to take some of the people who had accumulated on the beach. They were quickly rounded up—about fifty of them. Of those, about twelve or fifteen wanted to stay and wait for their relatives, who were coming to get them from the U.S. The balance came with me.

After the initial confusion, Fidel's plan was put into motion. Those applying to leave registered at the Office of Immigration and were ordered to go to one of several catchment centers where they were made to wait for processing. The *Abreu-Fontán*, a former military club from the Batista era, was one of those centers. People were then taken to a beach camp near Mariel to be sorted with the ones Fidel was deporting, the prisoners, mental patients, homosexuals, and prostitutes.

Ricardo Ochoa, a former bureaucrat in Cuba, had been waiting for fifteen years to leave Cuba. In 1965 Ricardo's brother had filed for a visa for him, but he did not receive permission to leave before the exits were closed. He had survived the past fifteen years as an agricultural worker.

Ricardo Ochoa: I got the call from my brother on May 3. He had arrived by boat and he was going to Immigration to ask that I be allowed to join him. By this time, about 100,000 people had applied. I don't know that for a fact, but that's the way it seemed to me from the crowds I saw.

First we were sent to *Abreu-Fontán*, a large club in Marianao, Cuba. It is now in the hands of a worker organization. It is all run down. People can take vacations there if they belong to a worker organization. It had a nice beach, but it was always full. When my wife and I got there, it was like a cattle drive. You know what it reminded me of? You know those pictures and documentaries of Nazi concentration camps during World War II? This looked just like it. About 6,000 people were standing around or sleeping on the bare ground. No food except what you could buy at exorbitant prices—a slice of ham and two pieces of bread for $5 or $10, after waiting in line an hour. Women and children were just out in the open for four, five days, with-

out food, only some milk for the children if you could afford it. We stayed there five days.

The people from Immigration—some were decent
people—but there were also sadists from the revolution.
They were only too happy to keep us there captive, hungry, and abused. All of us at Abreu-Fontan were part of
the group of people who were leaving voluntarily when Fidel said all who wanted to go could leave. There were other
groups—the convicts, the political prisoners—but not at
Abreu-Fontán; we saw them at Mosquito.

From Abreu-Fontan we were sent to Mosquito Beach,
a military installation in a cove, with high bluffs on all
sides. I think they called it Mosquito because of the mos-
quitos all around. There was a tent for each group, like a
circus tent—a tent for the convicts, a tent for the *lumpen.*
That's what they called them; they were all in a tent. The
escoria, the prostitutes and pimps and other assorted *escoria,* and us.

This was like a gathering center. From here we were
going to be taken by bus to Mariel and put on board a
boat. We stayed a day in Mosquito. The military had attack
dogs and machine guns and trigger-happy fingers. No one
said anything. You had to go to the beach and get in the
water if you wanted to go to the bathroom. There was no
food.

At Mosquito, they took all our money away. The prostitutes were very unhappy because no one had any money.
The boat had five or six people who were absolutely crazy,
and a few more who were candidates for the nuthouse. It
was a big sailboat, and it took twenty-four hours to come
across the ninety miles.

My family is still back there, and I don't know how
I'm going to get them out. I'm going crazy over that. Things
are much worse now for them in Cuba. I can no longer
help them out like I used to. This will be my first Christmas away from them. Here I met a man who hasn't spent
Christmas with his family in ten years. I'm afraid that will
also be me.

The Third Time Upon the Shores of Liberty

Lieutenant Francisco Bazán is a Cuban in the U.S. Army Reserve. He had been in Vietnam in the early seventies as a paratrooper and rose to the rank of Lieutenant in field combat. Now in civilian life he is on the security staff of a major Miami bank. Behind him in his office at the bank he has a glass display containing his medals—the Purple Heart and the Army Bronze Medal.

Lieutenant Francisco Bazán: I was detailed to Key West after the April 21 arrival of the first group of Cuban exiles, and I stayed there until the last major arrival in June of 1980. I met and interviewed most of those who arrived in Key West. I could not help but remember my own arrival in 1960. The first thing I noticed about the refugees was how they related to me. The uniform caused a different reaction in them than in other people stateside. People approached me with fear, dealt with me very tentatively. I tried to be friendly. They seemed to appreciate it.

My first day in Key West, a Cuban doctor arrived in a camper with his family and nurse and set up office. Many people were suffering from overexposure; some were very sick. The hospital in Key West couldn't handle all the people who needed medical attention.

I remember the first person I talked to who seemed to be mentally ill. He reminded me of that character in Havana, *El Caballero de París*. I used to live close to El Prado [Boulevard] where he would hang out. This man reminded me of *El Caballero de París*, and sure enough, he was nuttier than a fruitcake.

El Caballero de París was the pseudonym of a man who in the 1950s lived a very public life in Havana's El Prado Boulevard. The manner and gestures of this man, who was in his early sixties, were those of an eighteenth century Frenchman. His mostly incoherent conversation would at times contain a gem of intellect, captured as an aphorism, such as, "There is no such thing as an officer *and* a gentleman." He mixed remarks like these with a babble of obscure baroque poetry, geography lessons, endless repetitions of lists of names, and long, quiet, introspective moments in which, sitting by himself in Paseo del Prado, he concentrated on his folded hands.

El Caballero de París always wore white tie and tails—an outfit given to him by one of his many female admirers. He never took the suit off. He slept in it on the doorstep of a church and took his customary "rain shower" in it. Later he acquired a fine silk cape with which he covered his deteriorating clothing. He never asked for charity, always maintaining the *de rigeur* stoicism of nobility. But he survived because of the charity of people he saw regularly. He would often exchange labor for food, and his favorite form of labor was to write a poem on a pad of paper and hand it to the charitable soul who had offered to feed him.

In memory of the wisdom he shared so liberally, the amusement he brought to children and adults alike, and for the sake of those of us who have never met El Caballero de París, let me introduce you to his Cuban-American counterpart, El Galán de Galicia.

I am introduced by a Master Sergeant who pronounces El Galan's name almost right, in spite of the Sergeant's deep southern accent. I ask my collaborator . . . "Galán de Galicia, if you would be so kind, would you tell me the antecedents of your distinguished name?"

El Galán de Galicia: As a way of introducing myself, I want you to know that I am certifiably insane and that I know it, which means that I am quite sane to understand it and not become nearly crazy over it. You see my point?

He is sitting on a wooden bench inside the barracks at Eglin Air Force Base in Florida, where he is awaiting psychiatric evaluation. He's wearing Army fatigues and a baseball cap with an American flag pasted on it.

El Galán de Galicia: I am very pleased with the change from living in Guanabacoa to living in this marvelous air force base, where people are so generous. But I miss my friends—Pato and Redundel and Mario Romero—I miss them and the park where I used to spend most of my days. There is no park here and people do not speak Spanish. Another thing, I'm like a patient here in this facility. I haven't got the heart to tell these people that they shouldn't waste their time treating me like a patient. All I need is a park. They put me in a park when I first got here [Tamiami Park]. It was not as good a park as could be found, I am sure, but better than here, where there is no park. There are also no ladies. Without the ladies, I do not feel well any day; not even if I could go back to Guanabacoa. Without the ladies, I am not well.

I know how to make cigars from green leaf and from cured leaf. Fidel. There's no more leaf for Fidel.

I am El Galán de Galicia. [He gets up and bows.] Now, in the fateful moment that we meet, I am of reduced circumstances—ragged suit, decrepit look. I am nonetheless a noble man, a son of a noble man, and from Galicia, the land of the noble men. Blessed be the King and Queen of Galicia. May Thee live long, *Avemariapurísima* [Blessed Virgin]. Fidel has nothing. The king is good. [He has been talking into space. Now he turns and addresses me directly.] Do you know if any of my letters have reached the king? Will you take a message to the king for me? To King Juan Carlos, Galician king, Casa de Borbón, Spain. Your Majesty: I write to you about Fidel, King of Havana, who is not doing a good job. He sent me to the United States. He put me in a hospital. I respectfully advise the king that Fidel is not a true king. Long life for the true king. Death to the false king. Signed, El Galán de Galicia. Do you know if I will be able to go back soon?

A gentleman who came to see me last week told me that there is a park in Miami full of Cubans. Can I take a bus from here and get there? No transfers. I took the *Guanabacoa* bus to Parque Maceo; I didn't have to change buses.

I get confused if I have to change buses. [He slaps his fore-
head.] I think I am still in Cuba. Of course, in the United
States no one needs to change buses. Right?

The center of Cuban-American activity during the Third
Wave was the sleepy, tiny island of Key West, which was totally
unprepared for the off-season avalanche of Cubans from both
the north and the south. The Cuban-Americans occupied every
available hotel room and slept in cars and vans parked everywhere, even in the shadow of the magnolia trees on the grounds
of Ernest Hemingway's former house. In the midst of the chaos,
the Truman Annex became the southernmost office of the
Immigration and Naturalization Service.

Over 5,000 Cuban people sought refuge in Key West during the first week—an exodus that broke the record for a single
year established in 1966 by the Second Wave. And the Cuban
government estimated that another 250,000 Cubans had applied
to leave the country.

The Cubans in Key West had leased ten buses to handle
the traffic to the mainland. Boat "charters" were organized for
$1,500 per person by anyone who had a boat and dared to make
the trip. Others paid as much as $15,000 to persuade a Key West
captain to make the trip to Cuba. The U.S. government, alarmed
at the size of the flotilla heading for Mariel, and the uncertain
quality of its cargo, sought to stem the flow. The State Department condemned the flotilla, and other federal agencies threatened fines [up to $1,000 per refugee], five years in jail, or both
for anyone who brought Cuban citizens into the United States.
The day after these sanctions were announced, 3,300 Cubans
arrived in Key West and 200 boats left Miami ports. Clearly,
matters were out of control.

Control had shifted to the hands of Fidel Castro. Everyone
had forgotten about the Peruvian Embassy, had forgotten the
arrival in Costa Rica of the "brave exiles," had forgotten the
diplomatic reversal that had embarrassed Fidel. Now the world
concentrated upon Carter's reaction to Fidel's challenge to the
United States: "We have a completely open door. Now let's see
how you are going to close it."

Nicasio Lopez-Puerta: We moved on Washington right away, because we could see what Fidel was attempting to do and we were afraid the Carter people wouldn't know how to handle it. We had midnight meetings at the Hay-Adams Hotel and strategy sessions with the political aides. Nothing helped very much. Our position was that the United States shouldn't do business with Fidel directly but should go through the Swiss. The State Department was in a mess. U.S. diplomatic leadership was preoccupied with Iran, as far as I could tell, and the Swiss were more reliable. We couldn't convince the State Department. So we took independent action and encouraged our people in Miami to go ahead and pick up the cargo in Mariel. We couldn't make a policy. Only Carter and his people could do that, and they were all paralyzed. Damned if you do, damned if you don't. There was a moment there when I thought no one had control of things in Miami. I could see Carter's people had no control of things in Washington either. I said to myself, "That son of a bitch Fidel Castro, he's done it to us again."

Sylvia Gonzalez: I look at Cuba and the antics of Fidel, and I want to cry. I can no longer get angry and try to fight back. He has sapped my energy with his callous disregard for the humanity of men, for his denial of reason. When Mariel began, I was feeling all of my years . . . I knew I had to do something to help . . . and yet my soul only wanted to spit on his face. Nicasio Lopez-Puerta and Maxi Pons were involved, as they always like to be. The energy they had came to me, and soon we were all pulling boats in, knowing what the son-of-a-bitch Fidel was up to, and yet having to respond to the call once again and grab ahold of the rope and pull the boats in.

Rodrigo Ochoa is Cuca Plata's grandson born in the U.S. and a radio announcer in Miami. He donated his time to a WQBA "around-the-clock" broadcast of the exodus. He is tall and very slender with the clipped modulated voice of the trained announcer.

Rodrigo Ochoa: Well, of course, the big crowds did not begin to gather at the station until that Sunday—Palm Sunday. After church, people came by with *guano bendito* [blessed palm leaves woven into a cross] and everything else: clothing, food, medicines, money, cars, boats, house trailers. One man brought his gargantuan house trailer and parked it outside and said he was donating it to a homeless family from Mariel. Monday . . . Tuesday . . . Wednesday. We began to receive *Los Liberados* [members of the Third Wave]. And they continued coming until almost a few days ago [November 1980]. The radio station kept on going only during May and June: every hour on the hour, the arrivals report; every hour on the half-hour, the telethon fund-raising report. Do you know that by the end of April this community had raised $2 million for *Los Liberados?*

Sylvia Gonzalez: I was very surprised. We never thought there would be so many Cubans giving so much to any cause, least of all to feed and clothe people they probably didn't like very much and wouldn't have given the time of day to on a street in Miami. I didn't know my people very well until Mariel put us into contact with what must be, collectively, the most generous group I have ever encountered.

   The Cubans, yes, but not just the Cubans. The Puerto Ricans too. The telethon in Puerto Rico raised over $100,000. We had offers of homes coming in from small towns and villages up in the mountains of Puerto Rico. One Puerto Rican businessman, a friend of Maxi, gave us a blank check and said, "Don't let anyone go hungry for lack of food or money." Can you believe that? I feel things very deeply. This man reached me totally with his generosity. We organized a telethon. The Mexican-owned, Spanish-language television network in the United States aired the telethon, and so did hundreds of radio stations. The Mexican people were marvelous. They have to be extra careful of Fidel, who would love to swallow them alive, oil wells and all. They also have a very powerful intellectual left in Mexico, and Mexican presidents play to them with their policy of co-operation with Fidel. But even the Mexican left was with us on this one.

Nicasio Lopez-Puerta: The *Marielitos* [a deprecating name for those who were deported by Fidel] brought a great number of things to a head. First, they exposed the sham of the Cuban utopia. Not even the most naive of American reporters could ignore this.

Second, they brought us together. Up to that time, the Cuban-Americans had been out in the American continent, trying to survive and thrive, and maybe even keeping a low profile. Now people were looking at us as the group to respond to the *Liberación*. This expectation undoubtedly brought us together and put us in touch with one another through acts of personal generosity. These are probably the most favorable of all circumstances for people to meet again and cooperate. The West African phrase for it, which came to Cuba and somehow got into the vocabulary of my father, is *harambe*—pulling together. We were doing that.

The third thing that happened—and it was negative—was Fidel's plan. Fidel has always seen the Cuban-American community as a threat to him, and well he should; he's got an enemy right here. [He points to himself.] He has done much to ruin community relations for us in Miami, Puerto Rico, and New York. This time, he tried to get the American people to turn against us by sending us his jailed criminals, his prostitutes, his worst social beings to pollute the image we had so carefully cultivated. He succeeded, and that's one more reason why he is my enemy. He has caused the human tragedy of Mariel; I am as aware of it as anyone could be. I have relatives who came in from Mariel. I am aware of the suffering and the sacrifice. That's not new. What is new is that our relationships with other communities in Miami deteriorated, and xenophobia reared its ugly head.

Cuban-Americans, the U.S. government, and every religious or charitable group with resources to contribute prepared to receive the bewildered and anxious exiles in the Third Wave. As they were processed by the authorities and before being placed—either in the care of relatives or under investigation—they were moved from makeshift camps to air force bases to

open-air circus tents in order to make room for new and expected arrivals.

This was a continuation of the tragedy that had begun for
some of the new exiles at the Peruvian Embassy a month before
and for others at the Cuban Immigration in Havana fifteen years
before. But they were happy to be in the United States, even if
behind bars. They had faith in the law and in their own fate,
which had brought them to the United States alive. They were
going to experience *Libertad,* they said; many of them had been
born under Fidel, and so would be experiencing it for the first
time. They could wait a few more hours or days or even weeks.
Meanwhile, the authorities were courteous and the food plenti-
ful. Hopes abounded.

At Eglin Air Force Base, a group of 128 men, women, and
children arrived by air on May 4th. They were greeted with
roses, smiles, and hugs by fourteen members of the local Hispanic Heritage Society. After these greetings, six blue air force
buses transported the exhausted refugees to their new homes.
They were driven to the Fort Walton Beach Fairgrounds, fifty
miles east of Pensacola on the Gulf Coast. There they were
housed in newly-built, open-sided barracks built on red clay.
That afternoon, the Air Florida flight that had brought them to
Eglin returned to Key West to pick up another load, and then
another.

The scene at Fort Walton Beach was typical of refugee camps
around the world; in some ways it was probably better than other
camps, but it was still confusing and traumatic. In tents dozens
of battle camp kitchens set up by the air force served pork and
beans to each arrival. For most it was the first hot meal in two
or three days. Then the exiles were taken to a shower tent and
offered—while it lasted—the standard issue of an army private.
Said one, "I could have eaten for six months on the money I
would have gotten in Cuba for the boots they gave me. I couldn't
believe it." The sleeping tents segregated the men from the
women and children. The refugees filed in and lay down on the
cots covered with army blankets. Within an hour after arriving
at the fairgrounds, only three-year-old Lazaro was awake in the
tent and crying. Everyone else was asleep.

Sitting by himself at one end of the Eglin barracks is a young
man who is making flowers out of copper wire. He has been at Eglin

since his arrival in May. It is now December. His name is *El Chulo Lopez* and he has an open, friendly face.

El Chulo Lopez: I don't want anyone to know my real name. Even if you say you will change the name for the book, I don't want *you* to know my real name, either. Just call me *El Chulo* [the cute one]. I am that, am I not? [He stands up and turns around to display his body.] I have been a queen since I was fifteen. I became a queen when I was sent to a school in the Escambray Mountains to rehabilitate me for socialist service. I have been put in jail twice in the last five years for being a homosexual. They had a treatment facility in Matanzas [a city on the northern coast of Cuba], where they beat you up if they caught you loving another man. I was beaten regularly. It is like a sadomasochistic novel—these men watching other men so that they won't have sexual contact. They beat you up with a piece of solid rubber. The guards have a hard-on when they beat you. And they say *you* are the sick one!

My family was with Batista at some point, and most of them left shortly after Fidel came to power. I stayed behind with my brother Carlos, who was then eleven, and our grandparents. I was twelve. Our parents went to the United States. They were supposed to bring us over, but they died in an automobile accident within the first few months of exile. My brother and I were not told about it until seven years later. We used to write letters and get letters from them, which were actually written by my aunt. All this time, we thought they just couldn't get us out of Cuba.

School changed after Fidel. I used to go to a private Catholic school in Camaguey, but it closed in 1961. Then I went to a public school. The material was changing. The Cuban history they taught us and even the economics began to change. The way they brainwash you is to tell you as children that the socialist movement is responsible for everything that's good. They have to change history and everything else. The teachers in school changed, and the revolutionaries did the teaching. They were terrible. I began to get into trouble. [He looks at me mischievously.]

I once lit a fire in the room where the *Pioneros* [the Communist Youth Club] were meeting. They caught me and sent me to the Escambray for rehabilitation. I was fifteen. There I was raped by an older man who was in charge of the barracks. He took me into his room and forced himself into me. I didn't let out a sound. When he was through, he let me stay in his room, and I became his queen. He protected me against the others and brought me food. He didn't put me through the same paces he put everyone else through, clearing the land with machetes and picking coffee beans. I got to stay behind, but I had to be his queen. Eventually I fell in love with him. I left the camp when I was nineteen and went back to live with my grandparents. That's when I learned that my parents had died. I was empty for a very long time.

In Hialeah the Cuban-American community was in charge of a massive relief effort for the Third Wave. The city offered the use of the newly constructed Goodlet Recreation Center, which had yet to be officially inaugurated. The 1,000-seat stadium served as a holding area, and the eleven [still unused] tennis courts were soon filled up with portable kitchens, where pots of black beans, rice, meat stew, and fish soup were kept warm. The food was brought in from Cuban-American homes in the surrounding area. The interior of the center was packed with cots, mattresses, and an infirmary.

At the height of the bustle to accommodate thousands of refugees, the city manager of Hialeah, Richard A. Burgin, began receiving telephone calls from the non-Cuban residents of Hialeah, who were afraid the *Liberados* would spoil the surface of the tennis courts and delay the opening of the center scheduled for two weeks later. The head of the tennis program, Mike Jula, demonstrated his support of the relief effort by volunteering his services at the center. He was put in charge of monitoring water usage in the shower. "People outside, Americans mostly, cared more about the damage to the surface of the tennis courts than the people there, who were very, very needy," he said. "It was disgusting to watch people complaining on TV and protesting on the streets of Miami about the refugees."

Unlike the fairgrounds group, the Hialeah Center refugees were immediately urged to meet their own needs and those of the new arrivals. After the official business was over and their documents had been stamped "Cuban entrant: Status Pending," the business of starting a new life in the work-oriented culture of the Cuban-American community began.

The Cuban-Americans also had some adjusting to do. They often came face-to-face with the reality of the communist indoctrination and its effect upon the values and attitudes of the Third Wave. Often this realization came from the most insignificant of the day's events. On the third day of operations at Goodlet Center, a six-year-old boy who had just arrived wandered away from his mother and toward a Hialeah city policeman, Roberto Cruz, standing by the door. The little boy was absentmindedly holding his new toy gun. Cruz remembers the event. "I saw him coming and headed toward him to take him back to his mother. Suddenly he saw me approaching. He looked quite alarmed, but he just stood there, challenging me with his toy pistol and shouting, 'You are a Yanqui, I'm going to have to kill you.' Look what they've done to those kids."

Mariano Medina, a former officer in Fidel's army, arrived in Key West in Jesús María Laserie's boat, wearing a ragged shirt and torn pants. A few hours later he was sent to Hialeah.

Mariano Medina: I was taken to the Goodlet Center in Hialeah in a bus. When we arrived, there were a few people by the door. I could tell they were Cubans. The only thing I could think of at that time was the mob which Fidel had parked outside the Peruvian Embassy. They had thrown stones at us. One stone hit a little girl in the face, and I took her in my arms and walked out. Many stones hit me. For some reason, I thought these people were going to throw stones at us. Instead, they opened their arms and took us inside the center. They fed us, gave us clothing and a bed. I slept for about seven hours on a cot before somebody woke me up to help prepare for another contingent of people. It was incredible to be with these people—the Cuban exiles, I mean.

Some of them—like Jesús María Laserie—were like my relatives. We spoke the same way and understood each other. But some of them were not like us. They were just like the people who had run Cuba before Fidel—probably the same people. My thinking about them has changed a little bit since then. I can now see that they feel no ill will toward me and may even want to help me, but they can't help me come to grips with the twenty years I've spent in Cuba. They don't understand how I feel; I am beginning to understand what they feel.

I decided to leave Cuba many years before I was able to leave. I had been sent to Angola. I was a military officer and volunteered for duty in Angola, hoping I could escape and live in a free country. I was hoping to go to Nigeria or Swaziland—maybe reach the United States. But there was no opportunity to escape. In Angola we were always under heavy attack. We spent the whole winter in a guerrilla offensive. The only way to escape was to do it in a coffin. We had many casualties but won the conflict. I don't believe we won so much as the Africans lost. Before I knew it, I was being sent back to Cuba, and I didn't get a chance to escape.

I waited for my time, and it came to pass. I crashed the embassy gates with an army truck full of people. I couldn't get out on the flights to Costa Rica because there were other people who had priority—sick people and people with relatives in Costa Rica. I had no relatives anywhere. I am single and an orphan. Finally, I got on a list to go on one of the boats that were coming to pick up people. Then—after two weeks of waiting on the beach—I was told to get into a large tugboat. A very beautiful boat—the most beautiful boat in the world. A man in Miami [Jesus Maria Laserie], whom I had met but didn't know well, bought the boat to pick up people like me. That's the most beautiful man I know.

The Cuban Armed Forces have been training for tropical and subtropical guerrilla warfare since Ché first formed the special units in 1963. The Cuban special units have been in Chile, Peru, Bolivia, and Panama, and in Africa, the Middle East, and I don't know where else. If you say Mexico, I wouldn't put it past them. My loyalty to the Communist party had been under question, according to the political officer of the special unit to which I belonged. As a result, I was not sent overseas until Angola. My job for ten years had been to train guerrilla personnel, living in the mountains along with them, with one month's leave a year. The food was good, but the control was total. I felt like a beast of burden in someone's yoke.

I must have trained 10,000 guerrilla infantry in my ten years with the special units. I say this with no pride. They are the best mercenaries around. I saw that in Angola. Russia controls them, but I trained them. My men can shoot any rifle made, disable people with one hand, and live in a jungle for three years with no supplies or loss of aggressiveness. There is no weapon against these men, except other men like them.

As a black man, I felt a special pull to Africa and the campaigns there, but I really was looking for a chance to get out of doing what I was doing. I was sick of myself. I wanted to live someplace else. Do something else. Not kill people or train others to kill people. Even though they didn't trust me, they needed me in Angola because I was a black man. When I volunteered, I made a little speech about liberating the ancestral land of the Afro-Cubans. They took the line and the bait and sent me to Africa.

The largest group of unprocessed refugees was gathered at Tamiami Park in southwest Miami. Again, the government agencies simply kept order and provided security; the welfare of the exiles was totally in the hands of the Cuban-American community. Said one organizer at Tamiami Park, "The first few days we had a branch of Burger King in here. About 5,000 hamburgers were brought in from the company's stores each day— free of cost, mind you—with french fries, shakes, and cokes. By the beginning of the first week, we were unloading ten, twelve trucks a day coming from Miami restaurants and stores: ice cream by the garbage-pailfull, and clothes."

In a small trailer at one end of the park, CIA and FBI agents interviewed all new arrivals, looking for members of the Cuban intelligence forces. Another similar screening would await arrivals at Eglin. By May 8th, the FBI had identified twenty Cuban spies and was preparing to reinterview another fifty Cubans whom they suspected of espionage.

The Cincinnati Reds baseball team was looking for Cuban prospects to sign up at another end of the park. With the help of Reds Coach Sal Arteaga, Chief Scout George Zuraw set up tryouts outside of the building where the Third Wave was being processed. He had already identified three men—Carlos Martinez, Rogelio Mediaviela, and Julio Soto—as being in condition to play. When Baseball Commissioner Kuhn ordered the entire matter stopped, the Milwaukee Braves and the Baltimore Orioles were already setting up their own tryouts at Eglin.

In another corner of the park, rumors had it, ten female refugees had organized a *zona de tolerancia* [red light district] away from the lights and under the palm trees. For some, this was a welcome return to normality.

El Chulo Lopez: Of all the things that were going on at Tamiami Park and at two air force bases where I was sent, the sanest was probably the prostitutes going back into business in the *zona de tolerancia,* as they called it in Tamiami. I recognize today much more than I did then. When I arrived, I was not aware of what Fidel was doing, sending people like prostitutes and spies to the United States. I had always wanted to leave Cuba, but for one reason or another could not go. Now I could go if I said I was a queen, a *lumpen.* As far as I'm concerned, that has never been a secret. I decided to go to Immigration and say "I am a queen, take me." But only very recently did I become aware of my place in all of this, how the people here think of me—as someone who Fidel has sent to hurt them [the Cuban-Americans]. I am one of them. I would have left Cuba a long time ago if my parents had not died. I would have been one of them, smoking a cigar and driving a big car down Flagler Street. Maybe I would have been *macho* [straight] if I hadn't been sent to reform school. Well, maybe not.

J.J. Jimenez, M.D., helped give physical exams at Tamiami during his spare time. He was also working full time doing autopsies in Key West.

J.J. Jimenez: As a forensic doctor consulting with the County of Monroe, where Key West is situated, I was called to perform autopsies on ten victims of the Mariel stampede. Most people died while crossing the seas—some of carbon monoxide poisoning from being crowded in boats with diesel engines, and some of weak hearts, exhaustion-induced cardiac dysfunctions, and other similar causes. Three people died shortly after arriving in Key West. One of them—a sixty-eight-year-old woman—died of no special physical illness, as far as I could determine. She was so physically deteriorated that she could have died of a dozen different progressive conditions. She was like a woman of ninety, and her blood pressure, kidneys, liver, stomach, and muscle tissue showed the effect of prolonged malnutrition, which is like an acceleration of the organism's decline. She must have been a diabetic for over ten years.

The others I examined had varyingly progressive stages of the same symptoms. I became aware of how calorically reduced the Cuban diet was. I say the Cuban diet, but I mean the diet of these [newly arrived] Cubans. I don't know how representative they are, but I do know that they were uniformly affected. They all belonged to that vast underclass which the Cuban Revolution has created—*los gusanos* [the worms] *y los contra Fidel* [and those against Fidel]. They are the ones who want to leave the country and are forced to stay and pay for their disloyalty by losing their jobs. I now see that they also suffer from malnutrition. They are coerced into doing "volunteer" work on farms or in sugar factories. People don't know that this class of people exists in Cuba.

Fidel's Gulag is not just inside prison where, according to Amnesty International, he holds 40,000 people. No, no. Fidel's Gulag is the subculture. These half a million to a million people, who have applied formally to leave the country and have had everything taken away from them, are allowed to do only the most menial work, in some cases for fifteen or twenty years. In return for this, they get a diet of 1,100 to 1,600 calories per day, which is not enough to thrive and yet not so little that the organism dies. On this amount of nourishment one simply vegetates in a depressed mood, becomes more pliant, and never stops being hungry.

El Chulo Lopez: Of all the bad things that happened to me in Cuba, the worst was lack of food—not enough to keep you strong and healthy. People in Cuba live on practically nothing. Ask any of the *Marielitos*. Many of them, like me, were sent from place to place before they arrived in Key West, without food for three or four days at a time. Then they had a hot dog and nothing more for the rest of the week. The *Marielitos* will tell you that they survived the malnutrition of the trip and the beaches because they can live on nothing.

Adela Cisneros was a prisoner at an army base at the time of our interview. She is forty-one years old, but malnutrition has made her look much older. We sit in a common area of the prison compound a few feet from her cell, and I ask how she went from being a nun to being a political prisoner. As she answered, her eyes were clear and her manner decisive.

Adela Cisneros: Within the first year of the revolution, my father began to feel the pressure to take sides politically on the orientation of his newspaper. He was the publisher of a Cuban daily. Then he was told to show his loyalty to the revolutionary party by siding with Fidel on an issue he firmly opposed—the establishment of closer ties with Russia. He did not give in to the demands. But as a compromise, he did not publish editorials against the treaties. This posture was sufficient for a while. For several months, my family debated whether or not to leave the country.

My uncle was with the Cuban government, and he urged us to stay. My father and mother continued to work for the revolution, which to us meant independence from outside influences in our conduct as a nation, freedom to speak and write, and responsibility for that freedom. We tolerated the man who said no to elections [Fidel Castro], because he was pursuing the path of revolution and freeing us from the entanglements of economic dependency on the United States. My mother and father were with him on those issues, but not on the close association with Russia. My father feared the United States more than he feared Russia. He used to say, "The United States is closer and thinks of us as its imperial property." But he also feared the Russians very much, because "they don't know freedom." [She gets up to find an editorial written by her father, then comes back, disoriented.] I thought I was at home in Cuba, and I was going to go get a set of clippings of my father's editorials, which I kept in a drawer in my bedroom. I guess we will have to do without the references. There is much we have to do without. [She recovers fully.] In any event, we went as far as we could in accommodating the changes in the philosophy of the revolution. And then we were all put in jail without warning [1961].

I was staying at home. The cloister had closed because of the policies of Fidel, and almost everyone had been sent home. The G-2 came and took us with just the clothes we had to a theater in Marianao. My father was then placed in jail, and my mother and I were detained at the theater. That was the last time I saw my father. We discovered the next day that we had been collected and imprisoned because of the Bay of Pigs attack. We, my mother and I, were released the day after *Cochinos* was over. We started looking for my father, but no one would tell us where he was. He got word to us, somehow—I don't remember how—that he was at Principe, a maximum-security prison for political prisoners in Havana. We tried to see him but could not. They wouldn't acknowledge that he was inside. I decided that the best thing I could do to help him was to join the revolution.

I renounced my vestments and took a job in the National Bank, which was run by Ché Guevara. I knew that if I could get close enough to him, he could get my father out of prison. If Ché wanted it, it would happen. I worked for a year before I caught Ché's attention. Ironically, he was not then in charge of the National Bank but was involved in a revolution in Latin America. He was an injurious man, a cold-blooded assassin. But I became a very close ally of Ché [she makes the sign of the cross] and began to work on his staff, and eventually I got him to inquire about my father. Ché told me my father was alive and well, and promised me that he would be treated well and released someday. I worked for the government until 1975 without ever being able to see my father.

In 1975 the government was purged of all those who had relatives in jail and other people who were simply not entirely convinced about the revolution, and I was among them. I was never given a trial, although that wouldn't have made any difference. I was charged with participating in a plan to kill Raul Castro, but really I was just being purged. I had survived other purges—one at the National Bank after Ché left nearly took me—but this one I could not avoid. I was imprisoned for five years.

Then on May 9, 1980, the guard came and told us that our sentence would be commuted—everyone's in Cell Block 13—if we agreed to leave for the United States immediately. I'd been trying for twenty-one years to get out of Cuba. I didn't believe them, but I went along cautiously. When they put us in the truck to take us to Mosquito, I was sure they were going to shoot us and say we were trying to escape, but they didn't, and we wound up in a tent on Mosquito Beach. The tent was only four to five feet high. Everyone had to sit down on the dirt floor. There was no room to walk around. The tent had a big sign. It said *ESCORIA* [scum]. The other tents had other signs. Soon I discovered that all the rest of the women were prostitutes who had been picked up off the streets. I was classified as a prostitute for several weeks in Tamiami Park. I cleared that point up when I told them I had been a political prisoner. That was worse.

From Tamiami, we were sent to a military base, and finally to here. I don't have any relatives in the United States, but it wouldn't help anyway, since I am still imprisoned here. The attorney says that the claims I made to being a political and not a criminal convict have to be proven before I can be released. It will take some time, but I am not complaining. I have food, shelter, and human dignity. Maybe someday I can have *libertad*.

When I arrived in Key West I said, "Freedom at last." But here I am in jail in the United States until they figure out whether or not I was a political prisoner or perhaps another 5'1", 120 lb., mass murderer, who would, if set free, stalk the back streets of Philadelphia. I hope they find out soon and set me free. I would like to return to the cloister and just be a nun.

Gonzalo Ponce sat outside the lower-middle-class Hialeah home he occupies with his wife and talked about his efforts to adjust to this new *libertad*.

Gonzalo Ponce: After we got settled in the house in Miami which my brother [Pepe Ponce] bought and gave us rent-free, I began to look for a job. That was very hard. In Cuba if you wanted a job—and you were not an undesirable—all you had to do was go to a government office, and they would put you to work. I was a driver in Cuba. I drove a truck which was broken more often than not, so I also repaired the truck. It was a good job, an easy job. I wanted a job like that when I began to look here. I had a driver's license, but I couldn't find anything like that. People were getting on my back after a week, telling me to take any job. My best job possibility was trucker's helper. That way, if something happened to the driver and he couldn't drive, I could be the driver. That hasn't happened yet. I load refrigerators and washing machines at one end and unload them at the other end. We make six or seven trips a day. In Cuba, because the truck was broken or we had no gas, we used to make one or two trips a day. The work here is very hard. Prices are very high. My life here is better than in Cuba, but not much better. If I get a different job and if my wife gets a job, it will be better.

People around here—other Cubans who have been here longer—like to put out a greater amount of effort than people who have just come from Cuba. I'm not talking about everybody, but most people. In Cuba there was little incentive to work hard. Here, if you don't work hard, you can barely make it. The *liberados* will have to adjust to that.

Late in May, almost two months after the exodus had begun, the United States had still not announced a policy toward the Third Wave. Maybe, as Nicasio Lopez-Puerta says, it didn't have one. The old Immigration and Naturalization Service policy that had failed in the First Wave and worked badly in the Second Wave was revived for the third time.

Sponsors were sought, first within the Cuban-American community and then elsewhere. Refugee assistance centers were opened to receive exiles in Boston, New York, Los Angeles, and San Francisco. Religious and charitable organizations screened potential sponsors and advised the Miami immigration headquarters how many refugees they were prepared to accept. By the beginning of June, 18 relocation centers had processed 10,000 men, women, and children; 50,000 were still without sponsors. The Cuban and Haitian Refugee Emergency Assistance Act passed by Congress partially alleviated the bottleneck by making relocation and emergency relief funds available.

This group of exiles, unlike previous immigrations from Cuba, contained an "undesirable" element. Its proportions, however, were unknown. High on the list of undesirables were convicted criminals and spies for Fidel. The Immigration and Naturalization Service, the FBI, and the CIA were all searching for them among the thousands who arrived in Key West each day, and they were falling behind. Soon there was no more room at Tamiami, Goodlet, and the fairgrounds near Eglin for the suspects and the unsponsored. At that time, American authorities decided to open the former Vietnamese resettlement camp at Fort Chaffee, a barren army base in western Arkansas.

On the night of May 26, about 200 refugees at Fort Chaffee went AWOL and entered the rural community of Jenny Lind, where the local citizenry, armed and on rooftops, proceeded to fire at them. Several hundred rounds were fired that night. No one was hurt. Later, a group of hooded Ku Klux Klansmen carrying torches appeared at the gates of the fort to protest the refugee camp with signs that said, "Kill the Communist Criminals." The fence around Fort Chaffee became the patrol perimeter for a group of armed Jenny Lind residents, who cruised around the camp in their pickup trucks.

Lieutenant Francisco Bazán: In June, right after the so-called riots of May 26–31, I was sent to Fort Chaffee. The purpose of my detail was to organize activities which would engage the refugees in positive and constructive work and recreation. It was like putting out a fire with spit. Before I got there, some of the men who had been held for about fifteen days without any word about their future began to explore outside the fort, many with intentions of finding a job or something that would free them of government control.

Among the exile group were those who had been positively identified as linked with Cuban Intelligence. But the majority who wandered off that night were not considered undesirables when the investigation was completed. The problem, really, was communications. Some of the people being held had sponsors in the United States. Many of them had relatives who had traveled to Fort Chaffee and had filed all the necessary papers. But no one told the refugees that it would take at least a week for their papers to be approved in Washington and returned so that they could leave. The fences were short, relatives and freedom were outside, and I guess some people thought it wouldn't hurt to go for a stroll.

The locals were not very hospitable, and some had reason not to be. They did not feel adequately protected by their police, and they were being told daily by television, newspapers, and radio that these Cuban refugees right at their doorstep were potentially dangerous people, and not under control. We [the army] did not get the order to act as security police until a few days after I arrived, and then we had to be very careful, using minimum restraint and maximum caution with both the citizens and the refugees. The problem was, in my opinion still is, the lack of one central body to coordinate and provide service.

The job of coordinating services for the Cuban refugees and reporting to the President fell into the hands of a small federal agency, the Federal Disaster Assistance Administration (FDAA). The FDAA was in charge of directing the work of the Defense and Civil Preparedness Administration; the Federal Emergency Management Agency; the Immigration and Naturalization Service; the Department of Health and Human Services; the Federal Protective Service; the Departments of State, Justice, and

Interior (as Fort Chaffee was protected by the U.S. Park police); the Department of Defense; and the General Services Administration. Because President Carter had declared a state of emergency, several agencies that had no role in the process were pressed into service, further complicating the relief task and taxing the available human and physical resources. The Federal Insurance Administration, the Federal Emergency Manpower Agency, and even the Federal Fire Administration were told to help, although not a single fire broke out during the entire incident.

Lieutenant Francisco Bazán: When I got to Chaffee, the first thing I was told was that the Cubans were very hard to deal with and that I'd better revise my assumptions about them. At Key West I had developed a view of the new immigrants which was totally different from what I saw here at Chaffee. The *Marielitos* at Key West were very cooperative, wanting only to feed and house themselves. Though they were emotionally distraught, they seemed pleased to be treated with dignity and generosity. At Chaffee the men, at least, were like caged animals. I had processed many of them at Key West, and I couldn't help but notice the change. It was like night and day. Of course, here they were imprisoned and uninformed. This, plus the community's reaction and the Klansmen, had a great deal to do with how they were behaving. My first act was to introduce news bulletins on what was going on at Chaffee. This worked.

Estanislao Menendez: When I saw Lieutenant Bazán, I embraced him. He had been in charge at *Cayo Hueso* [Key West] when I was brought in. I was proud to be a Cuban when I saw this handsome, young military man in the American forces behave as a gentleman from Cuba behaves—good manners, intelligence, and control. In the sun at Fort Chaffee, he seemed to shine even more. He remembered me. I told him we had problems here—fights every day. No one knew what the hell was going on. A criminal element had taken charge and gone over the fence, and there was fear of what would happen next. I had even heard talk of a massive escape with guns and armored trucks, perhaps that same night I first saw Lieutenant Bazán. He knew what to do. He began to give us news and to help with small matters, like getting a visitor's pass. He also talked to everyone all the time, in person. Except for the *ñangaras* [communists], everyone paid attention to him. He never promised anything he couldn't do, but he did much more than he promised. We were put to work building barracks and taking care of our own needs.

I was taught as a child to respect the law and the military—first *La Guardia Rural* [the Cuban Rural Police, 1922–1959], and then the revolutionary army [which took over in 1959]. I would never do what the others were doing, make fun of the young privates who played ball with us at Fort Chaffee. Perhaps they were raised differently from me. I would never do that. But I can see that there was a reason for what they were doing—throwing stones, running away—and the reason was that we were not free, and we did not know what was going to happen to us.

Lieutenant Francisco Bazán: A system of governance began to evolve at Fort Chaffee. We offered rewards [such as a bigger sleeping area] to those elected to leadership. I was amazed at the behavioral conditioning of these Cubans. Positive and negative reinforcement worked very well. They took to democracy right away. There were new elections all the time, because the barracks leaders would find sponsors and leave. People needed help at very basic levels. A man who was separated from his family wanted to know where they were. Another wanted to recover the possessions he'd left behind at a previous stop. It occurred to me that the experience of dealing with the Cuban bureaucracy had taught some how to get around it and that this would be useful experience in dealing with our [army] bureaucracy. My hunch was correct. I had a number of refugees who could help solve problems for others through army channels. [He shakes his head in disbelief.]

I can't help but make a comparison between the Cubans and the Vietnamese who had been at Chaffee five years earlier. The Vietnamese barely altered their environment while they were here. They were model citizens but didn't do anything to the barracks to personalize them or improve the water supply. That is what a couple of Cubans set out to do one day, when they took some pipes that had been stacked at one end of a barracks and installed wash-basins in the barracks under construction. No one told them to do that, but they were changing things to make their life better, totally unlike the Vietnamese when they were here.

Finding sponsorship for Cuban immigrants was becoming a problem. The volunteer agencies, which had been so efficient in raising funds, now found it difficult to locate sponsors for the Cubans. The publicity given the incidents at Fort Chaffee created the impression that the *Marielitos* were mostly criminals and spies. Fewer families offered their homes to the new arriv-als than had offered financial support. U.S. law required official sponsorship before a refugee could be released, and few quali-fied official sponsors could be found. Those Cubans who were being sponsored had close ties to relatives already living in the United States. Many *Marielitos* found that distant relatives were unwilling to take on the responsibility of sponsorship. At that time disappointment, uncertainty, and lack of freedom were the forces behind the discontent at Fort Chaffee. Today [1981], nearly a year later, there are still over 10,000 refugees waiting at Fort Chaffee for sponsors. Disappointment has turned to bitterness; uncertainty has turned to pessimism about the future. When they left Cuba, they lost their past. Now they have nothing. Only their lack of freedom has remained unchanged.

Estanislao Menendez: The irony of it all hits me every day when I wake up. I risked my life. For what? To gain free-dom. *Libertad,* that's all I wanted. And here I am inside a compound surrounded by armed guards—not in jail, but not free. I can't find a sponsor. I don't know why. I am fifty-two years old. I have always worked the land. I don't want handouts from anyone. I know how to feed myself, from planting a seed of corn to making corn bread. I don't need to be fed or watched by anybody. I can't say bad things about the people out there. They are not bad people. Do they know we are here?

In spite of the difficulties some refugees have had finding sponsors, 84,000 have been sponsored by Florida residents, and 69,000 of them live in Dade County. The balance are spread throughout the United States, with significant numbers in New York, New Jersey, and California.

Those in Dade County have begun the process of integration into the Cuban-American community. The process is similar to that experienced by the Second Wave when it integrated with the First Wave. But there are important differences. Many members of the Third Wave (42 percent) are single males and females, whereas in the earlier waves families were the norm. This is responsible for the different lifestyles of the new arrivals. Another important difference is the large number of homosexuals (12 percent) among the newest arrivals. There is an element of rejection of the homosexual in the social life of the Cuban-American community in Miami, and suspicion of each male *sin peste a macho* [without male scent] who walks down the street or asks for a job.

Then there are the street people who came to the United States with the Third Wave. Like all urban societies, communist Cuba bred its own version of the disenfranchised, and the street people are part of this group. Fidel labeled them *peligrosidades*, which literally means "dangerous people." They are prostitutes, petty thieves, con men, *vividores* [hobos], and pimps. There is a whole litany of prejudicial adjectives that Fidel has deposited upon these people.

Now they have been sent against their will to another society, where another litany of prejudices and insults is being hurled at them. They are far from welcome, and we simply don't know what to do about them. Some have found sponsors but have clashed with them over differences in values and attitudes. They have been put out of their sponsors' houses or have left voluntarily. They wandered around Miami, looking for freedom, finding loneliness, hunger, and abuse.

And, finally, there are the people with criminal records who, at the date of publication of this book, are still being held without charges in federal prisons in Atlanta and elsewhere. Various sources place their number at between 800 and 1,500. Some have not committed crimes as defined by American law. They are political and "social" prisoners, like the man from Oriente who was convicted and imprisoned in Cuba for being an entrepreneur. Clearly, he doesn't belong in jail in the United States. Some of the Third Wave refugees still being held are dangerous people with established criminal histories.

Marco Soto is a forty-one-year-old convicted murderer. He is 6'2" and weighs 280 lbs. He is in Federal Prison in Atlanta.

Marco Soto: I killed my wife and was sentenced to life imprisonment. I have served twenty years. My life is not worth the trouble people are taking. I've been in jail since I was twelve, for stealing and beating people up, for selling drugs, twice for murder. The first time I got off. I was only sixteen and the judge kept me out of jail.

This jail is just like any other. The showers and toilets are better; the food is worse. People don't mess around with me. I liked the boat ride over. Wouldn't mind doing it again.

If Marco Soto belongs in prison, clearly Adela Cisneros does not. But both the dangerous and the endangered wait anxiously in federal prisons for their human rights to be granted by American society. Thus far, the United States has begged the question.

A Walk Around Miami

On December 2, 1980, I spent a hot winter's evening walking around Miami. I was looking for *Marielitos*. I began at the Café Versalles, which is the center for *el exilio* according to Omar Betancourt. It was 1:00 AM and the place matched his description of it. Among the usual after-midnight crowd were a group of musicians, young people coming from parties, and a well-known senator from the North. When the senator got tired of acknowledging requests for autographs and turned his back on the curious, I looked around for *Marielitos*, but there were no obvious ones there. I decided to take a walk.

Outside the overly air-conditioned Versalles, Miami rested under a blanket of warm Caribe moisture. A gentle wind blew from the east to the north. I walked down 8th Street against the wind. The salt air felt good on my face and reminded me of the wind I knew as a child in Cuba. I walked toward the sea. I walked for a long time, until my shirt was moist from humidity and perspiration. Then I sat down on a bench in front of the public library on Biscayne Boulevard to rest for a while and cool off. In front of the library, facing the boulevard, temporary scaffolding held up the bleachers where in a few days people would sit and watch the Christmas parade. I saw something move. Beneath the scaffolding, covered by newspaper and almost totally

out of sight, were three or four men. I couldn't make out exactly
how many were there, nor could I tell what they looked like in
the dark, but I could hear their voices.

The sound of fresh *Cubano* floated across to me in the quiet
of the night. The sound of *Cubano* is unmistakable. It is a pho-
nological pattern imposed on the Spanish language which makes
speech go twice as fast as it usually does when Mexicans or
Puerto Ricans talk. It sounds like music to my ears. But the *Cubano* one usually hears in the United States is a bit stale. It is
often spoken by someone—like me—who left Cuba fifteen or
twenty years ago. Since then the language has gotten mixed up
with English and the Spanish of other Hispanics, and it doesn't
sound quite like it used to. This *Cubano* I was listening to was
fresh. I moved closer to the men.

They were playing dominoes on a folding checkers board
and talking about another man, who was asleep on the floor.
*"Caballero eso no tiene madre, que su propia hermana, su misma
sangre, como se dice, lo eche pa'la calle, sin na'ni na', pa' la calle,
que cosa mas grande,"* I heard. Apparently the man asleep had
been kicked out of his sister's house and had no place to sleep.
"Que desgracia este país chico. Que venga uno a descojonarse acá."
[What a disgrace. To come to this country to lose your balls like
that.] The man speaking let the phrase hang in disbelief. I approached. There were four of them. Cato, the one who had spoken first is a former boxer who has kept his body in shape.
Miguel was wearing army fatigues and a Red Sox baseball cap.
He had been a policeman in Havana's supposedly nonexistent
red light district. Ramos, a toothless old man, was dozing, and
Chalo was soundly asleep on the floor. They had some food in
a shopping bag and a thermos full of Cuban coffee, a gift from
a Cuban woman who worked at the library.

Cato is a mulatto with a red, white, and blue tattoo on his
right shoulder. It is a recent tattoo, showing the American bald
eagle's resolute stare and clenched claws over a background of
stars and stripes, the date of April 29, 1980, and one word in
Gothic lettering: *LIBERTAD*. The tattoo occupies nearly all the
muscular shoulder. It cost, he said, $50. Miguel told me it took
two hours to make. Cato got the tattoo his second day in the
United States, with half the money given him by the radio station WQBA, "La Cubanísima." He met Miguel there, and in a
patriotic moment they both decided to get a tattoo. Miguel

showed me his. It is more modest, consisting of Cuban and American flags and the date, apparently all he could get for $10. Nonetheless he is very proud of it.

Ramos drifted in and out of sleep, leaning against some cardboard boxes, with a newspaper pillow placed against the metal scaffolding. Cato was the most talkative.

Cato: I was in jail in Cuba for hitting a militiaman on the mouth with my fist. [He shows me an enormous right fist.] The *degenerado* [degenerate] had taken my daughter Carmen. She is twenty now, but when she was fifteen, he took her to the back of his house and showed her his penis. Carmen told me about it when I got home. I went over to his house and waited for him, and when he showed up, bang! [He smashes a fist into the four-by-six board above us.] I hit him right on the mouth. He swallowed two teeth. Then I began to take his pants off, because I wanted to crush his balls too, but the neighbors came and a policeman. I was put in jail. I got five years.

[He turns to show me his tattoo again.] You see this? I promised the Virgin that if I became a free man I would not go back to jail, and I didn't. I didn't know half the time out there [he points toward the ocean] whether we were going to live or die. I promised the Virgin that if I got here safely, I would do a tattoo to my day of *Libertad*. I wanted to do a picture of the *Virgin del Cobre,* too, but I didn't have enough money, and the tattoo man had nothing to copy from. You know, he wasn't a Cuban or anything. So I said, "The hell with it. The Virgin will understand. Do the Eagle. That is me. The Eagle."

Chalo woke up with a start when Cato banged his fist on the board. He noted my presence without much enthusiasm and tried to go back to sleep but was kept awake by our conversation. He finally woke up and asked for the thermos with the *café*. He poured himself a cup and drank it, making a face and complaining. "*Está tibio, tibio.*" [It is only lukewarm.] He offered me coffee, and I declined, telling him it keeps me awake at night. It was 3:30 AM. Cato, Miguel, and Chalo laughed at the small joke. Chalo asked me who I was. I told him. He wanted to know what I was doing there. I explained. He was still unconvinced and asked me if I was with *Imigración*. I told him he asked too many questions. That seemed to put him at ease. Then I asked him how he had wound up sleeping outdoors; he didn't look like he'd been out there a long time.

Chalo: No. This is my first night. My only night, I hope. To-morrow I will sleep in a hotel. [He offered me some soggy crackers from a paper bag.] But I don't mind it out here. It is not too cold, and the library stays open until 10:00 PM. Then there is the bus station and the restaurant, if you want to drink something. I don't speak English, so I don't go to the restaurant. But I stayed inside the library until it closed and read some *novelas* [novels]. Shit like that.

Cato: He got kicked out of the house by his brother-in-law.

Chalo: Who asked you? [He shouts at Cato.]

To ease the tension between Chalo and Cato, I asked the tooth-less old man if he had a job.

Ramos: I run errands for a flower shop on the corner. I earn my money.

Cato: [Referring to Chalo.] His sonofabitch brother-in-law kicked his sister down the stairs, and Chalo goes for the guy's throat. The poor bastard got hit. Show him, Chalo. [He grabs Chalo's shirt and begins to pull it up. Chalo stops him.]

Chalo: That's enough, Cato. I don't go around talking about your easy-ass daughter and the *miliciano.*

Cato: I already told you that her ass was as easy as yours will be if you don't pull your mouth shut. Anyway the man knows. I told him all about it while you were dead to the world.

Miguel: [Interrupts.] I found a sponsor—a lady who was lonely and wanted company. I lived with her for a few months, but she wanted to run my life, so I left.

Cato: I didn't get sponsors. My boat arrived here in Miami Beach. I've been living around here since May. No papers.

Chalo: My brother-in-law was my sponsor. He thought he was
doing me a favor by letting me work with him. He didn't
get along with his wife—my sister. I didn't like seeing that.
She said she wanted to stay with him, so I left.

Chalo's voice dropped suddenly, his eyes narrowed, and he
looked past me, trying to see through the spaces in the scaffold's network of metal tubing. I looked in the same direction and saw a single
car, lights off, moving slowly behind the trees, in the park's footpath.
"Ahi están lo' de anoche" [There they are, the ones from last night],
said Cato, identifying the police car that had stopped here and bothered them the night before. *"Calabaza, calabaza, cada uno pa' su casa."*
He asked everyone to leave. The four men stood up and began moving
in different directions, shielded from the view of the police car by the
library building and hidden by the night.

Early in the morning—or late at night, depending on the end of
the cycle you find yourself in—Miami wakes up first as a group of
artisans and construction workers, truckers and taxicabs; then it arises
as a middle class to go to jobs downtown; and finally the day begins
for families, when they take their children to school.

By 5:00 AM I was standing at the corner of Ponce de León Avenue and Biscayne Boulevard. A truckful of painters arrived at a construction site too early to be let inside by the night watchman. They
sat around behind their truck and in the shade of a magnolia tree.

Two of the men—Rodolfo Dominguez and Arturo Mendieta—are
recent arrivals from Cuba. The third man, who employs the others, is
from the Second Wave. His name is Aureliano Sanchez Cero.

Rodolfo Dominguez: In Cuba almost everyone knows how to
do something to a house—lay a floor or build cabinets or
do the plumbing. The question is not whether you know
how to do it, but whether you know how to do it really
well. I like finishing carpentry. This is what I do. [He shows
me an unpainted and incomplete kitchen cabinet inside the
van.] Of course, it looks much better when I have real wood
instead of this processed stuff and when I finish it with real
lacquer. There's no real wood in the United States and no

real lacquer in Cuba. So I guess you'll never really see what a *Marielito* can do! [The group laughs with him.]

Arturo Mendieta: Rodolfo and I got together on the boat. We met at Mariel and sailed across together, and we remained together at Tamiami. We built barracks and tables at Eglin and Chaffee together. We got sponsors together, and we came out together to the same job.

Rodolfo Dominguez: And I have been trying to get rid of him ever since. [They laugh and offer me coffee, which is hot this time, and which I decide to accept.]

Aureliano Sanchez Cero: These two are the best workers I have ever had. You see them like this, happy to be working and outside. Free. People say the *Marielitos* are this and that. Lazy. Fidel made them lazy. I don't know who those people are talking about. These guys are the *Marielitos*. I can hire anyone I want to work for me. I hired these two.

Rodolfo Dominguez: One thing I find not easy to adjust to is everybody who talks down at you. I know I am not educated or sophisticated and haven't been as lucky as them, but some Cubans don't want to give you the time of day. The class thing. In Cuba, before Fidel, we had the upper class and the lower class. With Fidel, some of that went away.

We work for a builder who is the owner of all this property you see under construction here. He is a Cuban refugee just like me. He just got here a few years before me, and he is the smartest man I have seen working in construction. But he doesn't care about anything but making money.

Arturo Mendieta: We don't have our families with us. We hope the exits will be opened again so that our relatives can come and join us. Rodolfo has a wife and three children. We both have wives and children left behind. We thought we were going to come here, get a boat, and return to pick them up. We didn't know they were going to bounce us around from place to place. By the time we got out of Fort Chaffee, we couldn't get a boat to return. We were broke, and the Coast Guard was putting people in jail. We had to go to work. We hope we can get our families out before they starve to death in Cuba.

Later that day, on the same street that Martha Losada recalled on her first day in the United States nineteen years ago, I saw in the distance three lovely young women, their high heels pounding a beat on the sidewalk to the melody of a song, *Tres Lindas Cubanas,* emanating from the record store which now occupies the building that was Café Hunan. They were coming to meet me.

They are officially classified as "Cuban entrants." Permanent immigration status is being withheld from these young women pending possible charges of moral turpitude. Their attitude about their uncertain status and future is typical of many inhabitants of Little Havana. They are not fazed, either by their immigration problems or by the idea of the possibly injurious label of moral turpitude.

We sat on a park bench, and the young women told me about themselves.

Josefina: I am eighteen years old. I have never been a prostitute. I was very poor and lived in *San Lázaro,* a section of Havana to which the revolution has not come. They rounded us up, the three of us, from our homes. They labeled us *peligrosidades* and sent us to Mosquito and Mariel. We spent the first week in Miami at the Club Olympo, right down the street. Then we found a sponsor for the three of us—a very good family here in Miami.

Elena: I didn't like having to show identification wherever I went. The police are everywhere in Cuba. Anytime anyone asks you, you have to prove who you are and what you are doing there. I didn't want to go through that the rest of my life. I wanted to come here and was glad when they took us away.

Micaela: In *San Lázaro,* there were prostitutes everywhere. The police thought we were prostitutes. They treated us like scum and didn't feed us for ten days while we were waiting to leave.

I found a job here as a waitress in a good restaurant. Good tips. People still think I'm a prostitute sometimes, but here I just ignore them and they don't insist. They certainly don't put you in a boat and send you to Argentina! The problem is the loneliness. We have each other, but we've lost our family and friends. It is difficult to make new friends.

The young women said good-bye to me and headed on to their respective jobs, walking down Flagler Street, engaging the interest of every passing male along the way. After lunch at a cafeteria on 8th Street, I walked toward a Cuban-American-owned health clinic, which was established in the early 1960s. I had an appointment to meet Dr. Eduardo Cepa, the chief clinician and a member of the First Wave. I wanted to ask him about particular health problems of the new arrivals, but he took the initiative.

Dr. Eduardo Cepa: You want to know about the *Marielitos?* Come with me. [He guides me through a maze of small examination rooms and into one.] We have here a young Cuban male, about ten ["Eleven," says the patient on the examining table], with a mild case of malnutrition, anemia, loss of muscle fiber, loss of some reflex action. But he is not really sick. He got here six months ago. In two years he will be back to normal height and weight.

Dr. Cepa reaches into the pocket of his white coat and produces a stick of chewing gum for his patient. Before handing the child the candy, he points at the label and asks him to repeat what it says. "Sugarless," says the doctor. "Ugar-eh," says the patient, imitating the inflection, if not the sound, of the letters. The patient gets the candy anyway. The doctor shrugs his shoulders and turns to me.

Dr. Eduardo Cepa: It is hopeless. I try to teach people that sugar is bad for them. But how can you persuade a Cuban that sugar is bad? We have grown up with sugar all around. His mother will give him lots of it to fatten him up and maybe turn him into a mild diabetic.

We walk into another examination room where another doctor is asking a male patient clinical questions. Dr. Cepa introduces me to Dr. Rosalia Perez, a *Marielita* who appears to be in her early thirties. She is helping at the clinic until she takes the State Medical Licensure Examination in the spring.

Dr. Cepa takes over the patient's examination, and Dr. Perez and I go to another room. There she and her husband, Alejandro Perez, who is also a physician, tell me how they decided to leave Cuba.

Dr. Rosalia Perez: We have been all over the world as envoys from Cuba. My husband is a respiratory and heart specialist, and I am an internist. We went to Angola, Ethiopia, Afghanistan, Jamaica, and Nicaragua. We were more like public relations people—goodwill ambassadors—than doctors, but we were supposed to practice medicine if needed. There was always much need wherever we were sent. In Nicaragua we decided that we didn't want to go on with the revolution, but you ask Alejandro about that.

Dr. Alejandro Perez: What can I say to you that is new or that no one has said to you before about my reason—or reasons—for leaving Cuba? We were not free. We could not do as we wanted to, or say, or even think anything that was against Fidel or critical of his way of thinking. My wife and I had it much better than everyone else we knew. We had a big house and a car. We always went out to dinner. We traveled around the world, and we were highly respected. Maybe there is nothing more to life than that, but I doubt it. I doubt that people have to be malnourished to be good citizens. I doubt that people have to be killed to be silenced. I doubt that I have to deny the existence of God, if I feel Him inside me, or risk being called anti-revolutionary because I believe. I doubt that peace around the world is gained by helping violence flourish. I don't even know all the questions I could ask. But I want the freedom to ask them and have my government answer them. I am a product of revolutionary Cuba. I was ten when

Fidel took over. I was in school when the revolution took over the educational system. I am not supposed to ask questions. These are the questions of a traitor and a scum, according to Fidel.

The revolution has outgrown Fidel. The consciousnesses he has raised are now higher than his. I expect to go back to Cuba before I die. The people will take over from Fidel. The revolution will make Fidel useless, and he will be tossed aside. Then we will return to work for human dignity and freedom. Human freedom. I hadn't thought much about it until Nicaragua. Free people are better people. It is better for the organism. We will never stop the pursuit of freedom. *Libertad*. We can no longer do without it.

Conclusion

As we come to the end of this inquiry I am aware of having found an answer to the principal question the immigrant asks about himself as a member of a group within a society. The question for the immigrant is, "Where do I belong?" and my answer is now quite clear.

I belong to a group of Americans who share a common birthplace, Cuba, and to the group formed by their sons and daughters regardless of birthplace.

We live here, in the United States, and we are similar to many people already here. But we are different. We possess certain symbols through which we give our life meaning and interpret the reality we face. In varying degrees we recognize that we are a product of the historic interaction of three cultures: Spanish, African, and Yankee. And the fact of our immigration causes us to share in the wisdom and apprehension which are common to other groups who have similarly immigrated in search of survival.

As I came face to face with those I interviewed, the phenotypic and cultural characteristics I saw most often were those of our Spanish heritage. This heritage is also the source of the meanings we extract most often from events in our private lives, regardless of phenotype, and the source of the language we all share, Spanish, which is the carrier of our common understanding. Our Spanish heritage is a source of prestige in our culture and an element which ties us to other Hispanics in North, Central, and South America.

Second in frequency and observed impact upon my collaborators are the characteristics of our African heritage, coming from the plains of Zaire or the mountains of Zulu, through slavery in Cuba, and eventual freedom only in the twentieth century. Our African heritage is the source of symbols through which we practice our own versions of Catholicism and Protestanism. The carriers of our black racial heritage, the Cubans who are phenotypically black, appear to find a degree of resonance with the North American black cultural group. We see some evidence, to be discussed below, of links between the two groups in the North American environment we now inhabit.

And least in frequency but foremost in economic and social value to the group is the Yankee culture, introduced to us dramatically by Theodore Roosevelt and maintained until the beginning of Castro's revolution through media, music, and economic ties. Since we now share the environment which gave birth to the Yankee culture, this element grows stronger every day.

Economically, Cuban-Americans are spread across every social class in the United States. About 10 percent of us earn over $45,000 a year and are thus considered upper middle class. About half of us are middle class, and approximately 40 percent have incomes below the poverty line. Of this last group, about one-half are "working poor," and the other half (or about 20 percent of our total population) are too old, too sick, or otherwise unable to work. The Cuban working poor constitute a large majority of the seasonal workers in tourism and services in Miami. They are also agricultural workers in Florida and Louisiana. In New York and New Jersey thousands are employed "off the books" doing factory work in the same sort of sweatshops that served as the only source of income for the immigrants of the nineteenth century.

Our poor can be grouped in two categories: formerly middle-class Cubans who came to the United States in the First and Second Waves and who have been unable to surmount the social and linguistic hurdles of living in the United States, and the members of the Third Wave. The First and Second Wave poor have retained their middle-class values from Cuba, as evidenced by their living style—poor but virtuous—and the lack of Cuban slums in the United States. They live in isolation from the middle-class Americans and other Cubans, and have retained the attitudes and political philosophies that caused them to escape from Cuba in the first place. They show an inflexible, right-wing, conservative approach to Fidel and an intolerance of Cuban and American liberal ideas. It is no surprise that the greatest intracultural clashes take place when Third Wave Cubans come to live in the low-income neighborhoods already inhabited by members of the First and Second Waves.

The Third Wave constitutes the other category of Cuban poor. The new arrivals have experienced an environment and cultural indoctrination in Cuba different from that of the other two waves. They bring to the Cuban-Americans a fourth cultural element, which I will label Marxist, because it was described by Marx in *Capital*. "The process of changing man's nature," Marx had said. This element is not a philosophical belief in Marxism, but the behavioral outcome of having lived under Marxist rules. It is too recently acquired to be considered primal, and it is too dependent upon Marxist-reinforced environment to last very long. Nonetheless, the Marxist element is present in the Third Wave, particularly among the young. The two groups of poor Cubans thus interact uneasily, sharing little more than a common birthplace and a common turf and disagreeing about almost everything else.

The Cuban-American middle class is mostly white (92 percent) and is therefore able to align itself with the dominant cultural groups in the United States. It used to be said that certain immigrants could "pass," and indeed these do. They have not suffered from patterns of restrictive housing, school segregation, or job discrimination. These Cuban-Americans feel that they are pretty much able to do as they please and to live the life they most desire for themselves and their children. They share many of the cultural views of the host culture and acquire new ones every day. They seem willing to ignore the apparent prejudices they find in the American society, less willing to fight for equality than to recognize the inherent inequality thrust upon the immigrant classes as natural and accept it.

Many of the middle class (39 percent) live in Miami and have daily contact (economic and social) with other Cubans who are in the process of acculturation but are still mainly Cuban. These Miami Cubans are the most faithful carriers of the Spanish cultural element. The reasons for this are historical, as well as economic and social.

Being predominantly Catholic, their family values have remained different than those prevailing in the predominantly Protestant environment in which they settled, and their Catholic value structure is sustained by the positive and powerful role of the Catholic church in the daily lives of this middle class. The churches were the first to come to the aid of the refugees and have benefited from their loyalty over the past two decades. The values of feudal Spain, in particular those concerning sin, punishment of sin, and absolution from sin, prevail in church teachings.

It is important to note that the middle-class Cuban-Americans of Miami need not depend upon the host culture for their economic and social survival. They have their own core group able to provide the basic social resources—money, power, and prestige—and to do so in a language and style which reinforce their world view.

Some 80 percent of my Miami-based collaborators in this social category work for, with, or through another Cuban. (Incidentally, I have also found this factor of working "for each other" the most reliable predictor of social and economic success among Chinese, Vietnamese, and Italian immigrant groups.)

The upper and upper-middle class, even those who live in Miami, are the most obvious carriers of the Yankee element—Maximiliano Pons called himself an "American aspirant." This is very descriptive. Most of them have prestigious secondary affiliations acquired through schooling in the United States or Europe or through intermarriage with well-to-do families in America (North and South) and Europe. Psychologically they are the least restricted group and financially the best able to acquire new wealth and political standing. Their current interest in Pan-Americanism involves trade with Latin America, the growth of international banking, and their role as interlocutors between U.S. and Latin interests. Their psychological health comes from the fact that, of all the Cuban-Americans, they have had the least devaluing to do.

Everyone has done, to one extent or another, some cultural

devaluing in the process of acculturation to the United States. Learning a new culture and making it your own means devaluing the old. This devaluation leads to behavioral uncertainty, self-doubt, and in some cases to loss of self-control. Upper- and upper-middle class Cubans feel comfortable with their dual cultural identities, and their early success in the United States has dispelled any self-doubt.

The psychological dimensions of our immigrant experience act as a stronger bond among Cuban-Americans than any other facet of our lives as we seek a place for ourselves in American society. The most significant difference between Cuban-Americans and Cubans in Cuba is this immigrant experience and its impact on our cultural identity.

American society has acculturated us in very much the same way that it has acculturated all other immigrant groups, as sociologist Milton Gordon wrote in the definitive text on the subject (1964). He said that assimilation takes place in stages, which coincide with the stages of enfranchisement to the core social group in the host society, and that all immigrants go through these stages before they become members of the core group themselves. These stages (or landmarks) of enfranchisement are as follows:

1. *Learning the language of the core group.* In the United States the social group is monolingual, English-speaking, and, as described by sociologist Joshua Fishman (1961), composed of "white, Anglo-Saxon, middle-class clay to which all other particles adhere."

I can't estimate from available data how many of us have crossed this initial barrier. Of the group I studied, only those who immigrated in their forties remain monolingual, and many who were older when they immigrated have learned the language. My sample is insufficient to draw conclusions in this area. It is true that many hundreds of jobs in Miami and New York do not require knowledge of English and this makes it possible for Cuban-Americans who remained monolingual to become partially enfranchised to the U.S. economy. But these people remain forever locked at this level of participation in U.S. society.

2. *Acquiring the habits of the core group*—eating, dressing, hairstyles, dance, habits. This is also called extrinsic cultural change.

In progressing through the second stage, we have been helped by our Yankee contacts and aspirations. We have not, however, become acculturated to most extrinsic cultural characteristics, even in areas of the country where only the mainstream culture is practiced. In Dade County the whole environment has adapted to us, so that our Cuban habits have become the source of some popular mainstream cultural manifestations. This can be judged to be an artifact of the social class that immigrated from Cuba. Their ability to replace the extrinsic cultural characteristics which might have been lost or lain dormant during the first few years of the immigration, was praised by many of my collaborators as evidence of the inherent strengths of those characteristics. This, however, does not preclude us from adopting those habits and cultural forms we found here, and it is obvious that some of what we have adopted is now part of what we believe to be "ours."

3. *Joining the institutions of the mainstream,* including universities, large corporations, and clubs.

This stage of acculturation has been somewhat more difficult to reach. While we have created many of our own institutions—not only financial and commercial, but also educational, cultural, and social—admission to the institutions controlled by the core group has been very limited.

There are many Cuban students and professors at universities throughout the United States, and Cuban academic traditions have continued somewhat under the sponsorship of foundation grants and fellowships. Cuban-American professorships are mostly held in "ethnically-bound subjects," such as Spanish and Latin American history, where the American tradition is to import the expertise. But for the most part, academic departments in the social and behavioral sciences, the quantitative sciences, and the professions (with the exception of education) remain out of our reach as do foundations and research institutes. Social and cultural discrimination prevents this stage from being realized.

Commercial enterprises of the mainstream have been quicker to allow us access. In these institutions we are primarily playing a role as interlocutors with Central and South American markets. But increasingly, in top and middle management levels, the well cultivated talents of the Cuban-American entrepreneurial class are being put to use.

4. *Acquiring a "sense of peoplehood"*—feeling American and sharing in the dreams and aspirations of the American people. This is also called intrinsic cultural change.

This stage was, for us, an easy one. We came to the United States because we already shared a "sense of peoplehood" with the Americans. In a way our notion of American peoplehood was naive, simplistic, and perhaps the product of our own wishful thinking. Perhaps we resemble El Galán de Galicia, who has the utopian vision of a United States in which all buses go where you want them to go, and "no one needs to make transfers." America right or wrong is the battle cry of thousands of our people even today, after the Bay of Pigs, Watergate, and the American policy on further immigration to the United States. Of course, there are thousands of Cubans who reject American peoplehood, and who perhaps question the wisdom of what we do in the name of America, without totally rejecting the basic themes and aspirations of American society. Some of these Cubans immigrated at a young age, brought here by their parents against their will. They face a different set of "cultural possibilities" than the older group and thus have experienced a different America in which competition for the scarce resources of society is sometimes accomplished through prejudice and discrimination.

Yet we share in the dream of a society composed of free people, whose ideals seem to be the basic blueprint for their actions and, like Americans of all types, we also share in the hopelessness of not ever achieving the dream. If this book had any other title it would be *Libertad* [Liberty]. This is the strongest bond that unites the very individualistic Cuban-Americans to each other and the rest of the Americans.

5. *Intermarriage.* According to Gordon, the final stage of cultural and racial assimilation of an immigrant group to its host society.

This is a curious phenomenon in modern American society, because while cross-cultural intermarriage takes place quite freely in the U.S., it is seldom accomplished interracially. Italians marry Irish, and Cubans marry Irish and Italians, but they are all white. We have imitated the U.S. pattern quite well. For example, in 1980, 15 percent of all marriages performed in Dade County were between Spanish-surnamed whites and English-surnamed whites, 8 percent were between Spanish-surnamed blacks and English-surnamed blacks, but only 4 percent were between Spanish-surnamed blacks and Spanish-surnamed whites. Nonetheless, a 15 percent rate of intermarriage appears very high for an immigrant group, the bulk of whom have barely reached the second decade of immigration.

The high rate of intermarriage will have the predicted social effect—assimilation—only at the price of the group's identity in the future. It represents a growth of the affiliational ties with the Yankee element. There are figures on intermarriage between Cubans and other Latin Americans in New York City which corroborate a high rate of exogenous intermarriage. During my research I observed a high incidence in a trip through Texas, New Mexico, Arizona, and California, where over 300,000 Cubans live with over 6 million other Latins. This trend will produce some gains for the Spanish cultural element in these areas. It will also increase our heterogeneity and make a future study of the Cubans a much bigger job.

In all areas of social enfranchisement it appears as if we are following in the footsteps of other immigrations before us, but we are still imbued with a strong and separate self-perception.

Self-perceptions are nourished by moving among and using symbols. Our architecture, sometimes a bit gaudy and grandiose for my taste, looks faintly odd, or as Betancourt says, "a copy of a copy." It is French- and Spanish-inspired and functionally adapted to American architecture. Our music is our most obvious aesthetic realization. Cuban music became popular in the United States during the 1920s, when a generation of international ballroom dancers made it their own. The demand for *sones, congas,* and *rumbas* elicited numerous songs composed for the foreign market. The poignant African tradition expressed in the *són* was dressed in a Spanish wrap (for mainstream Cuban consumption) and made "lighter" for the fox-trot style of the American dancer. And that's how the Afro-Cuban *bembé* led to the worldwide popularity of Xavier Cugat and how the "country-club rumba" evolved from the serious and hauntingly beautiful "Ali-ba-ba" of Ernesto Lecuona. When the First Wave of Cubans began arriving in the United States after 1959, Cuban music was no longer popular; it had gone underground, and was kept alive in the jam sessions of jazz musicians, and the protest songs of the 1960s counterculture.

I heard "Guantanamera" from the lips of a youthful blond refugee from middle America at a protest rally in Berkeley in 1968, and he had heard it in Cuba a few weeks before. He asked me to help with the verses which came from the *Versos Sencillos* by José Martí. George Santana, a Mexican-American musician at the rally, had just cut a record that was a mixture of jazz, *sones, congas,* and *rumbas.* He called it *salsa,* because he liked hot sauce, and what he played was the musical equivalent. I told him that *salsa* was a name given to similar music performed by Cuban orchestras (Aragón, La Sonora Matancera) playing on the East Coast and in Latin America. He looked at me incredulously and asked, "No shit?"

Indeed not. *Salsa* was born in Puerto Rico, where the local aesthetic is similar to the Cuban, and became a U.S. product in New York's East Harlem theaters. But Harlem audiences are different from the Cugat audiences. They do not dance at country clubs to the *rumba-fox;* they are brown and black, and they respond to the African aesthetic. Curiously, the Spanish aesthetic of Cuban music found a market among the mountain people of Kentucky, Tennessee, and West Virginia. Willie Nelson blended the rigid structure of a *danzón* with his own bluegrass style, and the resulting song worked its way to the top of the charts and was featured in a movie called *Honeysuckle Rose.*

But the key to the emotional closet of the Cuban culture lies in the words, the tools of Fidel Castro. Two great Cuban writers have established the poles of Cuban-American literature: Alejo Carpentier, baroque and erudite, and Guillermo Cabrera-Infante, intuitive and brilliantly playful. Carpentier remained in Cuba, but his words escaped the Sugar Cane Curtain and came to live in the words of the new Cuban poets, short-story writers, and novelists living in the United States. Cabrera-Infante wrote from Europe about Cuban themes which recreated actuality in Havana. This infuriated Fidel and his work is banned in Cuba. Yet the gifted writers among the members of the Third Wave seem to emulate his style and strive for his visual clarity. Among these are René Cifuentes, Ismael Lorenzo and Delfin Prats. The language is still predominantly Spanish, but to reach a large audience some writers have turned to English.

At first our literary focus was upon *allá* [there] in Cuba: "Some said, centuries ago to God: 'When I am with you, *Allá en la Patria'* [there in Cuba]. But now, only death could relocate me." (Núñez, 1970). Then the focus shifted to *aquí, el exilio* [life in the United States]. We became more introspective: "Shall we taste the fruit of this existence, and having known it, shall we ever want ours again?" (Ciros, 1976). The words appear in music: "The orphan's loneliness gnaws at me. At times I have no idea who I am." (Allied Music, 1972). The music touches everyone, and words carry the moral principles that have survived the first few years of displacement. They are, in turn, reaffirmed in the words, and yet they change.

The moral principles. Fidel wrote a family code which defined the state's responsibility for children and their parents' duties to the state. These moral principles are still totally rejected by the immigrant group. They prefer the Spanish/Catholic family structure, with assignment of roles by age and sex. This structure has survived two decades of acculturation during the rebirth of the American feminist movement. In great measure it survives because the church survived and adapted to the demographic and linguistic changes that immigration brought to southern Florida. The values are less prevalent among Cubans living in other parts of the United States. A curious phenomenon obtains as a result of this strong value orientation, at play with the African cultural element and the economics of the environment. Namely, in the late 1960s wealth again became a symbol of spiritual salvation for the group. At first it was an extension of the church-inspired preoccupation with images, jewels, and religious offerings. Then it encountered *Santerismo*, coming from the African heritage, and turned into a symbolic interaction of object and salvation. This movement took place in the context of rapid economic expansion of our main environment, in Miami.

As a result, differences among classes, which immigration had all but blurred, began to emerge once again. Exclusive schools became popular status symbols, and children who were expected to "make good" themselves became status symbols for their parents. A new period of secularization might have developed, but the church adapted again. The church moved into a charismatic phase in Miami, and the Cuban young marrieds responded to the moral and aesthetic pull. At the end of this period our culture is rewarded. The "Cuban success story," which has received national attention, feeds back to the self-image of the community, and this changes community life.

Sociologist Daniel Bell (1980) defines community as a consciousness, as well as a primordial cultural link. "Community," he says, "consists of individuals who feel some consciousness of kind which is not contractual, and which involves some common links through primordial cultural ties. Broadly speaking, there are four such ties: Race, color, language, and ethnicity."

It is very difficult to find convergence among the Cubans in three of the four "ties" proposed by Bell. Only language gives a majority convergence. The Spanish language became our ethnic common carrier and the issue at stake in our first effort at community control. The Spanish language was made part of the program in public schools as a result of community involvement at the beginning of the Second Wave. At first parents wanted children to remember their language, so that when they returned to Cuba they would be able to resume their education. As the years passed and the preoccupation with returning to Cuba faded, Spanish-English bilingualism was pursued as a vehicle of economic and social survival. Today most Cuban-Americans agree bilingualism is a prerequisite to continued social and economic success, and Spanish is still the central unifying force in our community.

Ethnicity, however, is a new concept to Cubans. Viewing ourselves as an ethnic group puts us into a category of people who in the United States are known by various and sometimes injurious names: Hispanics (sharing in the Spanish central element), Latinos (more to our liking), Spanish-speaking (descriptive), Spanish-surname (limited), Spics (no comment). Ethnicity as a communal tie will have to wait for further geographic expansion of the Cuban culture and may never be a useful tie. It is a Yankee perspective on us. Yet *ethnos* in the Greek sense, a group, a clan, a tribe, is a useful political tool for those of us who are most interactive with other Latin Americans. Some of the sons and daughters of Cuban immigrants have become politically active, often in a way contrary to their parents' philosophy. Their self-identity is emerging from answers to the questions: Why am I here in the United States? Why couldn't our family stay in Cuba, where we were not second class and where a new society is being shaped?" The dream of nationhood revised and revisited.

The nation. No matter how we feel about Fidel and the revolution, the word Cuba is never far from our lips. (In randomly selected ten-minute recordings of my interviews, "Cuba" was the single most frequently used proper noun.) The fantasy of the nation, either as it was (*la Cuba de ayer*) in our rose-colored memories or how it will be in our lavender-colored myths of the future, is alive in all of us. Yet many of us belong to two nations now. Officially we are citizens of the United States (68 percent to 46 percent depending on estimates chosen), and circumstantially we are an important part of recent U.S. history. In brief, we are as American as the previous immigrants and Cuban to the last!

Our search for political and social equality started with American citizenship. Before becoming U.S. citizens, we viewed ourselves as invited guests, willing to demand fair treatment but conscious of our alien status. The search for the "central value of the American system and its legitimating agent"—equality—is something for "Americans" to do. Along the way we encounter Mexican-Americans, Puerto Ricans, Central Americans, blacks, Chinese-Americans, and we embrace democracy—U.S.-style democracy as a means of attaining institutional equality. Our own view is somewhat more jaundiced, nurtured in the totalitarianism of our heritage. Ironically, our struggle for equality is helped along by the progress made already, before inequality was actually perceived. This struggle will occupy our attention in the decades ahead, as our *ethnos* becomes part of our self-identity.

What will become of us here in the United States? What will become of Cuba? If Cuban society changes, will we be part of that change? When, if ever, will we stop feeling Cuban?

These and other questions remain to be answered in the fullness of time. Omar Betancourt and Luis Losada look at the future as an extension of what they see today. I leave you with their words as an epilogue.

Epilogue

Omar Betancourt: I see two very different destinies for the Cubans in the United States: one for those who have obtained riches from this country, the other for those who have not. For both I see a gradual loss of their own language and culture, which is already happening.

The *bourgeoisie* will continue to assimilate until their hair is blonde, their eyes blue or green, and their names Jones, Smith, or Kennedy. They will lose more of their culture than any other group, and the language will be retained only by those who see it as a business or political necessity. Traditions and facts about Cuban ancestry will be the object of curiosity and conversation at cocktail parties. These people will be total radicals, to the right of William Buckley, but not as bright and cheery. Or they will be apolitical, having decided that politics is bad for business. Relations with Cuba will affect them only to the extent that a changed posture toward Cuba might do harm to their business in Miami.

Then there will be the poor, the dark-skinned, the high school dropouts. Theirs is not going to be an easy lot. They will continue to be marginal, will continue to polarize. Can you imagine what the United States looks like to someone who risked life and limb to come here, only to wind up in jail, in some army installation, or in the streets?

The real test for us *cubanos* is still ahead. It has been twenty-two years since Fidel kicked the first of us out. Yet the real test is still ahead. I can feel it in my bones. I don't know what it will be, but how much worse can it be than it has already been?

Luis Losada: Now we are faced with the *Marielitos,* and everyone is saying it could be trouble. It could be. If we don't move to integrate them, they will become isolated, because no other element of American society will welcome them. But they have also helped us come together. They are our counterpoint, our Cuban-American counterpoint. They are proof of what we have always said about the situation in Cuba.

Now the world can see the farce of Fidel and understand what needs to be done. No more Fidels. The *Marielitos* will divide themselves into those who *abren surcos* [plow straight furrows] and others who *abren zanjas* [open sewers], just like the rest of us. They will continue to be suspected, but prejudices against them will be reduced over time. They are too much like us not to become a permanent part of our community. They are tobacco, and we are sugar.

Who can tell what the future holds for us, *los cubanos,* here in the United States and in Cuba, Nicaragua, Angola, wherever we are? We have a certain fate it seems. To make the world participate in our affairs, or have governments want to sway or influence or eclipse our people's power. There are only 10 million of us in the world. Why should Russia, the United States, and China care? We have no oil, no gold, no diamonds. Why is it that so much happens around us? Perhaps because we dare to pursue freedom. That is an intolerable offense for human societies. Imagine that! It is the very desire to pursue freedom that enslaves us to our fate.

Who's Who

The following characters were composed from the 187 Cubans whose stories have shaped this book.

First Wave

Carmen Bolaños is Cuca Plata's daughter-in-law and the mother of Mario Bolaños. She works with her husband Mario in their retail business in Tampa.

Mario Bolaños was a political science student in Cuba at the time of the First Wave and is now a professor of political science at a New England university. He is the grandson of Cuca Plata and the son of Carmen Bolaños.

Dr. Eduardo Cepa is a partner in a prepaid medical clinic in Miami.

Aureliano Sanchez Cero owns a contracting business that employs Rodolfo Dominguez and Arturo Mendieta.

Sergio Espinosa was a high school student when he left Cuba. He now owns a shoe factory in Florida.

Rafael Fernandez owns a jewelry store in New York City.

Esteban García is an adult illiterate who left for ethical reasons.

Sylvia Gonzalez is from an upper-class Cuban family. Kidnapped by Castro's forces at the age of fifteen, she is now a housewife in Key Biscayne.

Jesus Maria Laserie was a pit boss in a Havana casino. He is currently working as a bricklayer in Miami and is in hiding after testifying before a grand jury against his former Mafia employer.

Manolo Llerena, a former colonel in Batista's army, joined the Bay of Pigs invasion. He is now a security guard in Miami.

Miriam Llerena is Manolo Llerena's wife and a schoolteacher in Miami.

Eduardo Lopez is a fifty nine year old journalist working in N.Y.

Nicasio Lopez-Puerta is an investment manager and a political leader of the Cuban-Americans.

Martha Losada was a student from a middle-class family at the time of the First Wave. She is now a journalist in Chicago.

Francisco Maceo lived in the interior of Cuba. He and his family escaped on a small boat. He now owns a fish store in Tampa.

Miranda Martin is a politician in New England. She comes from an upper-class professional family and was a student at the time of the First Wave.

Teresa Martinez, whose husband was killed by a Cuban firing squad, works for an insurance company in New England.

Jorge Mendieta, a fifty-six-year-old former Cuban congressman, is now a professor of language and literature living in New York.

Cuca Plata is a ninety-four-year-old great-grandmother.

Maximiliano Pons is a manufacturing executive and a former production manager in Cuba. He is a forty-nine-year-old Cuban of Catalonian descent.

Ramon Puerto is a former sergeant in Batista's army who joined the Bay of Pigs invasion. He is now a manager of a fast-food store.

Amparito Sanchez vda de Mensa, a former Cuban socialite, is now living in a senior citizens' home in Miami.

Claudio Sanchez, a former Cuban bank executive, is president of a Miami-based international bank.

Porfirio Sanchez is a real estate developer in Miami and Maximiliano Pons's father-in-law.

Miguel Taboada was the chauffeur for Martha Batista, former First Lady of Cuba. He is a semiretired taxi driver in Los Angeles.

Second Wave

Omar Betancourt is a U.S.-educated social scientist who has written about the Cuban immigrants and lives in New York.

Antonio Chacon is a cartoonist now working for a Spanish-language newspaper in Miami.

Isaac Cohen is a Cuban-born rabbi who now owns an electronics business in Miami.

Carlitos Contreras is Rosa and Carlos Contreras's eldest son. He is a farmer in Adrian, Michigan.

Carlos Contreras is Rosa Contreras's husband. He manages an auto dealership in Michigan.

Rosa Contreras has taught school in Cuba and in Michigan. She and her husband Carlos will soon retire to their winter home in Florida.

Ismael Damasu is a psychiatrist living in California.

Luisa Gil is the real name of a Miami writer.

Alejandro Mederos is an orphan who is now general manager for a large Texas wholesale company.

Pepe Ponce is a researcher living in New England.

Antonio Wong is a Cuban of Chinese descent who owns a florist shop in Miami.

Third Wave

Francisco Bazan is a U.S.-trained dentist and a member of the U.S. Army Reserves working with the Cuban refugees of the Third Wave.

Cato, a mulatto with a red, white, and blue tattoo on his right shoulder, lives on the streets of Miami.

Chalo was kicked out of his sister's home for threatening her husband. He now lives on the streets of Miami.

Adela Cisneros is a former nun now in prison in Georgia.

Ramon Cisneros is a Cuban-trained psychologist who works as a rug salesman in Miami.

Rodolfo Dominguez works as a painter and carpenter in Miami.

Elena is a beautician in Miami.

Rustino Ferra was a Cuban employee of the Peruvian Embassy in Havana. Now he works at the Peruvian Consulate in Miami.

El Galán de Galicia, a mental patient at an army base, is believed to be suffering from delusions of grandeur.

Josefina is employed as a maid in Miami.

El Chulo Lopez, a former student and clerical worker in Cuba, is awaiting clearance to be released and moved to Miami. He is a self-proclaimed homosexual.

Mariano Medina, a former officer of the Cuban Revolutionary Army, is now a loading dock worker.

Arturo Mendieta is a carpenter working in Miami.

Estanislao Mendez, a Cuban agricultural worker, is being held until a sponsor can be found for him.

Micaela is a waitress in Miami.

Miguel lives on the streets of Miami because his sponsor was too demanding for him.

Ricardo Ochoa, a former Cuban bureaucrat and agricultural worker, works as a gardener in Miami.

Dr. Alejandro Perez is a Cuban-trained physician married to Rosalia Perez.

Dr. Rosalia Perez is a Cuban-trained physician who escaped by assuming another identity.

Gonzalo Ponce is Pepe Ponce's brother. He was a truck driver in Cuba and is now a trucker's helper in Miami.

Ramos, a man of about seventy, runs errands for a florist shop and lives on the streets of Miami.

Marco Soto is a forty-two-year-old convicted murderer.

About the Method

The method I used to gather these life stories is known as macro-ethnography, in which a purposively selected sample of a defined group is interviewed as the primary source of the data to be studied. These interviews are analyzed in the same way that cultural anthropologists approach their ethnographic data— that is, as a life-size slice of the group's most significant symbolic interactions.

The sample was selected to represent the referent group as a whole, using the following stratifying variables: date of arrival, income, race, age, sex, and education. The characteristics of the sample are summarized in the accompanying table. They compare very well with the estimates of total population available when I began the study in 1980, but not so well with the 1980 census. Presently the sample is skewed with respect to education and age but is roughly representative of the other variables.

Individuals were selected by consulting directories and making random number assignments to selected lists. Of course the tried and true method of asking friends to make suggestions was also used.

During each interview I asked only six predetermined questions and allowed the interviewee to lead the conversation into areas of his or her own choosing. My six questions were:

1. What is your last memory of Cuba?
2. How did you come to be in your _____ (job, career, course of study, neighborhood, social club, jail cell, Air Force base, as appropriate)?
3. What is your most powerful feeling about being here in the United States?
4. What has been the most important event in your life since 1959?
5. What do you think about us (Cubans) in the United States?
6. What will be our future, twenty years from now, in the year 2000?

During one interview, my very first question elicited the individual's whole story, filling four cassette tapes before I was able to ask question 2! Sometimes, in contrast, I was unable to extract anything more than a superficial answer. Over and over, emigrés have been asked by the native-born, "So, tell me, why did you leave Cuba?" Most of us have developed an Americanized version of our life to relate in such instances. We still guard our memories very carefully, and this stereotyped reply blocks access for the questioner interested in a deeper response.

Gradually, I began to identify certain patterns of symbolic interaction in the interviews. Questions were asked in succeeding interviews to explore the components of these patterns. For example, one pattern of memories and feelings concerns the Bay of Pigs invasion. When I began the study, I had no preference for including opinions about the Bay of Pigs. However, the responses to questions 3 and 4 made it obvious that *Cochinos* was, and is, an important symbol for the First Wave. Therefore, as I interviewed, I probed the role of *Cochinos*, and many of the life stories selected for the book reflect the responses to these questions.

Analysis of survey data was used to inform the inquiry. At times my collaborators would deliver erroneous data in the form of a statement I wanted to print. In those cases I looked up and presented the correct data in my narrative immediately following.

All the characters who speak in the book, with the exception of Fidel Castro, Luisa Gil, and José Yanes, are composite figures. Their names are pseudonyms for one, two, or often three different collaborators with comparable characteristics. I assembled, translated, and edited the composite interviews and sent them to each person interviewed. Each person interviewed was asked to approve both the translation of the interview (if the individual was bilingual) and the composite as a whole. Four individuals (represented in two characters) wanted to make changes in the narrative which were not acceptable to the others, so those composites were left out.

There are certain known limitations to the study. In analyzing the data and arranging it chronologically, I discovered that there was less material, fewer life stories, from the Second Wave than from the others. Another limitation is that no etic analysis is provided. Anthropological linguists and other social scientists make a distinction between ethnographic analysis done by an "etic" person (that is, a person from outside the group under study) and an "emic" person (who like me is within the group). They maintain that perceptual differences between etic and emic observers tend to influence findings.

I am fully aware that this book constitutes a word picture of a group, drawn by a person who is "within the frame" himself. I have tried to overcome this limitation in perspective by submitting the manuscript to outside review by social scientists who are "etic" to the group. In some cases they have contributed analyses which I have incorporated.

Characteristics of Sample (Stratified Variables of Sample)

| DATE OF ARRIVAL | NUMBER | % RACE | | | | DISTRIBUTION IN PERCENTAGES | | | | | | | | EDUCATION | | |
| | | W | B | M | O | % INCOME | | | % SEX | | % AGE | | | | | |
						I	II	III	M	F	I	II	III	I	II	III
First Wave (1959–62)	74	94	6	—	—	20	50	30	70	30	60	30	10	61	30	9
Second Wave (1969–73)	66	80	10	5	5	5	50	45	60	40	50	40	10	30	30	40
Third Wave (1980)	47	60	20	15	5	0	35	65	80	20	30	40	30	10	50	40

Age
I—over 45 years
II—21 to 45 years
III—under 21 years

Income variables
I—over $45,000 a year
II—between $15,000 and $45,000
III—under $15,000

Education
I—over 12 years
II—6–12 years
III—under

Bibliography

Addesa, Dominick Joseph. "Refugee Cuban Children: The Role of the Catholic Welfare Bureau of the Diocese of Miami, Florida, in Receiving, Caring for, and Placing Unaccompanied Cuban Refugee Children." M.S.W. thesis, Fordham University, 1964.

Aguirre, B. E. "Ethnic Newspapers and Politics: Diario Las Americas and the Watergate Affair." *Ethnic Group* 2 (1979): 155–165.

"Aid to Cuban Refugees: Refugee Problems." *America* 104 (February 1961): 655–656.

Alexander, T. "Those Amazing Cuban Emigrés." *Fortune* 74 (October 1966): 144–149.

Allen, Mary, and Goock, Karen. "Ethnocentric Characteristics of the American and Cuban Aged in Public Housing Projects, Miami, Florida." M.S.W. thesis, Florida State University, 1969.

Almeida, José, M.D. "The Massive Cuban Immigration: A Psychological View, Comments on the Group's Dynamics." Paper presented at the Annual Meeting of the American Psychiatric Association, May 6, 1969, Miami.

Alvarez, Carlos M. "Relationship Between Locus of Control as a Personality Variable and Neurosis: A Cross Cultural Study." M.A. thesis, University of Florida, 1971.

Alvarez, Carlos M., and Pader, O. F. "Cooperative and Competitive Behavior of Cuban-American and Anglo-American Children." *Journal of Psychology* 101 (March 1979): 265–271.

————. "Locus of Control Among Anglo-Americans and Cuban-Americans." *Journal of Social Psychology* 105 (August 1978): 195–198.

Arca, Manuel Porfirio. "Influence of Cubans in Present Expansion of the Sugar Industry in the Central Florida Area, Around Lake Okeechobee." M.A. thesis, University of Miami, 1962.

Argüelles, Maria de Lourdes R. "Cuban Political Refugees in the United States: A Study of Social Mobility and Authoritarianism." Ph.D. dissertation, New York University, 1970.

Azcárate, Eduardo. "Influence of Exile in the Psychopathology of Cuban Patients in the United States." Paper presented at the Annual Meeting of the American Psychological Association, September 6, 1970, Miami.

Balbona, Manuel. "Causal Factors in Cuban Exodus." Paper presented at the Annual Convention of the American Psychological Association, September 6, 1970, Miami.

Bardsley and Haslacker Inc. "Profile of the Latin Adults in Dade County and the Households They Live in." Palo Alto, October 1967.

Batista, Laureano. "Political Sociology of the Cuban Exile." M.A. thesis, University of Miami, 1968.

Bell, Daniel. "Ethnicity and Social Change." In *The Winding Passage: Essays and Sociological Journeys.* Cambridge, Mass.: Abt Books, 1980.

Bell, Paul W. "The Education of the Spanish-Speaking Child in Florida." Paper read at the Teaching English to Speakers of Other Languages Conference, New York, March 1966.

Benes, Bernardo. "The Impact of Cuban Exiles on the Economy of South Florida." Speech delivered before the Economic Society of South Florida, Inc., Miami, September 17, 1969.

"Blunted Arrow's Head." *New Republic* 148 (April 1963): 6.

Boone, Margaret S. "The Use of Traditional Concepts in the Development of New Urban Roles: Cuban Women in the United States." In *A World of Women,* edited by Erika Bourguignon, n.d.

Butterwick, John Teasdale. "A Dimensional Comparison of the Political Cultures of Cuban and American Community College Students in the Miami Area." Ph.D. dissertation, University of Miami, 1963.

Carballo, Manuel. "A Socio-Psychological Study of Acculturation/Assimilation: Cubans in New Orleans." Ph.D. dissertation, Tulane University, 1970.

Carballosa, Evis Louis. "Attitude of the Refugees Toward Economic Changes in Cuba Since Castro." Ph.D. dissertation, Texas Christian University, 1970.

Carmenate, Ruperto. *Problema del niño cubano*. Brooklyn: Editorial Ebenezer, 1971.

Casal, Lourdes. "Cubans in Exile: Social and Sociopsychological Studies." Paper presented at the Annual Convention of the American Psychological Association, Miami, September 6, 1970.

Casal, Lourdes, and Hernández, A. R. "Cubans in the U.S.: A Survey of the Literature." *Cuban Studies/Estudios Cubanos* 5 (July 1975): 25–51.

———. "Cubans in the United States." *Nueva Generacion* 3–4 (December 1972): 6–20.

———. *Cuban Minority Study*. Statistical Report Series, Nos. 2, 3, 4, 8, 10, 11, 12 April 1973.

Cejas and Toledo Inc. "Needs Assessment: The Prevention of Spanish-Speaking Dropouts in the Large Areas of Little Havana and Wynwood (Grades 7–12), Final Report." Miami, January 1974.

Chi, Peter Shen-Kuo. "Inter- and Intra-Group Income Inequities of Racial and Ethnic Groups in the United States." Brown, 1972.

"Chicagoans Welcome Refugees from Cuba." *Christian Century* 79 (April 1962): 418.

Clark, Juan M. "The Exodus from Revolutionary Cuba (1959–1974): A Sociological Analysis." Ph.D. dissertation, University of Florida, 1975.

———. "Selected Types of Cuban Exiles Used as a Sample of the Cuban Population." Paper presented at the Annual Meeting of the Rural Sociological Society, Washington, D.C., August 1970.

Clark, Juan M., and Mendoza, Manuel G. *The Spanish Speaking Elderly of Dade County: Characteristics and Needs*. Final Report presented to the Cuban National Planning Council Inc., Miami, May 1974.

Cohn, Michael. "The Cuban Community of Washington Heights in

New York City." Occasional Papers in Cultural History No. 12. New York: Brooklyn Children's Museum, 1967.

Copey-Blanco, M.; Montía, P. A.; and Suarez, L. L. "A Study of Attitudes of Cuban Refugees Toward Assimilation." M.S.W. thesis, Barry College (Miami), 1968.

Cortes, Carlos, ed. Cuban Exiles in the United States: An Original Anthology. New York: Arno Press, 1981.

"Cuban Doctor's Dilemma." Time 101 (June 1973): 104.

"Cuban Success Story: In the U.S." U.S News & World Report 62 (March 1967): 104–106.

"Cubans Take Off on SBA Test Run." Business Week (June 21, 1969): 41.

"Cuba's New Refugees Get Jobs Fast: Opportunities in the United States." Business Week (March 12, 1969): 69.

Davis, J. Michael. "The Relationship of Selection Factors in the Cuban Teacher Retraining Program to the Effective Classroom Performance of Cuban Refugee Teachers." Ph.D. dissertation, University of Miami, 1969.

Dominguez, Jorge L. Cuba: Order and Revolution. Cambridge, Mass.: Harvard University Press, 1978.

Dowd, Donald Jerome. "A Comparative Study of Attitudes, Goals, and Values Between Negro American, White American, and Cuban Refugee Groups in a Large Southern City." Ed.D. dissertation, University of Florida, 1966.

Egerton, John. Cubans in Miami: A Third Dimension in Racial and Cultural Relations. Nashville, Tenn.: Race Relations Information Center, 1969.

"Embittered Exiles." Economist 207 (April 27, 1963): 324.

"End of the Freedom Flights." Time 98 (September 1971): 34.

Fagen, Richard R., and Brody, Richard A. "Cubans in Exile: A Demographic Analysis." Social Problems 11 (1964): 389–400.

Fagen, Richard R.; Brody, Richard A.; and O'Leary, Thomas J. Cubans in Exile. Stanford: Stanford University Press, 1968.

Femee, M. M. "Employment Without Liberation: Cuban Women in the U.S." Social Science Quarterly 60 (January 1979): 35–50.

Fineman, C. "Attitude Toward Assimilation: Its Relationship to Dogmatism and Rigidity in the Cuban Refugee." M.A. thesis, University of Miami, 1966.

First Research Company. *Latin Market: 1970 Report, Dade County, Florida.* Miami, 1970.

Fishman, Joshua. "Childhood Indoctrination for Minority Group Membership." *Daedalus* 90, No. 2 (Spring 1961): 329.
329.

Florida Industrial Commission. "Characteristics of Cuban Refugees in Dade County, Florida." Tallahassee, March 1963.

Florida International University, Cultural and Human Interaction Center. *Emergency School Aid Act: Project Review, 1973–74.* Miami, 1975.

"Florida's New Cosmpolitanism." *Florida Commentary* (Summer 1975): 40–41.

Fox, Geoffrey E. "Cuban Workers in Exile." *TRANS-ACTION* 8 (September 1971): 21–24.

"Free for All Cubans." *Economist* 217 (October 1965): 155–156.

Gallagher, Patrick Lee. "The Cuban Exile: Socio-Political Analysis." Ph.D. dissertation, Saint Louis University, 1974.

García Tudurí, Mercedes. "Resumen de la Historia de la Educacíon en Cuba; Su Evaluacion: Problemas y Soluciones del Futuro." *Exilio* 3–4 (Fall 1969/Spring 1970): 109–143.

Garzón, Carolina G. "A Study of the Adjustment of 34 Cuban Boys in Exile." M.S.W. thesis, School of Social Service, Florida State University, 1965.

Gibboney, Joseph Dominic. "Stability and Change in Components of the Parental Role Among Cuban Refugees." D.S.W. dissertation, Catholic University of America, 1967.

Gil, Rosa María. "The Assimilation of Problems of Adjustment to the American Culture of One Hundred Cuban Refugee Adolescents, Attending Catholic and Public High Schools, in Union City and West New York, New Jersey, 1959–1966." M.S.W. thesis, Fordham University, 1968.

"Glimmer of Sense." *Economist* 217 (November 1965): 713.

Gomula, Wanda Wallace. "Common Patterns of Nonverbal Behavior Among Selected Cuban and Anglo Children." Ed.D. dissertation, Indiana University, 1973.

Gonzalez, Esther B. "Annotated Bibliography on Cubans in the United States, 1960–1976." Mimeographed. Miami: Florida International University, 1977.

Gonzalez, Isabel. "The Cubans—From Political Exile to U.S. Citizen." *INS Reporter* 25 (1976–77): 43–46.

Gordon, Michael W. *The Cuban Nationalization: The Demise of Foreign Private Property.*

Gordon, Milton. *Assimilation in American Life.* New York: Oxford University Press, 1964.

Grupo Areito. *Contra viento y marea.* New York: Ediciones Vitral, 1978.

Gutíerrez de la Solana, Alberto. *La Investigación y la Crítica Literaria y Linguística de los Cubanos en el Exilio.* Montclair, N.J.: Senda Nueve de Ediciones, n.d.

Harrison, Polly Fortier. "Changes in Feminine Role: An Exploratory Study in the Cuban Context." M.A. thesis, Catholic University of America, 1974.

Harrison, R. J. "Catalan Business and the Loss of Cuba, 1898–1914." *Economic History Review* 27 (August 1974): 431–441.

Haskins, James. *The New Americans: Cubans.* Hillside, N.J.: Enslow Publishers, 1982.

"Havana, Florida." *Newsweek* 74 (September 1969): 59.

"Havana-in-Exile." *Economist* 228 (August 1968): 33–34.

Hernández, Andrés R., ed. *The Cuban Minority in the U.S.: Final Report on Need Identification and Program Evaluation.* Washington, D.C.: Cuban National Planning Council Inc., 1974.

Hernández, Carmen M. "Use of Community Mental Health Facilities by Cubans: A Survey of the Washington Heights–West Harlem–Inwood Area." Paper presented at the Annual Convention of the American Psychological Association, Miami, September 2–8, 1970.

Hilsman, Roger. "R.F.K. on Cuba: An Insider's Analysis." *Commonweal* 99 (November 1968): 273–275.

Horowitz, I. L., ed. *Cuban Communism.* 2d ed. New Brunswick, N.J.: Transaction Books, 1972.

"How the Immigrants Made It in Miami." *Business Week* (May 1971): 88–89.

Illinois State Advisory Committee to the U.S. Commission on Civil

Rights. *Bilingual/Bicultural Education—A Privilege or a Right?* Washington, D.C.: U.S. Commission on Civil Rights, 1974.

"Iowa, Si! Training Programs for Spanish Teachers." *Newsweek* 62 (August 1963): 75.

Jaco, Daniel E.; Hagan, Robert J.; and Wilber, George L. "Spanish Americans in the Labor Market, Lexington, Kentucky." M.A. thesis, University of Kentucky, M.A. thesis June 1974.

Jacoby, Susan. "Miami Si, Cuba No." *New York Times Magazine*, September 29, 1974, p. 28.

Joyner, Genevieve Czepiel. "The Role of the Family in the Adjustment of Cuban Refugees." M.A. thesis, University of Florida, 1972.

Kennedy, Edward M. "The Immigration Act of 1965." *Annals of the American Academy of Political and Social Science* 367 (September 1966): 137–149.

Laosa, Luis. "Socialization, Education and Continuity: The Importance of the Sociocultural Context." *Young Children* 32 (July 1977): 21–27.

Latin Chamber of Commerce. *The Latin Community of Dade County, 1975.* Miami, 1975.

Lavernia, Angela Cristina. "The Cuban Refugee Assistance Program: A Study of Mothers' Reaction to Training for Independence." M.S.W. thesis, Barry College (Miami), 1968.

Lazaga, José I. "La Juventud del Exilio y la Tradición Nacional Cubana." *Exilio* 3–4 (Fall 1969/Spring 1970): 51–81.

Lima, Facundo P., M.D. "How the Miami Community Dealt with the Cuban Refugees." Paper presented at the Annual Meeting of the American Psychiatric Association, Miami, May 6, 1969.

Linehan, Edward J. "Cuba's Exiles Bring New Life to Miami." *National Geographic Magazine* 144 (July 1973): 68–95.

Linn, M. W. "Differences by Sex and Ethnicity in the Psychosocial Adjustment of the Elderly." *Health and Social Behavior* 20 (September 1979): 273–281.

Lombillo, José, M.D. "The Initial Crisis of the Cuban Refugee: Coping and Adaptive Mechanisms." Paper presented at the Annual Meeting of the American Psychiatric Association, Miami, May 6, 1969.

Lopez-Blanco, Marino; Montiel, Pedro A.; and Suárez, Luis A. "A Study of Attitudes of Cuban Refugees Toward Assimilation: Selected Attitudes of Cuban Refugees in the Miami Area." M.S.W. thesis, Barry College (Miami), 1968.

Maier, Francis. "Nation in Our Midst: The Cuban Diaspora." *National Review* 33 (February 20, 1981): 148.

Marcus, Pamela T. "Social Integration and Attitudes Toward Return to the Homeland of Cuban Political Refugees." M.A. thesis, University of Florida, 1971.

Mayer, John Charles, "Women Without Men: Selected Attitudes of Some Cuban Refugees." M.A. thesis, University of Miami, 1966.

Moncarz, Rául. "A Study of the Effect of Environmental Change on Human Capital Among Selected Skilled Cubans." Ph.D. dissertation, Florida State University, 1969.

―――. "Effects of Professional Restrictions on Cuban Refugees in Selected Health Professions in the United States, 1959–1969." *International Migration Review* 8 (1970): 22–30.

―――. "Professional Adaptation of the Cuban Teachers in the United States, 1959–1969." *International Migration Review* 8 (1970): 110–116.

―――. "Cuban Lawyers: Ten Years Later." *International Migration Review* 10 (1972): 109–114.

Montori, Susana. "Study of the Services Rendered by Christian Community Service Agency Inc. to the Cuban Refugee Population in Miami." M.S.W. thesis, Barry College (Miami), 1969.

Morrissey, R. F., and Naditch, M. P. "Role Stress, Personality, and Psychopathology in a Group of Immigrant Adolescents." *Journal of Abnormal Psychology* 85 (Fall 1976): 113–118.

Navarro, Carlos. "An Analytical Study of Three Hundred and Sixty-One Slang Forms Collected at Random from a Heterogeneous Group of Twenty-Six Cuban Informants." M.A. thesis, University of Miami, 1963.

Nicholas, J. C. "Racial and Ethnic Dissemination in Rental Housing." *Review of Social Economics* 36 (April 1978): 89–94.

"Now You Have to Swim." *Economist* 240 (September 1971): 36.

Nuñez, Ana Rosa, ed. *Poesía en Exodo: El Exilio Cubano en Su Poesía, 1959–1969*. Miami: Ediciones Universal, 1970.

Oettinger, Katherine B. "Services to Unaccompanied Cuban Refugee

Children in the United States." *Social Service Review* 36 (December 1962): 377–384.

O'Leary, Thomas James. "Cubans in Exile: Political Attitudes and Political Participation." Ph.D. dissertation, Stanford University, 1967.

Ortiz, Fernando. *Cuban Counterpoint.* New York: Alfred A. Knopf, 1940, p. 9.

Parker, Everett C. "Miami's Real-Life Drama." *Christian Century* 78 (October 1961): 1209–1211.

Peláez, Armantina R. "The Cuban Exodus." B.A. thesis, Ladycliff College (Highland Falls, N.Y.), 1973.

Penas, Graciela, and Marqués, José A. "Factors Precipitating Cuban Refugee Senior Citizens' Application for Public Housing." M.S.W. thesis, Barry College (Miami), 1969.

Portes, Alejandro. "Dilemmas of a Golden Exile: Integration of Cuban Refugee Families in Milwaukee." *American Sociological Review* 34 (August 1969): 505–518.

Portes, Alejandro et al. "Immigrant Aspirations." *Sociology of Education* 51 (October 1978): 24–60.

Prince, Maria Cristina. "The Cuban Family: A Comparative Approach." M.A. thesis, New York University, 1972.

"Professional Adaptation of Cuban Physicians in the United States, 1959–1969." *International Migration Review* (Spring 1970): 80–86.

Prohías, Rafael J., and Casal, Lourdes. "The Cuban Minority in the U.S.: Preliminary Report on Need Identification and Program Evaluation." Report prepared for Fiscal Year 1973, Florida Atlantic University, 1973.

"Refugee Cuban Children Need Homes." *Christian Century* 79 (April 1962): 417–418.

"Refugees from Castro." *Economist* 205 (December 1962): 1204–1206.

Richardson, Mabel Wilson. "An Evaluation of Certain Aspects of the Academic Achievement of Elementary Pupils in a Bilingual Program." Ph.D. dissertation, University of Miami, 1967.

Richmond, Marie. *Immigrant Adaptation and Family Structure Among Cubans in Miami, Florida.* New York: Arno Press, 1981.

Richmond, M. L. "Beyond Resource Theory: Another Look at Factors Enabling Women to Affect Family Interaction." *Journal of Marriage and Family* 38: 257–266.

Rinn, Frank Burton. "Some Problems of Teaching Spanish-Speaking Children in the Public School." M.A. thesis, University of Miami, 1961.

Rivas-Vázquez, Ana A. "Objective Differences Between American and Cuban Cultures and Their Subjective Importance for the Cuban Exile." Paper presented at the Annual Convention of the American Psychological Association, Miami, September 6, 1970.

Rodríquez, Leonardo. "An Exploratory Analysis of the Relationship Between the Application of Organization Principles and Financial Measures of Success in Cuban Owned Businesses in Miami, Florida." D.B.A. dissertation, Florida State University, 1975.

Rogg, Eleanor. "The Influence of a Strong Refugee Community on the Economic Adjustment of Their Members." *International Migration Review* (Winter 1971): 474–481.

————. "The Occupational Adjustment of Cuban Refugees in the West New York, New Jersey Area." Ph.D. dissertation, Fordham University, 1970.

————. *The Assimilation of Cuban Exiles: The Role of Community and Class.* New York: Aberdeen Press, 1974.

Ropka, Gerald W. "The Evolving Residential Pattern of the Mexican, Puerto Rican, and Cuban People in the City of Chicago." Ph.D. dissertation, Michigan State University, 1973.

Rumbaut, Ruben, M.D. "The Cubans: Historical and Psychological Background." Paper presented at the Annual Meeting of the American Psychiatric Association, Miami, May 1969.

Rumbaut, R. D., and Rumbaut, R. Y. "Family in Exile: Cuban Expatriates in the United States." *American Journal of Psychology* 133 (April 1976): 395–399.

Salter, Paul S., and Mings, Robert C. "The Projected Impact of Cuban Settlement on Voting Patterns in Metropolitan Miami, Florida." *Professional Geographer* 24 (February 1972): 122–131.

Schlise, Suzanne. "The Cuban Refugee Child: A Study in Parent-Child Separation." M.S.W. thesis, Barry College (Miami), 1971.

Servick, Charles V. "A History and Evaluation of the Teacher Retraining Program of the University of Miami, 1963–1973." Ph.D. dissertation, University of Miami, 1974.

Sheeley, Loran L., and Burck, Lee. "Operation: Adjustment." *Clearing House* 38 (October 1963): 80–82.

Sherwood, Charles Frederick. "A Paradigm for Teacher-Education in Reading Instruction Based Upon the Perceptions of Selected Elementary Teachers in Dade County, Florida." Ed.D. dissertation, University of Miami, 1972.

Shreiner, Charles. "Gloom over Miami." *America* 104 (February 1961): 664–665.

Smith, Jean Edward. "Bay of Pigs: The Unanswered Questions." *Nation* 198 (April 1964): 360–363.

Smith, Richard F. "Refugee." *Annals of the American Academy of Political and Social Science* 367 (September 1966): 43–52.

Spanish-Speaking Action (ad-hoc) Committee. "Strengthening Manpower Programs for Spanish-Speaking Americans in Dade County." Paper presented to the Metropolitan Dade County Manpower Area Planning Council, Miami, February 25, 1972.

Stevenson, James J. "Cuban-Americans: New Urban Class." Ph.D. dissertation, Wayne State University, 1973.

Stevenson, Russell. "Refugees Still Coming." *Christian Century* 78 (June 1961): 703.

"Stranded on the Beach." *New Republic* 144 (June 1961): 5.

Strategy Research Corporation. *The Dade Latin Market, 1974.* Miami, 1974.

————. *Prospectives of Dade County Growth, 1980.* Miami, 1975.

Strong, Sister Miriam, O. P. "Refugees from Castro's Cuba of Fish and Freedom." M.S.W. thesis, Fordham University, 1964.

Supervielle, Alfredo Fernández. "The Bilingual-Bicultural Communities and the Teaching of Foreign Languages and Cultures in the United States." Ph.D. dissertation, Florida State University, 1973.

Szapocznik, J. et al. "Comparison of Cuban and Anglo American Values in a Clinical Population." *Journal of Consulting Clinical Psychology* 47 (June 1979): 623–624.

————. "Cuban Value Structure: Treatment Implications." *Journal of Consulting Clinical Psychology* 46 (October 1978): 623–961–970.

"These Are Cubans . . . Why They Endure." *Atlas Magazine* 15 (May 1968): 52–56.

Tikhonov, D. "Experience of the Cuban Revolution." *Kommunist* 51 (1974): 95–106.

Trillin, Calvin. "U.S. Journal: Union City, N.J." *New Yorker* 51 (June 1975): 94–96.

University of Miami Center for Advanced International Studies. "Psycho-Social Dynamics in Miami." Report of a summer study conducted under the auspices of the University of Miami, 1969.

———. "The Cuban Immigration 1959–66 and Its Impact on Miami/Dade County, Florida." Report prepared by the Research Institute for Cuba and the Caribbean, 1967.

"Unsavory Plot." *Economist* 261 (November 1976): 58.

Vilá, José Jorge, and Zalamea-Arenas, Guillermo. *Exilio*. Miami: Editorial AIP, 1967.

Villalón, José R. "El Camino del Exilado Cubano." *Exilio* 3–6 (Fall 1969/Spring 1970): 255–277.

Walsh, Bryan O., Monsignor. "Cuban Refugee Children." *Journal of Inter-American Studies and World Affairs* 13 (July–October 1971): 378–415.

Walter, Ronald. "Uneasy Haven: The Cubans of Puerto Rico." *Nation* 216 (March 1973): 399–400.

Wenk, Michael G. "The Cuban Refugee Experience." *International Migration Review* 3 (Fall 1968): 38–49.

Williamson, David. "Adaptation to Socio-Cultural Change: Working Class Cubans in New Orleans." *Caribbean Studies* 16 (October 1976/January 1977): 217–227.

Williamson, David. "Cognitive Complexity and Adaptation to Socio-Cultural Change: The Case of the Cuban Refugees in New Orleans." Ph.D. dissertation, Tulane University, 1973.

Winsberg, M.D. "Housing Segregation of a Predominantly Middle-Class Population: Residential Patterns Developed by the Cuban Immigration into Miami, 1950–1974." *American Journal of Economics and Sociology* 38 (October 1979): 403–418.

Wolfe, Jerome A., and Cartano, David G. "A Study of Spanish-Speaking Drivers in Dade County, Florida." *Miami Interactions* 5 (Spring 1974): 21–26.

Wong, Francisco R. "Political Orientation and Participation of Cuban Migrants: A Preliminary Analysis." Paper prepared for the Panel on Refugee Politics at the Annual Meeting of the American Political Science Association, Miami, September 6, 1973.

————. "The Political Behavior of Cuban Migrants." Ph.D. dissertation, University of Michigan, 1974.

Yanés, José "La Habana es una Ciudad que espera" 1972, *En Cuba,* Ernesto Cardenal. Ediciones Carlos Lohle, Buenos Aires.

Yearly, C. K. "Cubans in Miami." *Commonweal 83* (November 1965): 210–211.

Zeitlin, M. "Political Generation in the Cuban Working Class." *American Journal of Sociology* (March 1966): 493–508.